Southern Colorado State College
Pueblo, Colorado

the OAS
and United States
Foreign Policy

A publication of the Social Science Program

of the Mershon Center for Education in National Security

of the Ohio State University

JEROME SLATER

the OAS

and united states

foreign policy

OHIO STATE UNIVERSITY PRESS

*

To Judith

*

*

Acknowledgments

THIS STUDY was made possible by a Brookings Institution
Research Fellowship for 1962-63 and by fellowships granted
by the Mershon Social Science Program in National Security
for 1963-65. For some of the material herein I have drawn
from my *A Revaluation of Collective Security: The OAS in
Action* ("Pamphlet Series of the Social Science Program of
the Mershon Center for Education in National Security,"
No. 1 [Columbus: Ohio State University Press, 1965]) ; "The
United States, the Organization of American States, and the
Dominican Republic, 1961-63," *International Organization,*
Vol. VIII, No. 2 (1964) ; and "Democracy vs. Stability: The
Recent Latin American Policy of the United States," *Yale
Review,* Vol. IV, No. 2 (1966) , copyright Yale University.

I am grateful to Professor Leon Gordenker of Princeton
University, who greatly encouraged this study at various
stages of its growth and read the manuscript in several versions, offering invaluable suggestions and criticisms. My col-
leagues in the Mershon Program, particularly Stanley J.
Michalak, Walter Goldstein, and Edward A. Kolodziej, provided intellectual stimulation and a most pleasant atmosphere in which to work. But most of all, I owe an immeasur-
able debt to the late Edgar S. Furniss, Jr., director of the

Mershon Social Science Program until his tragic death in the summer of 1966. Professor Furniss had an enormous impact on all of us who were fortunate enough to know him as mentor, colleague, and friend. The academic profession and the discipline of political science is the poorer for his loss.

My wife Judith not only painstakingly edited the entire manuscript but made many helpful substantive suggestions as well. Naturally, only the author is responsible for both the form of the presentation and errors of fact or interpretation.

JEROME SLATER

CONTENTS

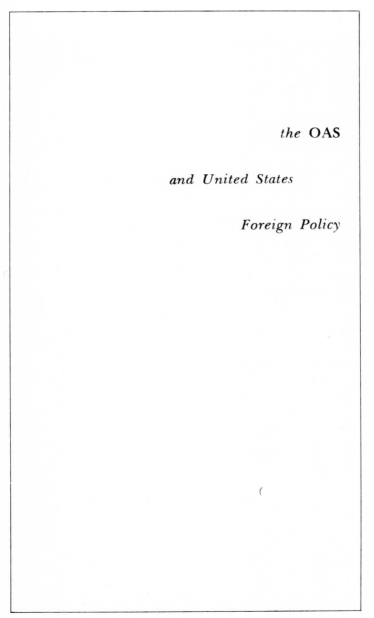

the **OAS**

and United States

Foreign Policy

*

Introduction

IN RECENT YEARS, after the embarrassing attacks on Vice-President Nixon in 1958 and the Cuban revolution of 1959 made it sharply clear that Latin America could no longer be taken for granted, the United States has begun to devote more of its attention and resources to its southern neighbors. The events of the late 1950's not only symbolized the failure of United States foreign policy toward Latin America, they also focused attention on the dismal state of scholarship on Latin American politics and inter-American relations. The topics that social scientists—especially political scientists—choose to examine are influenced mightily by the headlines of the day. With Latin America relatively quiescent, the attention of academicians as well as policy-makers was focused on more exciting and urgent areas.

In particular, rigorous political analyses of the Organization of American States (OAS) have been meager. The major purpose of this study is to partially fill one of the most obvious lacunae by examining the role of the OAS in United States foreign policy from 1947 through 1964. Hopefully, the discussion will also shed light on the general Latin American policy of the United States, the advantages and costs of multilateral diplomacy as a technique of United States foreign policy, the capacity of the OAS as an instrument for the management of political conflict in the Western Hemisphere, and the behavior of states in international organizations.

Since the study is centered on interstate political conflict in the hemisphere, the increasingly important role of the OAS in economic and social matters, notably in conjunction with the Alliance for Progress, is not dealt with. Nor is the Dominican crisis of 1965 discussed, since it occurred while the final draft was in process. Finally, although it falls within the time span of the book, the United States–Panama conflict of 1964 is dealt with only tangentially because practical considerations made impossible the extensive interviewing necessary for a detailed case study.

Before proceeding, it might be helpful to summarize the major arguments of the study and offer a brief overview of United States policies toward Latin America since World War II.

Since the enunciation of the Monroe Doctrine, the primary political objective of the United States in its inter-American policy has been the maintenance or attainment of political stability in Latin America. Stability, as understood by United States policy-makers, has three dimensions: internal Latin American political structures, interstate relations within the hemisphere, and the relationship of the hemisphere to the rest of the world. With regard to internal stability, the United States seeks to insure that no Latin American governments come to power, or remain in power, that represent a serious challenge to the security of the United States. In the context of the cold war, of course, internal stability refers to the exclusion of communism from the hemisphere. In its intrahemispheric dimension, stability requires the absence of serious interstate conflict. United States security can be best maintained in an atmosphere of tranquility; disturbances threaten the solidarity of the hemisphere under the leadership of the United States and may involve annoying expenditures of time, energy, and resources. Finally, stability requires the insulation of the hemisphere from undesirable external political influences (Nazi, Soviet, Red Chinese) and the preservation of the hemisphere as part of the United States "sphere of influence."

The policies the United States has followed in the OAS, then, have been designed to maintain or achieve hemispheric stability, as defined. Depending on the type of action considered most appropriate for the maintenance of stability in particular conflict situations, the United States has attempted to influence the OAS to play one of three roles — that of a collective security system, of an anti-Communist alliance, or even on occasion of an anti-dictatorial alliance.

The collective security function differs significantly from the alliance role. In collective security systems, all states agree to come to the assistance of any member that is attacked by any state, regardless of whether the aggressor is a member of the system or outside it, and regardless of the domestic political structures and ideologies of either the aggressor or the victim. Aggression, per se, is to be resisted. On the other hand, alliances are selective. They represent the agreement of some states to band together against specified others, who, for ideological, political, or military reasons, are considered to be threats to the alliance members. Moreover, unlike collective security systems, alliances do not necessarily exclude offensive action (aggression) against non-members.[1]

As the perceived requirements for hemispheric stability have shifted, United States policy has shifted, emphasizing first one role for the OAS, then another. When the primary threat to stability has been intra–Latin American conflict, the United States has pressed for collective security action. When the threat has been seen to be Communist infiltration of the hemisphere, the United States has sought to transform the OAS into an anti-Communist alliance. Finally, when the threat has been conceived to be the resistance of conservative dictatorships to political, economic, and social change, the United States has attempted to persuade the OAS to take action against its own dictatorial members.

A Review of Postwar Policies

United States policy toward Latin American since World War II has gone through three phases: the first from 1946–60, the second roughly coinciding with the Kennedy administration, the third beginning with the Johnson administration.

With the defeat of the Axis and the onset of the cold war, communism was seen as the major threat to United States security in the Western Hemisphere. Until the Castro revolution, however, the threat was not considered immediate—except for the short-lived Guatemalan crisis in 1954—and consequently there was thought to be little need to devote extensive intellectual and material resources to inter-American relations, particularly since the policy of world-wide containment of communism clearly demanded the heavy concentration of these resources in Europe and Asia. Political stability continued to be the primary objective of United States foreign policy in Latin America, but in the absence of an immediate outside threat, little positive action was required to realize it. Stability was sought through support of the status quo, *any* status quo, as long as it was non-Communist.

Defined in these terms, "stability" was not seriously threatened by the often violent Latin American domestic political conflict, whether the traditional "outs" versus "ins" variety, the conflicts between democracy and dictatorship, or modernization and traditionalism.

The maintenance of the status quo was reflected in United States diplomatic, military, and economic policies and was sought by both unilateral and multilateral techniques. The Latin American policies of the Truman and Eisenhower administrations, particularly after 1947, resembled each other far more than they differed.

Diplomatically, support of the status quo was implied in the decision of both administrations to avoid embroilment in Latin American internal affairs by working with any and all governments, democratic or dictatorial, leftist or rightist—a decision reached after the failure of the 1946 intervention in Argentine politics. In that affair, the Department of State and the United States Ambassador to Argentina, Spruille Braden, had openly attacked the dictatorial, pro-Fascist regime of Juan Perón in an attempt to influence the Argentine public prior to the 1946 elections. Perón, however, made use of the United States intervention to arouse nationalistic resentments and won the election by a wide margin.

The Braden episode marked the last direct United States intervention in the internal affairs of a non-Communist Latin American country until 1960. After 1946 the use of diplomatic recognition (and economic assistance) as a means of leverage over the domestic politics of Latin American regimes was abandoned in favor of the policy of de facto recognition of all (non-Communist) governments, regardless of their moral or constitutional validity. In addition, conservative, business-oriented ambassadors—both political and career—were appointed to most Latin American nations. It was no accident that such men normally had little difficulty in maintaining warm relationships with the Batistas, Somozas, Pérez Jiménezes, and Trujillos.[2]

The postwar military assistance program also served to bolster the status quo in Latin America. The Latin American armed forces, although occasionally siding with reformist elements, normally served as the major bulwark of the conservative ruling oligarchies against economic, social, and political change. Furthermore, the military was, and is, normally the single most powerful political force in Latin America, whether ruling directly, utilizing a thinly disguised civilian front, or acting as a veto group to prevent specific actions. In this context, United States military assistance could, it was hoped, serve a number of purposes: it could gain the friendship of a key political group, strengthen the military's capabilities for the maintenance of "internal order," and by preempting the military market, exclude non-Hemispheric and particularly Soviet-bloc suppliers and thereby preclude a potential threat to United States political leadership in the hemisphere.[3]

The economic assistance programs of the Truman and Eisenhower administrations were likewise primarily political instruments of the policy of support for the status quo. When the Mutual Security Program was developed in 1951, the Assistant Secretary of State for Inter-American Affairs acknowledged that the major purpose of the program in Latin America was to keep the hemisphere "economically and politically stable." In this respect, he pointed out, "the military program and the proposed technical-cooperation program are opposite sides of the same coin."[4] This was to remain the most important rationale for the program under the Eisenhower administration as well. For example, on several occasions the massive aid program to Bolivia kept the MNR regime from collapsing; United States generosity was not based on enthusiasm for the revolutionary policies of the MNR, of course, but on fear of an even more radical Bolivia if the MNR failed—at least the existing government was anti-Communist in its domestic politics and reasonably responsive to United States hemispheric leadership.

Finally, on the multilateral level, United States policies in the OAS were carefully designed to keep Latin America peaceful and quiet. To this end, the United States normally found the twin OAS principles of collective security and non-intervention quite useful.[5] The effect of the non-intervention principle, of course, was to insulate states against external pressures; i.e., it tended to preserve the status quo. Similarly, the emphasis of collective security on the maintenance of international peace inhibited the efforts of Latin American exile groups to bring about changes in their homelands. Thus, until about 1960, the main thrust of United States policy in the OAS was to uphold the principles of non-intervention and collective security as long as they were compatible with the maintenance of a non-Communist status quo. In the one case in which they were not—the Guatemalan situation of 1954—the United States took the lead in attempting to have the OAS act as an anti-Communist alliance rather than as a system of collective security.

The United States throughout this period was not only unconcerned with the democratization and modernization of Latin America, but its policies often constituted a major obstacle to Latin American economic, social, and political progress. Attempts to transform the OAS into an antidictatorial alliance by making respect for democratic principles and human rights a prerequisite for diplomatic recognition, economic assistance, and OAS membership were frequently blocked by the United States in the interests of stability. More importantly, on a number of occasions collective security and non-intervention directly clashed with the cause of democracy in Latin America, and on each the OAS, under United States prodding, gave priority to the former. In 1948-50 and again in 1959, for example, the dictatorial Nicaraguan and Dominican regimes were attacked by exiles based in sympathetic neighboring countries. Within the OAS there was considerable sentiment for looking the other way rather than allowing Somoza and Trujillo to be the beneficiaries of collective security action, but the United States successfully pressed for the activation of OAS machinery to discourage further expeditions.[6]

On these and other occasions, United States spokesmen denied any conflict between collective security and democracy, arguing that democracy could not be "imposed" from outside, but had to "come from within."[7] Since, however, the grip of the Somozas and Trujillos of Latin America could have been broken only with outside assistance, the United States position had the effect of stabilizing the power of hemispheric dictatorships. This is not to imply that under the Truman and Eisenhower administrations the United States necessarily had an outright preference for dictatorial or reactionary regimes, as has frequently been charged. The priority given to keeping Latin America stable simply dictated the acceptance of existing realities, especially when change could be brought about only by violence.

In 1958 and again in 1959 the United States received two severe shocks that were eventually to lead to major changes in its inter-American policy. The anti-Nixon riots in 1958 symbolized the extent of anti-Americanism in

Latin America, and the Castro revolution focused attention on a more important problem. Although the extent of rising mass dissatisfaction with the status quo in Latin America had been well known to serious hemispheric observers for years, its implications were ignored or not understood by United States policy-makers. But the revolt against Batista sharply dramatized this discontent, making it painfully obvious that rightist dictatorships, through their repression of all political opposition and their reactionary social and economic policies, were creating an environment ripe for Communist exploitation.

As a result, the primary objective of United States inter-American policy became the fostering of concerted hemispheric action to prevent further Communist gains in Latin America. This policy had two dimensions. On the one hand, the need for immediate measures to contain the Cuban revolution and check subversion in Latin America was stressed. To this end the United States sought, over the bitter opposition of the major Latin American states, to transform the OAS into an anti-Communist alliance. On the other hand, in order to eliminate the underlying conditions that might facilitate the spread of Castro-Communism, the incoming Kennedy administration also decided to press actively for democracy and modernization in Latin America. This, in turn, required an effort to transform the OAS into an antidictatorial alliance: "The failure of the democratic process in any one of the member states is a matter of concern to the entire community . . . [requiring] possible collective measures . . . to assure all the peoples of the Americas, within their own boundaries, of their freedom."[8]

The new policy, first manifested in a changing United States attitude toward Trujillo in 1960 and in the establishment of the Alliance for Progress in 1961, still had political stability in Latin America as its *ultimate* objective, but it was based on the assumption that the preservation of the status quo was a chimerical as well as an unworthy goal and that the wisest course for the United States would be to help guide Latin American revolutionary forces into reasonably moderate, non-Communist channels. Thus, as the keystone to its anti-Communist strategy, the United States became a powerful force for Latin American change.

The main thrust of the Kennedy pro-democratic program was a long-range effort to restructure gradually and to modernize Latin American political, economic, and social institutions—the Alliance for Progress. In the more immediate future, the Kennedy administration sought to create political conditions in Latin America that would facilitate the work of the Alliance. This required resistance to military coups against constitutional regimes and the favoring of moderate social democratic governments, such as the Betancourt regime in Venezuela, over traditionalist oligarchies. The use of diplomatic recognition as an instrument of policy was revived. Non-recognition, or more precisely the "suspension of diplomatic relations," accompanied by the discontinuation of economic and military assistance, was employed against rightist governments in the Dominican Republic in 1961; Peru in 1962; and Haiti, Honduras, and the Dominican Republic again in 1963, with varying degrees of success.[9] In the Dominican Republic, moreover, far more powerful measures were taken; after the assassination of Trujillo in May, 1961, the United States employed a wide range of diplomatic, economic, and even military pressures to pave the way for the holding of free elections in December, 1962.

The unsuccessful United States effort to bring down the Duvalier regime in Haiti in the summer of 1963 marked the high point of United States leadership in the fight for democracy in Latin America. Beginning in the last few months of the Kennedy administration, but not reaching fruition until the Johnson administration, United States hemispheric policy entered its third postwar phase: a partial and modified return to the "stability-first" posture of the Truman-Eisenhower period.

Several factors were involved. To begin with, there had always been a considerable amount of skepticism in the United States government, especially among the career foreign service officers in the State Department, about what was considered to be the naïve idealism of the Kennedy administration. By the fall of 1963, Kennedy himself was becoming disillusioned, and the traditionalists apparently gained the upper hand, thanks to the failure of United States pressures against Duvalier and, even more importantly, to the progressive deterioration of the position of the Bosch government in the Dominican Republic, culminating in the September military coup. Kennedy did not like being identified with losing causes or quixotic ventures, and he had begun to suspect that his administration had overestimated United States leverage over Latin American political processes.[10]

Even more fundamentally, the administration had begun to revaluate Latin American militarism. Borrowing from a well-known academic school of thought, administration spokesmen began pointing to the "changing nature" of the military. No longer was the military invariably the bulwark of the old oligarchies, they argued. Increasingly recruited from lower-middle groups and even the working classes, Latin American officers were now much more representative of their societies than in the past; and far from invariably acting in a predatory and reactionary manner, they were becoming increasingly honest, efficient, and progressive in their exercise of political power.

Thus, in the last few months of the Kennedy administration, evidence of a retrenchment mounted. The Ecuadoran military coup of July, 1963, was greeted with only *pro forma* resistance (although in part because of the administration's evaluation that the Arosemena government had been corrupt and inept and that the coup was designed to hasten modernization, not to block it). The Dominican and Honduran military coups in late September and early October, 1963, were vigorously denounced, and diplomatic relations and economic assistance were suspended; but far more powerful weapons, such as the suspension of trade or even military pressures, were not utilized as they had been a year earlier in the Dominican Republic.

The reversion to more traditional policies was rapidly accelerated after the assassination of President Kennedy. On December 14, 1963, diplomatic relations with the Dominican and Honduran juntas were restored, and shortly afterward economic assistance was resumed, although both regimes had made it clear that they would do nothing to hasten a return to constitutional processes. Two weeks later Edwin Martin, who had been closely identified with the earlier pro-democratic policy, was replaced by Thomas Mann.

A few months later Mann was reported to have said that in the future the United States would avoid involvement in Latin American domestic political crises (as long, presumably, as "communism" was not involved) and would stop trying to distinguish between dictatorships and democratic regimes in conducting its foreign policies.[11] Although the report was denied, its plausibility has been subsequently confirmed by the enthusiastic United States response to the Brazilian military coup of 1964, the resumption of "correct," if not cordial, relations with Duvalier in Haiti, and the token United States response to the Bolivian military coup of November, 1964—a coup that overthrew a regime closely identified with the United States for over a decade and considered to be a model of Alliance for Progress rectitude.

Within the Alliance itself there has apparently been some change from the earlier United States emphasis on long-range projects designed to alter existing social and economic structures to a more traditional concern with short-range financial measures designed to *restore* stability and order. Significantly, within six months of Johnson-Mann rule, Teodoro Moscoso, one of the architects of the Alliance, had resigned as its United States chief. Shortly afterward he was publicly charging that the Johnson administration had forgotten the political meaning of the Latin American revolution.[12]

It is now clear that the United States for a number of reasons has returned to a modified version of its postwar policies in Latin America, and although it is improbable that the extreme right will be openly embraced, as under Eisenhower, it is equally improbable that under Johnson the United States will actively foster change, as it did in the early years of the Kennedy administration. Like the Kennedy administration in its last few weeks, the Johnson administration is generally pessimistic—or as it likes to think of itself, "realistic"—about the ability of the United States to influence constructively internal Latin American political processes. Again like the Kennedy administration, the Johnson administration professes to see a change in Latin American militarism: according to Mann, "The [Latin American] military establishments are demonstrating an ever greater degree of social consciousness and political responsibility."[13]

In some ways, however, the Johnson administration differs significantly from its predecessor. For one thing, at the highest levels of decision-making for Latin America, the non-professional Kennedy appointees are gone. Men like Arthur Schlesinger, Richard Goodwin, Teodoro Moscoso, and Arturo Morales-Carrion have been replaced by Foreign Service officers, exemplified by Mann himself. The Kennedy men were deeply committed to liberal democracy and, perhaps because of the academic background most of them shared, were predisposed toward long-range general plans and programs, even at the cost of short-run setbacks. The career men, on the other hand, tend to be cautious and anti-"idealistic," concerned with the immediate crisis and the short-run, ad hoc solution. It is not merely that most senior career men were recruited in a relatively conservative era and from generally conservative backgrounds. More importantly, the very nature of their function, the roles they must play, tends to establish a pattern of behavior that eschews "ideological" foreign policies in favor of the protection of United States "interests," that gives priority to getting along with existing governments rather than undermining them. In short, the Foreign Service, for both sociological and structural reasons, tends to favor stability.

Secondly, while both the Kennedy and the Johnson administrations were concerned first and foremost with the prevention of the spread of communism in Latin America, the Kennedy administration viewed the threat primarily as long-term in nature, to be met by long-term measures. The Johnson administration is far more preoccupied with the allegedly immediate dangers of Communist subversion, making co-operation with the "anti-Communists" of Latin America, any anti-Communists, often seem necessary (e.g., the Dominican Republic, 1965).[14]

It now seems clear that in the oas, the Johnson administration is giving anti-Communist action the highest priority, thereby undercutting the Kennedy administration's effort to establish a role for the OAS in the struggle against reaction and, more generally, in the process of political development in Latin America.[15] As will be argued later, this policy is detrimental to the real long-term interests of the United States and is a grave threat to the inter-American system itself.

1. For a full treatment of the theoretical problems involved here, see my pamphlet, *A Revaluation of Collective Security* (Columbus: Ohio State University Press, 1965), I, Pamphlet Series of the Social Science Program of the Mershon Center for Education in National Security.

2. For example, George Messersmith, James Bruce, Stanton Griffis, and Ellsworth Bunker in Perón's Argentina; Thomas Whelan in Somoza's Nicaragua; Fletcher Warren in Pérez Jiménez' Venezuela; Arthur Gardner and Earl T. Smith in Batista's Cuba; and others.

3. The best-known analyses of the Latin American military are Edwin Lieuwen, *Arms and Politics in Latin America* (New York: Frederick A. Praeger, 1961) and *Generals vs. Presidents* (New York: Frederick A. Praeger, 1964). For an analysis of the United States military assistance program, see Edgar S. Furniss, Jr., *Some Perspectives on Military Assistance* (Princeton: Center of International Studies, 1957).

4. U.S. House Committee on Foreign Affairs, *Mutual Security Program, Hearings*, 82d Cong., 1st sess., 1951, pp. 1080-81.

5. Cf. a similar analysis by John Dreier in *The Organization of American States and the Hemisphere Crisis* (New York: Council on Foreign Relations, 1962), pp. 75-76.

6. For details, see Chapter II, below.

7. See, for example, a major speech by Secretary of State Acheson, in the *Department of State Bulletin*, September 26, 1949, pp. 462-66.

8. Assistant Secretary of State for Inter-American Affairs Edwin Martin, *Department of State Bulletin*, May 6, 1963.

9. The Dominican and Haitian cases are dealt with in detail in Chapters V and VI. In the Peruvian situation, in July, 1962, the United States suspended diplomatic relations and economic and military assistance to a military junta that had refused to allow a democratically elected government headed by the moderately leftist APRA party to take office. Under United States pressures the junta in the ensuing weeks agreed to respect civil liberties and to hold free elections in less than a year. In view of this promise and the apparent apathy of the Peruvian public to the coup, the United States soon resumed normal diplomatic and economic relations. The junta did in fact rule with moderation, and elections were held on schedule in June, 1963.

10. The comments on President Kennedy's attitudes during this period are based on several interviews with important State Department officials.

11. *New York Times,* March 19, 1964.

12. *New York Times,* February 18, 1965.

13. *Department of State Bulletin,* June 1, 1964, p. 858.

14. The differences between the Kennedy and the Johnson administrations with regard to the immediacy of the Communist threat in Latin America should not be overstated. The Kennedy administration was concerned enough to accept without much fuss the Argentine military coup of 1962 and the Ecuadoran and Guatemalan military coups of 1963, all considered to have forestalled a danger from the extreme left. Moreover, through its military assistance program, the Kennedy administration sought to strengthen the capabilities of the Latin American armed forces for the maintenance of "internal order." Since the Latin American armed forces historically have been prone to resist the very forces the Alliance for Progress was designed to encourage, the administration's long-term objectives collided with what were thought to be short-term exigencies. Still, it is clear that the Kennedy administration was considerably less preoccupied with the "subversion" danger than the Johnson administration and therefore felt considerably freer to oppose the extreme right as well as the extreme left.

15. By early 1966, there were some indications that the Johnson administration was revaluating its initial Latin American policies. Mann had been removed from direct responsibility for Latin American affairs, and there was evidence of a more liberal United States policy in the Dominican Republic. It was too soon to evaluate the over-all significance of these developments, however.

CHAPTER **1**

The United States and the

Development of the Inter-American System

THE INTER-AMERICAN SYSTEM has been in existence since 1824, when a number of the newly independent Latin American states met to discuss ways of protecting themselves against the revival of Spanish imperialism. Since its inception, the primary purpose of the inter-American system in Latin American eyes has been to protect the "sovereignty" of each state against external threats, whether from Europe, from the United States, or from within Latin America itself. During the nineteenth century, because of both their need for, and their fear of, the "Colossus of the North," the Latin Americans sought

United States participation in non-aggression, peaceful settlement, and mutual defense agreements. Neither the fears nor the potential benefits were reciprocal, however, and the United States refused to make any binding political or military commitments. Although the primary Latin American objective—the exclusion of European political influences from the Western Hemisphere—was clearly consistent with United States objectives as enunciated in the Monroe Doctrine, the European threat was not considered serious enough to warrant restrictions on the independence of United States policy. Thus, because the movement toward inter-American political co-operation in the nineteenth century did not for all practical purposes include the United States, the system remained largely ineffective.

During the early years of the twentieth century, the Latin Americans lost interest in building effective political machinery. With the central institution of the system, the Pan American Union, located in Washington, financed mainly by the State Department and almost always under United States leadership, it was feared that an inter-American system with political functions would merely institutionalize and legitimate North American domination of the hemisphere. At the same time, the United States for entirely different reasons continued its opposition to politicizing the system: in the era of United States imperialism in the Caribbean and Central America, it was feared that an effective organization might develop the capability of inhibiting United States unilateralism. Thus, ironically, there was general agreement on a 1928 resolution explicitly denying political functions to the Pan American Union.[1] Prohibited from dealing with the real problems in hemispheric relations, the inter-American system after a century had little to show but unratified treaties, verbose resolutions, and a million dollar palace in Washington whose primary function was to serve as a clearing house for commercial information, or, more unkindly, as "mailbox and dues collector."[2]

Beginning in 1933, a meaningful political role for the inter-American system gradually developed. Under Franklin Roosevelt's Good Neighbor Policy, amicable relations with Latin America became the keystone of United States foreign policy, and to this end the United States liquidated the remaining vestiges of its imperialistic ventures in Latin America and formally agreed to refrain from intervening in the domestic political affairs of its southern neighbors. A few years later, the development of the Nazi threat and later World War II itself gave urgency to the policy of inter-American co-operation. As a result, during the late 1930's and early 1940's the hemispheric states agreed to a series of co-operative efforts, including formal procedures for hemispheric consultation in the face of external threats, more vigorous efforts to solve inter-American conflicts, and multilateral policies for the co-ordination of hemispheric defense and the fight against subversion in Latin America.

All of this had proved possible because Latin American and United States objectives had become compatible. Although in United States strategy the object of the inter-American system was not the preservation of national sovereignty per se, but the maintenance of hemispheric stability, stability as well as sovereignty required the prevention of external threats to existing governments in Latin America and a general insulation of the hemisphere from external political influences. Throughout the nineteenth century and the first part of the twentieth, the United States had believed it could attain its objectives unilaterally, through the proclamation and enforcement, when necessary, of the Monroe Doctrine. But the magnitude of the Nazi threat and the subsequent development of the cold war convinced United States policy-makers that for both strategic and ideological reasons multilateral co-operation in the insulation of the hemisphere was essential.

The Major Principles of the Inter-American System

Throughout the first century and a quarter of its existence, the inter-American system had been based on a series of *ad hoc* resolutions and a number of overlapping, sometimes contradictory, and largely unratified treaties, with no central organization other than the primarily administrative Pan American Union. In 1945, as part of the strategy of preserving the regional system against the threat of its incorporation into the United Nations, the hemispheric foreign ministers agreed to draw together the historically developed political principles and operating procedures into a formal organization.

The four major principles or political ideals incorporated into the Inter-American Treaty of Reciprocal Assistance (Rio Treaty) of 1947 and the OAS Charter signed at Bogotá in 1948 were mutual non-intervention of hemispheric states in one another's domestic affairs; the "juridical equality" of all states; containment of intrahemispheric conflict—by peaceful settlement procedures if possible, by active collective measures if necessary; and the common defense of all hemispheric states against external aggression.

These principles reflected a still unresolved tension in Latin American attitudes toward the inter-American system, the tension between international co-operation and national sovereignty. On the one hand, the purpose of the system was to protect national sovereignties, but on the other, since the Latin Americans did not have confidence in their ability to do this acting independently, a certain amount of collective action (of necessity involving the subordination of national independence of action to an international decision-making body) was essential. The first two principles emphasized sovereignty, the last two co-operation; in practice they have often directly clashed.

For the Latin Americans, non-intervention has been the key principle of the inter-American system since its inception, for in its emphasis on independent state action it is well suited to the maintenance of sovereignty. At Bogotá, the Latin Americans succeeded in writing into the oas Charter the most sweeping prohibition of intervention ever included in an international treaty (Article 15):

> No State or group of States has the right to intervene, directly or indirectly, for any reason whatever, in the internal or external affairs of any other State. The foregoing principle prohibits not only armed force but also any other form of interference or attempted threat against the personality of the State or against its political, economic, and cultural elements.

If that was not clear enough, Article 16 added:

> No State may use or encourage the use of coercive measures of an economic or political character in order to force the sovereign will of another State and obtain from it advantages of any kind.

Although the hemispheric states had agreed at the Buenos Aires Conference of 1936 to prohibit the "intervention of any [American state] . . . directly or indirectly, and for whatever reason, in the internal or external affairs of any other of the Parties,"[3] Article 15 went even further, for it proscribed collective as well as unilateral intervention, thus excluding the OAS itself from involvement in the domestic or even the foreign policies of the member states, except in the case of aggression.[4] (Article 19 of the Charter provided that measures adopted for the maintenance of peace and security under the Rio Treaty would not constitute intervention.)

The meaning of "intervention," especially "indirect intervention," is quite vague, of course, and it has been convenient for the Latin Americans to keep it so. Almost any action by one state that affects the affairs of another—foreign aid, tariff policies, diplomatic representation, public statements—can be, and has been, considered intervention. Even non-actions can have interventionist effects, as in the failure to recognize new governments or to engage in favorable trade relations. Taken on their face, then, Articles 15 and 16 were obviously non-operational; they would prohibit not merely intervention in the normal sense—the direct use of power to obtain national advantages—but *influence* as well. In fact, they would prohibit the exercise of foreign policy itself, particularly by the United States, which has the greatest capabilities to influence the affairs of other states, intentionally or even unintentionally, by the exercise of its tremendous political, economic, and military power. But it is clear that the significance of these Articles lay not merely in these attempted proscriptions of future state behavior, but in their reflection of continuing Latin American distrust of the United States and unwillingness to engage in co-operative political action beyond that required to maintain international peace.[5]

Although there could be no mistaking the main target of the non-intervention clauses, the United States did not object to Articles 15 and 16 at Bogotá. Roosevelt had been willing to forego not only military intervention but the direct use of economic and political power in Latin America precisely because one of his major objectives had been the allaying of Latin American fear and distrust of the United States. Although the United States departed briefly from this principle during World War II to bring pressure on Argentina and Chile to co-operate in the hemispheric war effort, after the war, as will be shown, non-intervention again became compatible with—indeed, ideally suited to—United States objectives. But as the Argentine and Chilean affairs suggested, and the development of a Communist threat in Latin America would conclusively demonstrate, non-intervention would remain the rule in inter-American relations only as long as it was compatible with United States as well as Latin American purposes.

Juridical equality is, like non-intervention, an expression of sovereignty. It is institutionalized in the formal voting procedures of the system, which have always been based on the principle of one vote per state. As the former Secretary-General of the OAS put it,

> One of the sources of power of our Organization is the fact that all the member states are one another's peers; they have equal rights and identical obligations. In its assembly halls the foremost power of our times has but one vote, exactly like the vote cast by some of the poorest and weakest countries in the world.[6]

It is obvious, of course, that in many respects juridical equality is a myth, although a highly useful one insofar as it helps hold the system together. Regardless of the formal voting method, there is no equality in the decision-making processes of the organization: the votes of the United States and the major Latin American states clearly have more significance than those of the smaller states, for few collective measures could be taken without major power support. Moreover, the United States can almost always muster the seven or eight votes it needs to block unwanted OAS action.[7] There has not been a single important vote in which a majority of the Central American and Caribbean states, so closely tied both politically and economically to Washington, has broken with the United States.

The principle of juridical equality is not *merely* a myth, though, for it is the basis of the unanimity tradition, which reigned supreme until the Rio Treaty established that collective action could be taken by a two-thirds majority, and even thereafter continued to have considerable importance. Although the tradition has been severely strained by the recent willingness of the United States to accept only a bare two-thirds majority for OAS support of its anti-Communist policies, most OAS decisions are still the outcomes of painstakingly constructed compromises in which, to avoid open splits, strong efforts are made to accommodate even the weakest and smallest states, and issues are rarely pushed to a vote before consensus is attained. Moreover, as in the United Nations, most OAS decisions are not mandatory but are put in the form of "requests" or "recommendations" to the members, leaving dissenting states free to ignore them, as, for example, a number of states have ignored recommendations for antisubversion measures.

Still another effect of the unanimity principle is to force decisions to be based on the lowest common denominator of agreement, even when the resulting consensus will not support significant action. The United States, for example, has often watered down its demands for collective action against Cuba in efforts to gain the largest possible majority, even when it had the votes for much stronger action.[8]

Peaceful settlement of hemispheric disputes has been an important principle of the inter-American system since the early nineteenth century, although the actual results have been mixed. By the end of the nineteenth century, most of the American states had formally agreed to refrain from the use of force in settling their conflicts, and in the first part of the twentieth century this principle was incorporated into a series of treaties providing for a variety of conciliation, mediation, adjudication, and arbitration services.

Despite some successes in settling a number of minor disputes, the failure of the inter-American peace structure to settle the Chaco dispute in the 1920's and 30's and the long delay in resolving the Letician boundary dispute between Peru and Colombia demonstrated that more adequate institutions were required. At the Mexico City Conference of 1945 the foreign ministers directed the Juridical Committee of the Pan American Union to reorganize the system and incorporate its main features into a single treaty. The resulting 1948 "Pact of Bogotá," however, was to founder on the issue of compulsory arbitration. The original draft of the treaty provided only for binding arbitration of *legal* disputes. In this form, the treaty had the support of most hemispheric states (including the United States, which in keeping with its general predilection for unilateralism had heretofore remained generally aloof from the peace system), for states wishing to avoid arbitration could always claim that disputes were "political" rather than "legal." To close this loophole, a group of Latin American states led by Mexico insisted on more stringent procedures, and a new version of the draft treaty provided that *all* controversies were to be arbitrated when other methods failed. It was in this latter form that the pact was approved, but it was a

Pyrrhic victory for the Mexican group, since seven states, including the United States, signed with reservations that vitiated the compulsory settlement procedures. Furthermore, only ten states subsequently ratified the pact, all of them except Mexico among the smallest and least powerful hemispheric nations.[9] Thus the Pact has been a dead letter from the start and has played practically no role in inter-American political disputes. Instead, as will be discussed below, the Inter-American Peace Committee and the Council itself have emerged as the primary organs for peaceful settlement.[10]

The establishment of a formal system of collective security at Rio in 1947 was the logical outcome of the gradual politicization of the inter-American system, given impetus and urgency by World War II and the formation of the United Nations. Although as early as 1847 a number of the Latin American states had formally agreed to come to one another's assistance in the event of foreign attack, it was not until 1936 that the United States agreed that "every act susceptible to disturbing the peace of America affects each and every American State."[11] This principle was reaffirmed in more precise and forceful terms during the war, although no multilateral procedures for its implementation, beyond the agreement to consult, were established.

As the end of the war approached and negotiations for a postwar international organization progressed, the American states were faced with the question of whether they should go beyond their wartime arrangements and create a permanent system capable of dealing with hemispheric political problems, or whether the inter-American system should be "integrated" into a universal system of collective security that would hopefully be created within the structure of the United Nations. Members of the Roosevelt administration were known to be divided on this question,[12] but by 1944 the balance seemed to have swung toward universalism. At the Big Four Conference at Dumbarton Oaks, the United States agreed that the proposed UN Security Council should have the major responsibility in matters pertaining to international peace and security, utilizing regional arrangements where appropriate but prohibiting enforcement action without the Council's prior authorization.[13]

The publication of the Dumbarton Oaks proposals alarmed the Latin Americans, most of whom favored an autonomous regional system. Thanks to the Good Neighbor Policy the governments of Latin America, most of them conservative and representative of the traditional elites, now feared the Soviet Union and the spread of Communist ideology more than United States interventionism, and were determined to insulate hemispheric political matters from external influences as much as possible. Along with influential members of the United States Senate, the Latin Americans were finally able to induce a somewhat reluctant State Department to meet at Chapultepec (Mexico City) in early 1945, just before the San Francisco Conference on the United Nations.[14]

It was clear from the Dumbarton Oaks proposals that the key feature of the UN would be a universal system of collective security. If, then, the inter-American system was to be saved and non-hemispheric states kept out of local conflicts, an effective hemispheric collective security system was essential. The Act of Chapultepec was in fact a long step toward the creation of such a system. The key clause stated,

> every attack of a State against the integrity or the inviolability of the territory, or against the sovereignty or political

independence of an American State, shall . . . be considered
an act of aggression against the other states. . . .[15]

However, the Act fell short of a true collective security
system, for although it provided that in the event of
aggression the member states would consult on the measures to be taken, it was silent on the specific procedures
by which the aggressor would be identified and the sanctions applied. Furthermore, the Act was to remain in
effect only for the duration of the war, after which a new
conference would be held to consider the establishment
of permanent procedures.

The issue of the future relationship of the inter-American system to the UN had not really been settled at
Mexico City, for at San Francisco the Latin Americans
had to fight to retain hemispheric autonomy against continued resistance by some high State Department officials
who still favored the merging of the system into the UN.[16]
It is generally agreed that the pressures of the Latin
Americans, enthusiastically supported by Senator Vandenberg of the United States delegation, were primarily responsible for the inclusion of Articles 51 and 52 in the UN
Charter, the loopholes under which the existence of regional collective security systems was supposedly made
compatible with UN responsibility for international peace.
Article 51 provided that "Nothing in the present Charter
shall impair the inherent right of individual or collective
self-defense if an armed attack occurs against a Member
of the United Nations." Article 52 specified that regional
organizations, where they exist, should have primary responsibility for pacific settlement of local disputes before they are referred to the Security Council.

On the other hand, Article 53 of the Charter specified
that "no enforcement action shall be taken under regional

arrangements or by regional agencies without the authorization of the Security Council." This would seem to indicate that only outright armed attack would justify collective resistance without prior authorization of the Security Council and that regional agencies could not independently impose economic, political, or military sanctions against forms of aggression other than armed attack.

Articles 51-53 of the Charter represented a compromise between the regionalists and the universalists, a compromise designed not to retain security functions for regional systems but to locate ultimate responsibility for international peace in the United Nations. Almost immediately, however, the compromise collapsed. The 1947 Rio Treaty completed the victory for the Latin American states and for the advocates of regionalism over universalism within the United States government. Article 3 of the Rio Treaty, which authorized collective resistance to an *armed attack* against any American state, was clearly consistent with Article 51 of the UN Charter. However, Article 6, dealing with aggression or threats *other* than direct attack could not be meshed with the Charter, for it provided that the oas would meet *immediately* to determine collective measures, making no reference to the provisions of Article 53 of the Charter. In view of the silence of Article 6 on the necessity for prior Security Council authorization,[17] Article 10 of the Rio Treaty, which specified that "none of the provisions of the Treaty should be construed as impairing the rights and obligations of the High Contracting Parties under the Charter of the United Nations," had very little significance. Article 6 obviously *did* impair the obligations of the American states to the UN, unless one accepts the recent rather strained oas "interpretation" that measures short of armed force do not constitute enforcement action within the meaning of Article 53.[18]

The course of international politics since the San Francisco and Rio conferences has insured the continued subordination of universalism to regionalism. The fear that the Soviet Union would use its veto in the Security Council to disrupt regional action has strengthened the determination of the American states to keep hemispheric problems out of the UN. The United States has used its influence, and if necessary could have used its *own* veto, to prevent the Security Council from actively intervening in the Guatemalan, Cuban, and Dominican cases. With both the United States and the Soviet Union subordinating the collective security functions of the UN to cold war exigencies, the OAS for all practical purposes has become completely autonomous.[19]

The Institutionalization of Collective Security

The establishment of a formal and enforceable collective security system at Rio in 1947 culminated the process that had begun with the nineteenth-century efforts of some Latin American states to band together in self-de-defense, had gained real momentum in the 1930's when the United States made multilateral co-operation the basis of its inter-American policy, and had been given the promise of permanence with the acceptance of the principles of collective security at Mexico City. Collective security had proved to be compatible with both United States and Latin American national objectives. It was well-suited to the maintenance of stability, for in its external manifestations collective security sought to insure a common front against any non-hemispheric aggressor and, more generally, the insulation of the hemisphere from outside political and military influences, while internally it would help preserve the political status quo by preventing armed attacks or subversion aimed at altering the internal political structures of the member states. It might have been possible for the United States to impose a Pax Americana on the hemisphere by unilateral action, but experience had convinced Washington that the preservation of stability by multilateral methods was more economical, more reliable, and more consistent with professed American values.

From the Latin American perspective, the primary effect of collective security would be to protect the independence of the member states. That the Latin Americans were willing to join with the United States in a system that would be inevitably dominated by that country indicated that they now felt the primary threats to their sovereignties were from the Soviet Union or from expansionist Latin American states, rather than from the north. In any event, the United States could dominate the hemisphere if it so chose with or without the inter-American system, while its solemn commitment to the system gave the Latin Americans at least some leverage over United States policies and some assurance of United States restraint.

Despite the Mexico City agreements, there was still some opposition at Rio to creating a true collective security system, and there were several proposals that, in effect, would have transformed the system into some form of alliance. Most of these proposals went to the crucial issue of the inclusiveness of the treaty. At whom should it be aimed—at *any* aggressor, as collective security required, or at Communist states, dictatorships, or simply non-hemispheric states, in which case the system would be an alliance?[20]

A major battle was fought over an Argentine proposal, initially supported by Venezuela and Peru, that would have reserved the use of actual force for non-hemispheric aggressors, leaving intrahemispheric conflict to be dealt with solely by peaceful means.[21] Argentina was undoubtedly motivated by its traditional resistance to a strong inter-American system dominated by the United States, and perhaps by expansionist plans of its own, rather than by a positive preference for an alliance instead of a collective security system. In any event, its proposal had little support. The Latin American states wanted a true collective security system, many of them precisely because they feared Argentine aggression and wanted the protection of the United States. The United States also opposed any distinction between inter- and intrahemispheric aggression, explicitly arguing that such a distinction would make the pact "appear" as an alliance directed against the rest of the world, which in the context of the times would primarily mean the Soviet Union.[22]

In the interest of unanimity, the conflict was resolved by a compromise, but one that was so much closer to the United States (and the majority) position that it amounted to little more than a face-saving device for Argentina. After Article 3 of the Treaty stated flatly that "an armed attack by *any* state shall be considered as an attack against all the American states" (emphasis added), the first part of Article 7 provided that in the event of conflict between American states, the other members would attempt to resolve it by peaceful means. The Article added, however, that such attempts would not "prejudice . . . the right of self-defense," and concluded with a warning that "the rejection of the pacifying action will be considered in the determination of the aggressor and in application of the measures which the consultative meeting may agree upon," clearly implying that if attempts at peaceful settlement should fail, sanctions would be applied, just as they would against non-hemispheric aggressors.[23]

A related problem dealt with the question of whether the pact should apply to attacks on overseas bases or territories of the member states as well as to attacks or threats directed at the Western Hemisphere proper. The United States initially argued for overseas coverage, but a number of Latin American states, led by Mexico and Argentina, wanted a more restrictive formula. The resulting compromise, reluctantly accepted by the United States delegation at the behest of Senator Vandenberg,[24] retained the principle of overseas coverage but was actually closer to the Mexican and Argentine positions. Article 3 of the Rio Treaty provided that an armed attack inside the hemisphere obligated all states to come immediately to the assistance of the victim, whereas an outside attack required in the first instance only consultation.

The official rationale for the distinction was that in an overseas attack the threat would be less clear and less urgent.[25] What was really at stake, however, was the reluctance of the Latin Americans to be automatically drawn into a European or Asian conflict involving United States troops. In one sense, the unwillingness of the Latin Americans to tie themselves too closely to United States security efforts overseas was a failure to accept the full implications of collective security under conditions of modern warfare. More plausibly, though, the distinction helped *preserve* the collective security features of the treaty. United States troops and bases overseas were, after all, not there to enforce collective security against *any* aggression, but were explicitly designed to contain Soviet expansionism and were therefore a part of the anti-Communist alliance of Western nations that was soon to become institutionalized in NATO.

Another important issue at the conference was the question of whether the inter-American system should act as an antidictatorial alliance. Guatemala, Uruguay, and Venezuela proposed that the treaty provide that "violations of the essential rights of man or the departure from the democratic system shall require joint and solidary action."[26] They found little support. The United States was opposed, ostensibly on the grounds that since the purpose of the conference was to conclude a treaty as soon as possible, controversial issues ought to be left for later conferences.[27] As has already been pointed out, however, the United States had decided that hemispheric stability required support for all existing governments, and this undoubtedly was a far more important consideration. The antidictatorship proposals were rejected in committee by a show of hands,[28] undoubtedly to spare the delegates the embarrassment of having their opposition to a pro-democratic proposal officially recorded.

Thus, the framers of the Rio Treaty rejected proposals that in effect would have created an anti-Communist or antidictatorial alliance. They did, however, leave the door open for a *later* transformation of the OAS into an alliance. The manner in which aggression is defined in a collective security system is crucial, for it determines the circumstances under which the system will be activated; yet regardless of what definition is chosen, an essentially irresolvable dilemma is created. If the definition is precise, certain types of international actions that are aggressive in intent and effect (such as subversion and political infiltration) may be excluded; on the other hand, a vague and general definition lends itself to short-run political uses.

The United States argued for a very general definition at Rio, proposing that aggression be defined merely as "every attack of a State against the integrity or the inviolability of the territory, or against the sovereignty or political independence of an American State."[29] The conference adopted an only slightly more restrictive compromise: Article 9 specifies that *armed* attack by one state "against the territory, the people, or the land, sea or air forces of another state" constitutes aggression. The same Article also, however, authorizes the Organ of Consultation to characterize "other acts" as aggression as well. Moreover, Article 6 of the treaty, dealing with aggression other than armed attack, is even more flexible, authorizing collective action in the event of any "fact or situation" that affects "the inviolability or the integrity of the territory or the sovereignty or political independence of any American State." Aggression, then, in effect, is defined as whatever a two-thirds majority of the American states choose at any given time to so characterize.

The vagueness of Articles 6 and 9 enabled the OAS to later use the Rio Treaty to legitimate action that was essentially anti-Communist or antidictatorial in nature, rather than merely antiaggression.[30]) There is little doubt that the United States negotiators at Rio had in mind the possibility that the inter-American system might later want to characterize subversion as a form of aggression, as was indicated by the State Department's comment that advance definition of aggression was undesirable "at a time when the forms of aggression are less foreseeable than ever."[31] There was no inherent conflict between the United States position and the requirements of collective security though, for it certainly can be plausibly argued that subversion is indeed a real form of aggression. Moreover, the United States insistence on treating internal and external aggression alike, and its refusal to engage in anti-Communist oratory or go along with the proposal of some states that the Communist issue be placed on the agenda,[32] indicated that Washington was not yet resigned to the cold war and wished to avoid turning the inter-American system into an anti-Communist alliance.

Nor were the majority of Latin American states interested in an anti-Communist alliance. In their eyes anti-Communist provisions would open the door to collective action based solely on the internal political structures of hemispheric states, directly countering the principle of non-intervenion; in particular, the relatively democratic states undoubtedly feared that action might be taken against progressive governments under the pretense of fighting communism.

Neither the United States nor most Latin American states wanted an antidictatorial alliance. The requirements of both hemispheric stability and the protection of sovereignty dictated the preservation of the status quo. Moreover, at least half the states represented at Rio were themselves more or less dictatorial and could hardly concur in measures aimed at their continued existence.

Thus, despite the loopholes left by Articles 6 and 9, the Rio Conference attempted to create a true collective security system; collective action would be taken to defend any hemispheric state, regardless of its ideological predisposition or internal political structure, against the aggressive action of any state, regardless of its geographical location. In a hemisphere divided between the left and the right, between dictatorships and democracies, collective security represented the lowest common denominator of mutual interest—the maintenance of the existing system.

The Political Evolution of the OAS, 1948–1964

The final step in the institutionalization of the inter-American system was the agreement on the OAS Charter at Bogotá in 1948. Some Pan Americanists in Latin America and the United States had hoped that the Bogotá Conference would create a true hemispheric community with a high degree of political, economic, and social content, but the foreign ministers, as at Rio, chose the far less ambitious aim of building a security system with capabilities for political action limited to the minimum required for the keeping of the peace. This was hardly surprising, given the continuing strength of Latin American nationalism; the desire of the United States to avoid large-scale commitments of economic aid to Latin America and to retain as free a hand as possible in formulating and executing its foreign policies; and the wide divergence between the United States and Latin America and among the Latin American states themselves in foreign policy objectives, military capabilities, internal political structures, and economic and social systems.

Since 1948, the extent to which the OAS should become involved in hemispheric political conflicts has remained a highly controversial issue, reflecting the continuing conflict between the principles of national sovereignty and interstate collaboration. With some important qualifications (to be discussed below), the minimalists have generally held the balance of power, at least in the sense that the OAS today still has no important mechanisms for centralized suprastatal decision-making, such as the European Economic Community or perhaps even the UN Secretariat under Hammarskjöld. All important decisions are made by the member states, responsible solely to their own interests and constituencies.

Over the years the United States has cautiously pressed for a broader political role for the OAS, primarily because of its own enormous influence in OAS decision-making processes. The general United States position has been that questions of OAS "jurisdiction" over political matters should be left flexible and treated as political rather than legal questions, to be decided according to the circumstances of each case and not on the basis of predefined rigid limitations.

On the other hand, the United States has not supported occasional Latin American proposals that would involve a *vastly* expanded OAS role in hemispheric political affairs. Not only might such an organization seriously constrain United States freedom of action on the international scene, it might even raise embarrassing questions about United States domestic policies, e.g., civil rights. In short, the United States would like to see some expansion of OAS political activities, but not too much.

Latin American views of the political scope of the OAS have been conditioned primarily by expectations of what action the Organization would take in specific situations. Several cautious generalizations are possible, however. First, the Latin American states as a whole have usually insisted on a more limited role for the OAS than has the United States. Secondly, however, the Latin American democracies, usually excepting Chile and recently Uruguay, have tended to favor a more liberal interpretation of OAS powers than have the dictatorships (and some times even the United States), particularly in recent years when the Organization has indicated some signs of a willingness to foster changes in the hemispheric status quo. (The Cuban case, however, especially until about 1962, was an exception to even this rule; for here the dictatorships argued for a flexible interpretation of OAS powers, and the democracies rediscovered that non-intervention was the cornerstone of the inter-American system.) Finally, and most importantly, the Latin Americans have allowed the OAS, through a series of incremental, *ad hoc,* and usually reluctant reactions to pressing problems, to play a generally increasing role in hemispheric affairs.

The Major Political Organs of the OAS

The Council, consisting of representatives of each of the member states, has become the major political institution of the OAS. This has been a relatively recent development for during most of its history the Council, or as it was formerly called, the Governing Board of the Pan American Union, was almost exclusively an administrative body.[33] The confinement of the Board to light housekeeping chores reflected the insistence of the Latin Americans on keeping the inter-American system out of hemispheric politics and, more specifically, their feeling that the Board was under the thumb of the State Department.[34]

At the end of World War II, as a result of the expansion of inter-American collaboratory activities and the effect of the Good Neighbor Policy in dispelling Latin American distrust of the United States, the Board was temporarily granted the sweeping political authority to take action "on every matter that affects the effective functioning of the inter-American system and the solidarity and general welfare of the American Republics."[35] By the time the Bogotá Conference convened, however, Latin American attitudes had changed, in part because of a resurgence of traditional hostility to supranationalism, in part because of renewed fear of the United States (stemming from the State Department's pressures on Perón's Argentina). The emphasis at Mexico City had been positive—on creating effective international machinery; at Bogotá, it was negative—on insuring that the machinery was not so powerful as to constitute a threat to the national units.

Prior to the Bogotá Conference, the Pan American Union

secretariat had prepared a draft Charter that would have retained for the Council the political authority invested at Mexico City in the Governing Board. Argentina and Chile led the opposition to the draft, arguing that a Council with political functions would turn the OAS into a "superstate."[36] In an effort to preserve a significant role for the Council without precipitating a major hemispheric split, the United States took a middle position, proposing that the Council be given the authority to

> take cognizance, within the limits of the present Charter and of inter-American treaties and agreements, of any matter referred to it by the Inter-American Conference or the Meeting of Consultation of Ministers of Foreign Affairs.[37]

This compromise proved acceptable and was embodied in the Charter as Article 50. Although the broad authority granted at Mexico was rescinded, the Council would retain the authority invested in it at Rio to act as provisional Organ of Consultation. More importantly, the door was left open for a future *ad hoc* role in hemispheric political affairs.

As has been indicated, since 1948 the Council in fact has developed into a politically significant body in response to the exigencies of hemispheric conflict. The major vehicle for the expansion of its activities has been the Rio Treaty, especially Articles 6 and 12. Article 12 grants to the Council the authority to act "provisionally" as the treaty's Organ of Consultation until a meeting of foreign ministers can be convoked. Although initially intended merely to insure immediate hemispheric action in the event of aggression, this provision has usually been "interpreted" as allowing the Council to function *indefinitely* during Rio Treaty action, thus avoiding the nuisance and possible political dangers of the full-scale conference.

Article 6, it will be recalled, provides for collective action in the event of a violation of the "integrity, sovereignty, or political independence" of any American state, or in the event of "any other fact or situation that might endanger the peace of America." Thanks to the vagueness of this language, the Council can, if it wishes, assume jurisdiction over "any matter which may affect the functioning and purposes of the Inter-American System," the mandate granted to it at Mexico City but rescinded at Bogotá. Article 6, however, leaves the Council much more latitude, for its language can be interpreted broadly or narrowly, depending on the political objectives of the majority in each situation.

To preserve this flexibility, a majority of the OAS members have consistently rejected attempts to formally broaden the Council's authority. For example, at the Caracas Conference of 1954 an overwhelming majority opposed a Colombian proposal to restore to the Council the jurisdiction given to it at Mexico City.[38] Later, in 1959, the United States found no response when it suggested that the Council's authority be expanded to fill the "important gap. . . in the powers of the OAS" created by the inability of the Council to take political action without invoking the Rio Treaty.[39]

Despite the continuing official restrictions, though, the Council has played a number of important roles in hemispheric political affairs. First of all, it has facilitated and stimulated consulation among the hemispheric states. The rhetoric of non-intervention notwithstanding, there is a general expectation that almost all interstate political conflicts will be at least discussed and usually mediated by the Council, if not always formally in public meetings then informally through normal diplomatic channels.

Officially, the major forum for inter-American decision-making is the full-scale "Inter-American Conference" or the "Meeting of Consultation of Ministers of Foreign Affairs." In practice, the Council has assumed this role, for if political matters could be dealt with only by the twenty-one foreign ministers, most of them could not be dealt with at all. Foreign ministers' meetings are expensive, inconvenient and time-consuming, making them practicable only for the most serious matters. By contrast, the Council is in effect in permanent session. It meets regularly twice a month, except during the summer, and since all countries maintain year-round representation in Washington, it can without difficulty be called into special session at the request of any member.

Council diplomacy has other advantages over conference diplomacy. The relative informality and lack of publicity surrounding most Council meetings result in the traditional by-products of "quiet diplomacy." The delegates see each other almost daily, developing personal friendships and smooth working relations that often pay off in a surprising degree of unofficial flexibility, within the sometimes vague limits set by national political positions. Most Council matters are worked out in off-the-record committee meetings or in even more informal diplomatic negotiations, public meetings generally being held only to ratify and formalize agreements reached in private. As a result, the pressure to take rigid stands aimed at pleasing domestic and usually nationalistic groups is reduced. In short, the atmosphere is far more conducive to conciliation, mediation, and compromise than that prevailing in gatherings of the foreign ministers.[40]

Second, the Council has served as an investigatory body. When political disputes have been brought before the Council, a small subcommittee normally will go to the scene of the conflict to obtain accurate information and locate responsibilities amid the welter of conflicting charges and countercharges, as in the Costa Rica–Nicaragua conflicts of 1948 and 1955, the Haitian–Dominican conflicts of 1950 and 1963, and others.

Third, in a number of ways the Council has helped prevent potential or existing conflicts from developing into actual armed hostilities. The Investigating Committee has served not only to bring out the facts but also to deter actual fighting and provide a cooling-off period during which bilateral negotiations have proceeded, as in the Ecuador-Peru border dispute in 1955, the Caribbean conflicts of 1959, and the United States–Panama dispute of 1964.

A related function of the Council has been to delay or bury issues that were not at the time susceptible of actual settlement. In this capacity, the Council plays a role analogous to an interagency committee in a pluralistic political system. By creating the impression that something is being done, the Council helps to reduce domestic pressures on harassed governments and spread the responsibility for unpopular actions or non-actions. This has been a very important function of the Council in the Cuban problem since the missile crisis. The endless round of Council meetings and the spate of largely meaningless and unenforced reports and resolutions on antisubversive and other measures, ostensibly designed to increase pressure on the Cuban government, have really served to obfuscate the unwillingness of the United States to take the drastic action that would be necessary to overthrow Castro.

Fourth, the Council has been able to obtain and enforce ceasefires in a number of conflicts in which armed hostilities have already begun, as in both Costa Rica–Nicaragua conflicts, both Haitian–Dominican conflicts, the Honduras–Nicaragua border clashes, and the Caribbean exile invasions of 1959. Sometimes this was accomplished merely by the "presence" at the scene of the conflict of the Investigating Committee. On other occasions more active measures were necessary— the establishment of an OAS land, sea, or air patrol, the authorization of armed assistance to the potential or actual victim of aggression, or the implicit or explicit threat of more massive collective economic or military sanctions.

Fifth, once peace has been restored, the Council has normally played an active role in the conciliation or mediation of disputes. The usual procedure is for negotiations between the disputants to be conducted with the assistance of the "Investigating" Committee. Moreover, in some cases the Council has gone beyond mediation to act in effect as arbitrator and specify the terms of settlement, as in the Costa Rica–Nicaragua cases, the Haitian–Dominican case of 1950, and especially in the 1961 settlement of the Honduras–Nicaragua territorial dispute.

Finally, the Council has often played an important post-dispute role by observing the fulfilment of the terms of the settlement and, if necessary, enforcing them. For example, in disputes involving illegal border crossings (Costa Rica–Nicaragua and Honduras–Nicaragua) a Council commission remained on the scene for some time after the cessation of hostilities to patrol the border and insure the compliance of both sides with specified measures designed to avert renewed conflict.

Second to the Council in political importance is the Inter-American Peace Committee. Officially created by the Havana Conference of 1940, the Peace Committee did not actually begin functioning until 1948. It consists of five states elected by the Council for five year terms; a rotational principle was established in 1956 when the Committee statutes were modified to provide that no state could be re-

elected until at least one year after its term had expired.[41]
In practice, a broad geographical representation has been
maintained. The United States is almost always on the Committee, at least one Central American or Caribbean country is included, and two or three seats are reserved for the
South American states. Apparently, also, an effort is made
to exclude the more disreputable states: the only unqualifiedly dictatorial state elected to the Committee so far has
been Cuba under Batista in 1956.

The mandate of the Committee is to maintain

constant vigilance to insure that states between which any
dispute exists or may arise, of any nature whatsoever, may
solve it as quickly as possible . . . [and to suggest] measures
and steps which may be conducive to a settlement.[42]

The role envisaged for the Committee was to mediate
minor disputes before they became major, relying on publicity, the collective prestige of the members, and the
presence of the United States and other major powers on
the Committee to insure success.

In theory, the Committee is an independent organ of the
OAS, but to all intents and purposes it has become an arm
of the Council, supplementing and making more flexible
the political authority of the larger body. The Council determines the Committee's jurisdiction and operating procedures and Council members simultaneously represent
their states on the Peace Committee. Thus, Peace Committee action is merely Council action in a different guise.

The general practice has been for the Peace Committee
to take jurisdiction over disputes that are too minor to
justify dramatic action under the Rio Treaty, as in the
Haitian–Dominican Republic dispute in 1949 and a number
of others during the 1950's.[43] On the other hand, sometimes the Committee deals with disputes that are so politi-

cally controversial and in which the existence of "aggression" is so dubious that invocation of the Rio Treaty would risk diplomatic escalation and a bad split in the hemisphere, as in the Panama Canal conflict of 1964. Lodging the problem with the Peace Committee helps bypass the disruptive "aggression" question, avoids the implication of possible sanctions implicit in Rio Treaty action, and provides a cooling-off period during which the dispute may either be settled or allowed to subside.[44]

More specifically, the Peace Committee has performed four major political functions. First, it has acted as hemispheric "watchdog," publicly focusing attention on potentially dangerous inter-American conflicts and creating international pressures on the states involved, as in the various Caribbean conflicts in 1948-50.

Secondly, it has supplemented the Council's investigating function, acting as a means by which the Council can examine charges of aggression without the necessity of prior invocation of the Rio Treaty. Peace Committee reports on the Haitian–Dominican case of 1949 and the Venezuelan charges against the Dominican Republic in 1960 provided the factual background and verified the need for later Council action under the Rio Treaty.

Third, the Peace Committee has often served as the vehicle by which the OAS has promulgated statements of general policy, later to be used as the basis for action in specific cases. For example, in 1949 the Peace Committee issued a report on the non-intervention principle, which served as the underpinning for subsequent Council action designed to dampen Caribbean tensions. In 1960 the Peace Committee issued several "studies" on the relationship between internal dictatorship and international tensions that were used to legitimate pressures on behalf of democracy in the Dominican Republic. In 1961 the Committee issued a report on Cuban subversion that served as the basis for the sanctions imposed on Cuba at the Punta del Este Conference of 1962.

Finally, the Committee has often acted as a channel of communication and as third-party conciliator and mediator in inter-American conflicts. When the disputants have been genuinely interested in settlement but were in need of a face-saving formula making concessions possible for both sides, the privacy and informality of Peace Committee mediation has facilitated solution, as in the minor disputes in the 1950's between Cuba and the Dominican Republic. Conversely, the Committee can focus international pressures on states reluctant to make concessions by making public its own "impartial" suggestions, as in the United States—Panama conflict.

Although ostensibly the Peace Committee has only "moral authority" and no mandate "to judge disputes or issue opinions upon the merits of a case presented to it . . . or propose formulas of settlement,"[45] the Committee has in fact often judged disputes and proposed such formulas. In view of its collective prestige and its unofficial but real relationship to the Council, moreover, the Committee's "suggestions" in some cases have had considerably compelling force. The best example of this was the highly active role of the Committee in the final settlement of the Honduran–Nicaraguan border dispute, in which the Committee drew up a number of detailed agreements, helped establish new boundary lines, and headed a border commission to supervise execution of its proposals. It was clear to both disputants that failure to comply with the proposals would probably result in Council action under the Rio Treaty.

Although the Peace Committee has played a quite useful role in hemispheric political affairs, there is a widespread feeling in the OAS that it should be equipped to do more. Under the Committee's present statutes, it can take action only at the request of states directly involved in a controversy, and the request can be granted only with the consent of all the concerned states.[46] Until 1956, any hemispheric state could initiate a request (in effect giving the Committee itself the power of initiative), and the consent of the interested parties was not required.[47] The more restrictive changes were instituted during the period when half of the Latin American states were under the control of military dictatorships, and when, consequently, the emphasis in the OAS was on non-intervention.

The new statutes have resulted in a sharp curtailment of the peaceful settlement role of the Peace Committee—from 1948 to 1956 the Committee was involved in nine such cases, from 1956 to 1965 only two[48]—although it has continued to issue useful general reports under a 1959 extension of its authority directing it to examine "methods and procedures to prevent any activities from abroad designed to overthrow established governments" and "the relationship between violations of human rights or the non-exercise of representative democracy, on the one hand, and the political tensions that affect the peace of the hemisphere on the other."[49]

The movement to restore to the Committee something similar to its original authority is being led by the United States which opposed the 1956 revisions),[50] the Secretary-General of the OAS, and the Peace Committee itself.[51] Having been stung by Panama's successful invocation of the Rio Treaty in the Panama Canal crisis of 1964, the United States now hopes to see the Peace Committee become the court of first resort in future hemispheric squabbles, the Rio Treaty being reserved for "serious" conflicts. It is probable that the proposed changes will eventually be adopted, for the misgivings of the United States are shared by many Latin American states, most of whom went along with Panama's request only reluctantly and out of the political need to support a small Latin American nation involved in a conflict with the North Americans.[52]

The Inter-American Defense Board, consisting of military representatives of all the OAS members, theoretically has a considerable military and therefore political role within the OAS, but in fact it has been insignificant. The official mission of the Board is to plan and co-ordinate hemispheric collective defense and advise the governments on measures to increase preparedness. No one takes seriously the likelihood of a direct external (Soviet) attack against the hemisphere, however, and in any event it has been well understood that "collective" defense for all practical purposes would be a unilateral responsibility of the United States. As a result, the Board has merely rubberstamped United States plans and preparations. In the Cuban missile crisis, the only situation since the creation of the OAS in which an external military threat actually materialized, the role of the Board, if any, was undetectable.

The Board could conceivably play a significant role in *internal* hemispheric military operations, particularly in the event of the creation of the much-talked-about permanent inter-American police force. There is little prospect for such a force in the foreseeable future, however, since most of the Latin American states would view it as a Frankenstein's monster that under the guise of "peace-keeping" would permanently enthrone the military as the arbiters of Latin American politics. Thus, the Board is left with neither an external nor internal military function.

Nonetheless, both the United States and most Latin

American countries find the continued existence of the Board to be useful. From the point of view of the United States, the Board's activities provide a measure of multilateral legitimacy for unilateral United States measures and bilateral military assistance programs. More importantly, the Board serves as an officers' club for the hemispheric military brethren, and thus it is a means by which high United States officers can develop close relationships with, and, hopefully, political influence over, Latin America's most powerful political group.

In the eyes of the Latin American military, the Board helps maintain the fiction that there is a genuine necessity for large national armed forces, legitimizing their demands for modern armaments and a large share of the national budget. From the civilian perspective, the Board is a convenient dumping ground for politically ambitious Latin American leaders who are too dangerous to be allowed to remain in their own countries.[53] Finally, the myth that each state has an important role to play in hemispheric defense, perpetuated by the continued functioning of the Board, gratifies Latin American nationalistic sentiments with their emphasis on the "sovereignty" and "equality" of all states.[54]

The oas Secretariat, unlike its United Nations counterpart, has not yet evolved into an important political organ, although there have been indications that it is beginning to assume some political responsibilities.

Prior to the Bogotá Conference of 1948, the draft Charter prepared by the Secretariat had assigned to the Pan American Union the vague but potentially significant duty of "strengthening the political, economic, juridical, social, and cultural relations among all states."[55] But at the conference many Latin American nations raised the "superstate" argument again, and insisted that the Pan American Union and the Secretary-General be excluded from any political role.[56] To allay fears that it would dominate the Secretariat,[57] the United States successfully moved to drop the offending portions of the draft Charter, and in addition proposed that the Charter stipulate that

> In the performance of their duties the personnel shall not seek or receive instructions from any government or from any other authority outside the Pan American Union . . .

and that

> every member of the Organization of American States pledges itself to respect the exclusively international character of the responsibilities of the Secretary General and the personnel, and not to seek to influence them in the discharge of their duties.[58]

As finally adopted, the Charter embodied the traditional view of the proper role for the Pan American Union, limiting the Secretariat to administrative, technical, and informational matters.

The first Secretary-General, Alberto Lleras Camargo, later to become President of Colombia, was a man of universally acclaimed ability and the highest prestige. Yet even he was so severely restricted in his mild attempts to play a political role—primarily through the drafting of working papers for the Rio and Bogotá conferences and analytical and sometimes critical reports on the results of these conferences and other OAS activities—that in 1954 he resigned in frustration. Later he was to charge that the Secretariat, because of the Council's negativism, had been reduced to producing

innocuous papers, unnecessary documents, recommendations

to which no one pays attention, all this with no sense of mission, no sense of the urgency of the task, and no sense of common purpose.[59]

Under the present Secretary-General, José A. Mora of Uruguay, a man with less prestige and allegedly less ability than Lleras, the Secretariat until recently has studiously avoided involvement in hemispheric political problems, ceasing to play an important role in conference preparations and confining its reports to strictly factual matters. Mora's conception of his role—or at least the conception he deems it wise to officially hold—is indicated by his statement:

> The Secretary General, by presenting with full objectivity to the organs of the Institution, to the Governments and to public opinion, the thinking and the action of the Organization, divorces itself from all national or political interests, and bases itself exclusively in the conclusions that have been approved through the competent organs of the Organization.[60]

In recent years, however, the Secretariat has begun cautiously to expand its political role, primarily by interpreting broadly its authority to grant "technical assistance" to countries requesting it. For example, the staff of the Pan American Union in effect governed a Nicaraguan province for some months during its transition in 1961 from Nicaraguan to Honduran control.[61] Also, the Secretariat and a technical assistance mission acting in its name played a significant role in preparing for and "observing" (i.e., insuring the honesty of) the Dominican presidential elections in early 1962.[62] Pan American Union electoral missions performed similar functions in the Costa Rican elections of 1962 and were to do the same in the Honduran elections scheduled for 1963, before the latter were "canceled" by a military coup.

Along with some Latin American states, the United States is hopeful that the Secretariat can continue to expand its political activities.[63] The possibility has even been suggested that the Secretariat could play a key role in temporary oas administration of hemispheric trouble spots (along the lines of the UN role in the Congo), as, for example, in the event of a chaotic situation in Haiti following a successful revolt against Duvalier.[64] It is more likely, though, that the political role of the Secretariat will develop less dramatically, in piecemeal fashion. In the final analysis, the role of the Secretariat depends on the role of the Council; if the balance of power in the Council should ultimately shift from the non-interventionist to the activist states, the role of the Secretariat will inevitably be greatly expanded.

1. J. Lloyd Mecham, *The United States and Inter-American Security, 1889-1960* (Austin: University of Texas Press, 1961), p. 102.

2. Edgar S. Furniss, Jr., "Recent Changes in the Inter-American System," *International Organization,* September, 1948, p. 456.

3. Quoted in Mecham, *op. cit.,* p. 132.

4. In view of Article 15 it is somewhat puzzling that some commentators (e.g. Laurence Duggan, *The Americas* [New York: Henry Holt, 1949], p. 154) have seen significance in the fact that the OAS Charter, unlike the UN Charter, contains no provision allowing states to reject collective action on their internal problems on the grounds of "domestic jurisdiction." Obviously, Article 15 serves precisely the same purpose, for under it states could and in fact often have prevented OAS inquiry into domestic matters.

5. Since Bogotá, there has been a general if tacit disposition to consider *intent* in defining intervention. In 1961, the Inter-American Juridical Committee, an advisory body of the OAS, noted that "intervention is commonly understood to mean the dictatorial interference by one state or group of states in the internal or

external affairs of another . . . presupposing a request or peremptory demand whose purpose it is to obtain a certain kind of action, positive or negative, a demand that may be direct or indirect." (*Opinion on the Legal Aspects of the Draft Declaration on Nonintervention Presented by the Mexican Delegation*, p. 9.)

6. Alberto Lleras, *The Inter-American Way of Life* (Washington, D.C.: Pan American Union, 1951), p. 2.

7. This does *not* imply that the United States can always have its way in the OAS, for it certainly cannot invariably gain the requisite *majority* for all its policies. See "Conclusions."

8. See Chapter IV.

9. The text of both draft treaties are reprinted in Bogotá Conference, *Report of the Delegation of the United States of America* (Washington, D.C.: U.S. Government Printing Office, 1948). Cited hereafter as *U.S. Report*.

10. In 1954, at the Caracas Conference, Brazil proposed that the Pact of Bogotá be revised to remove the "difficulties" preventing ratification, notably the compulsory arbitration features (Inter-American Conference, 10th, Caracas, 1954, *Chronological Collection of Documents*, Document 30 [Washington, D.C.: Pan American Union, 1954]). In view of the continued resistance of Mexico and its supporters to any weakening of the Pact, the matter was turned over to the Council for "further study." Finally, in 1957 a committee of the Council reported that the majority of the states favored keeping the Pact in its existing form, and there the matter rests (*Actas del Consejo de la Organizacion de los Estados Americanos*, March 6, 1957; cited hereinafter as *Actas del Consejo*).

11. Resolution of the Buenos Aires Conference, quoted in Mecham, *op. cit.*, p. 133.

12. Duggan, *op.cit.*, p. 121; Adolf A. Berle, Jr., *Tides of Crisis* (New York: Reynal & Co., 1957), pp. 68-71; Sumner Welles, *Where Are We Heading?* (New York: Harper & Bros., 1946), pp. 182-91.

13. The text of the relevant Dumbarton Oaks Proposals is in Mecham, *op. cit.*, pp. 255-56.

14. Edgar S. Furniss, Jr., "The United States, the Inter-American System, and the United Nations," *Political Science Quarterly*, September, 1950.

15. Quoted in Mecham, *op. cit.*, p. 262.

16. For an account of the split, see Inis L. Claude, Jr., "The OAS, the UN, and the United States," *International Conciliation,* March, 1964.

17. Initially the United States had proposed at Rio that collective measures in response to acts of aggression short of armed attack should be "subject to the provisions of Article 53 of the Charter of the United Nations." (Rio Conference, *Original Minutes and Documents,* Document CRJ/73, Revision of the United States Proposals.) Later this stipulation was quietly dropped in response to Latin American sentiment.

18. This interpretation was necessitated by the Cuban and Dominican cases, in which Security Council authorization of OAS sanctions would have carried the danger (and in the Cuban case the certainty) of a Soviet veto.

19. For discussions of the San Francisco Conference and subsequent developments in the UN-OAS relationship, see Mecham, *op. cit.,* pp. 268-77; Furniss, "The United States, the Inter-American System, and the United Nations"; Claude, *op. cit.;* Charles Fenwick, "The Inter-American Regional System: Fifty Years of Progress," *American Journal of International Law,* January, 1956; John A. Houston, *Latin America in the United Nations* (New York: Carnegie Endowment for International Peace, 1956).

20. See above, p. 5 for definitions of *collective security* and *alliance.*

21. Rio Conference, *Miscellaneous Documents,* Doc. CRJ/82 (Washington, D.C.: Pan American Union, 1947); Rio Conference, *U.S. Report* (Washington, D.C.: U.S. Government Printing Office, 1948), p. 17.

22. Rio Conference, *U.S. Report,* p. 17; Ward P. Allen, "The Inter-American Treaty of Reciprocal Assistance," *Department of State Bulletin,* November 23, 1947, p. 984.

23. Article 8 of the Treaty spelled out the type of collective measures that could be applied against aggression, including the breaking of diplomatic relations, partial or total economic sanctions, and the use of armed force. The Act of Chapultepec had specified the same measures but was silent on the question of whether all states, even those that did not concur, were obligated to join in collective action if voted by the Organ of Consultation. In a compromise settlement, Article 20 of the treaty provided that all sanctions except the use of armed force would be

obligatory. This represented a major concession for the United States, for it originally had proposed that all measures be non-compulsory. (Rio Conference, *Consultation on the Principal Points of the Treaty to be Signed at Rio de Janeiro,* Washington, D.C.: Pan American Union, 1947, p. 2.)

24. Arthur H. Vandenberg, Jr. (ed.), *The Private Papers of Senator Vandenberg* (Boston: Houghton Miflin Co., 1952), pp. 365-72.

25. In Rio Conference, 1947, *The Director General's Report on the Results of the Conference* (Washington, D.C.: Pan American Union, 1947), pp. 35-37.

26. This is the wording of the Uruguayan proposal, in Rio Conference, *Analysis and Comparative Compilation of the Projects* (Washington, D.C.: Pan American Union, 1946), p. 16. (Cited hereinafter as *Analysis.)* The similar Guatemalan proposal is in Rio Conference, *Original Minutes and Documents* (Washington, D.C.: Pan American Union, 1947), Doc. CRJ/82.

27. The United States position was argued by Senator Vandenberg in Rio Conference, *Original Minutes and Documents,* Minutes of Committee II.

28. *Ibid.*

29. *Ibid.*

30. See my discussion of the Cuban and Dominican cases below.

31. Rio Conference, *U.S. Report,* p. 23.

32. *New York Times,* May 25 and August 23, 1947; March 25, 1948. Also, Samuel Guy Inman, normally a harsh critic of United States anti-communism at inter-American meetings, noted with satisfaction that "At Rio, the United States Delegation succeeded in keeping the Communist issue out of discussion." ("American Issues at Bogotá," *Survey Graphic,* April, 1948, p. 212.)

33. For an analysis of the Governing Board, see John Dreier, "The Council of the OAS: Performance and Potential," *Journal of Inter-American Studies,* July, 1963.

34. This feeling was understandable, for until the chairmanship of the Board was made a rotating position in 1945, it had always been filled by the United States Secretary of State. Moreover, until 1923 the Latin American states could be represented on the Board only by their ambassadors to the United States, giving rise to the assumption that the delegates were generally reluctant to

prejudice the success of their main function by undue shows of independence. Although since 1923 the Latin Americans have been permitted to appoint special representatives, a number of small states, unwilling to incur the expense of two missions, have continued the original system. That this still rankles many Latin Americans was indicated in 1962, when Brazil, Mexico, and Chile announced that in future elections they would not vote for any candidate for Council chairman who was also the Ambassador "to the country in which the Council is located." (*Actas del Consejo,* November 21, 1962)

35. Resolution at the Mexico City Conference, Quoted in Mecham, *op.cit.,* p. 264. In fact, the Board was not to take action on any important political matter under this short-lived mandate.

36. Bogotá Conference, *Diario* (Washington, D.C.: Pan American Union, 1948), pp. 285-86.

37. United States Amendments to the Draft Charter, *Diario,* pp. 307-12.

38. Inter-American Conference, 10th, Caracas, 1954, *Diario* (Washington, D.C.: Pan American Union, 1954), Document 327, Minutes of the 4th Session of the Committee on Organization.

39. The United States suggestion, contained in a speech by Assistant Secretary of State Roy Rubottom (*Department of State Bulletin,* May 11, 1959), was made in the context of its growing concern with the Caribbean tensions that followed the Castro victory in Cuba. If the OAS was really as "impotent" in that situation as the United States charged, however, it was because it wanted to be, and not because it lacked authority. Clearly there was nothing to prevent two-thirds of the Council from characterizing the situation as "a fact or situation" endangering the peace. The constraint was political—the unwillingness of most Latin American states to take anti-Castro action—not juridical.

40. For a similar analysis, see Edgar S. Furniss, Jr., "The Inter-American System and Recent Caribbean Disputes," *International Organization,* November, 1950.

41. An attempt to extend this provision to a minimum of five years was defeated after the vigorous opposition of the United States and Mexico, at whom it was probably aimed. (*Actas del Consejo,* April 23, 1956.)

42. Inter-American Peace Committee, *Report to the Fifth Meeting of Consultation of Ministers of Foreign Affairs* (Washington, D.C.: Pan American Union, 1959), quoting Resolution XIV of

the Havana Conference of 1940. (Cited hereinafter as *Fifth Report.*) Some changes have been made in the original wording since 1940, but the mandate has remained essentially the same.

43. Cases referred to for illustrative purposes throughout this section will be dealt with in detail in subsequent chapters.

44. In the Canal conflict, however, the breakdown of Peace Committee action resulted in the later invocation of the Rio Treaty.

45. John C. Dreier, *The Organization of American States and the Hemisphere Crisis* (New York: Council on Foreign Relations, 1962), p. 38.

46. The statutes are contained in the Inter-American Peace Committee, *Fifth Report*, pp. 53-54.

47. The original statutes are in *ibid.,* p. 48-51.

48. Inter-American Peace Committee, *Report to the Second Special Inter-American Conference on Modifications of its Statutes* (Washington, D.C.: Pan American Union, 1965).

49. Meeting of Consultation of Ministers of Foreign Affairs, 5th, Santiago, 1959, *Actas y Documentos* (Washington, D.C.: Pan American Union, 1959), Final Act, Resolution IV.

50. *Actas del Consejo,* February 15, 1956.

51. The present United States position has been ascertained in interviews; the views of the Secretary-General were developed in a recent speech to the Council (*Actas del Consejo,* October 21, 1965); and the Peace Committee's own position is presented in its *Report to the Second Special Inter-American Conference.*

52. Interviews.

53. For example, in 1958, General Castro Leon of Venezuela was named as Venezuela's delegate to the Board after his involvement in an unsuccessful coup attempt against the Betancourt government. (*Hispanic American Report,* July, 1958, p. 385.)

54. The preceding discussion of the functioning of the Board has been partially based on Dreier, *Hemisphere Crisis,* pp. 43-48; and Edwin Lieuwen, *Arms and Politics in Latin America* (New York: Frederick A. Praeger, 1961), pp. 214-15.

55. Bogotá Conference, *Diario,* p. 308.

56. *Ibid.,* especially pp. 285-86.

57. Latin American attitudes had undoubtedly been influenced

by the fact that all Secretaries-General had been United States citizens, and until the post was made elective in 1945 had been appointed by the United States government, some of them even serving concurrently in the State Department. (Walter F. Cronin, "Some Basic Concepts of Inter-American Organization," unpublished Ph.D. thesis, Harvard University, 1949, p. 182.)

58. Articles 89 and 90 of the Charter.

59. The statement of Lleras' resignation is based on a number of interviews. Lleras' statement on the Secretariat is in William Manger (ed.), *The Alliance for Progress* (Washington, D.C.: Public Affairs Press, 1963), p. 10.

60. Quoted in Northwestern University, *The Organization of American States* (Washington, D.C.: Senate Foreign Relations Study No. 3, 1959), p. 230.

61. See Chapter II.

62. See Chapter V.

63. Interviews.

64. The Secretariat apparently was very active in the 1965 Dominican crisis, perhaps even performing quasi-governmental functions. At this writing, however, no detailed information is available.

*   *

CHAPTER **2**

The OAS as a Collective Security System

FROM 1948 TO ABOUT 1960, the United States was the leading OAS champion of the principle of collective security. During this period there were seven interstate conflicts involving armed hostilities. One of them was purely territorial in nature; the others, although partially manifestations of the classical Latin American "outs" vs. "ins" sort of political instability, were basically ideological, pitting the democratic left against the dictatorial right.[1] Since the United States was not concerned with the outcome of the democracy vs. dictatorship struggle per se, its objectives in the OAS were limited to the cessation of hostilities, the restoration of the status quo ante, and a return to inter-American tranquility. Collective security, an ideologically neutral principle, was ideally suited to United States aims.

63

Not all the OAS members considered the underlying causes of the disputes to be irrelevant, however. When dictatorships attacked democracies, other Latin American dictatorships were not enthusiastic supporters of OAS counteraction. More frequently, when dictatorships were attacked by forces seeking to establish more democratic regimes, a number of Latin American democracies attempted to block collective security action, seeking, in effect, to transform the OAS into an antidictatorial alliance. Only vigorous United States leadership kept them from succeeding.

The strategy of the United States was to emphasize the inviolable right of states to conduct their domestic affairs without external interference, an appeal to which the Latin Americans, of course, are particularly receptive. For years a weapon directed against the United States, the principle of non-intervention, ideally suited to collective security, became the major weapon in the United States effort to maintain the hemispheric status quo.

The Honduras-Nicaragua Territorial Dispute, 1957–1961

The intervention of the OAS in the century-old Honduras–Nicaragua dispute has been one of its most successful ventures, in part because the absence of ideological conflict, which has inhibited OAS action in almost every other major case, facilitated action by a relatively united OAS.

Over a four year period stretching from 1957 to 1961 the OAS interposed itself in a potentially explosive situation, averted major violence, drew up and in effect imposed the terms of a comprehensive settlement, and insured that it was carried out. Even more significantly, for six months an international "technical assistance" group under the auspices of the Pan American Union performed quasi-governmental functions, helping temporarily to administer a Nicaraguan province and thereby establishing a precedent and source of experience for possible future OAS trusteeships in the hemisphere.[2] This forceful and effective action would hardly have been possible without the full support and powerful leadership of the United States, which from the beginning stressed its "grave concern" with the situation and its intention to "participate fully" in any collective action necessary to settle the dispute.[3] Put on notice that United States power was available to the OAS, the disputants proved to be relatively compliant.

The circumstances surrounding the dispute were complex. When the Federation of Central America was dissolved in the mid-nineteenth century, the boundary line between Honduras and Nicaragua was not precisely demarked, leaving an area of about 8,700 square kilometers in dispute. In 1906 the matter was submitted for arbitration to the King of Spain, but Nicaragua refused to accept his decision supporting the Honduran claims.[4]

Until 1957 the dispute remained dormant, each nation exercising control over parts of the territory. Early that year, however, after the discovery of potential oil deposits, Honduras attempted to extend its control to the areas held by Nicaragua.[5] When Honduras moved troops into the disputed territory several armed clashes took place, and each country accused the other of aggression and requested OAS assistance under the Rio Treaty. Honduras claimed that its troops were exercising "self-defense," since they were merely taking over the territory ceded to Honduras by the 1906 arbitral decision; Nicaragua rejoined that it had never accepted the 1906 decision, as was its privilege under international law.[6]

Faced with these legal complexities, several states (led by Mexico, traditionally the Latin American state most reluctant to allow vigorous OAS action) initially argued that since no clear-cut case had been presented supporting either charge of aggression, the Rio Treaty could not be invoked and only the Peace Committee could handle the matter.

The United States, however, anxious for more forceful action than the purely voluntary mediation that the Peace Committee could provide, argued that there were really two aspects to the dispute: the legal issue could indeed be submitted to the Peace Committee, but first collective action under the Rio Treaty was necessary to maintain the peace. This view prevailed, and the Council voted unanimously to send an Investigating Committee (composed of representatives from Argentina, Bolivia, Mexico, Panama, and the United States) to the scene.[7]

The subsequent action of the Council went far beyond mere peacekeeping. After the Investigating Committee had brought about a formal ceasefire and a withdrawal of troops from the disputed area supervised by an OAS commission of military advisers, the Council unanimously voted to authorize the Investigating Committee to mediate a more permanent solution.[8] After a month of negotiations, during which OAS land and air patrols enforced the ceasefire and insured against the re-entry of troops, Honduras and Nicaragua agreed to the mediators' proposal to submit the dispute to the International Court of Justice for a binding rule. Under the plan, if the losing party should fail to comply immediately with the ruling, the other would request OAS action to consider "all the measures necessary to execute the juridical decision."[9] Shortly thereafter, the Council unanimously endorsed the plan, and thereby clearly implied willingness to take collective action to enforce it.[10]

In November, 1960, the Court upheld the Honduran claim that Nicaragua was bound by the 1906 arbitral decision. Once again, though, the OAS, acting this time through the Peace Committee, was forced to intervene. The new issue arose when the Honduran demand that the territory be speedily evacuated was refused by Nicaragua on the grounds that a "transition period" of unspecified duration was necessary to delineate the new boundaries and allow for the orderly resettlement of residents that did not wish to come under Honduran jurisdiction.[11]

In early March, 1961, both nations agreed to a Peace Committee plan under which Nicaragua would immediately withdraw its authorities in favor of an international commission consisting of representatives of Honduras and Nicaragua under the chairmanship of the President of the Peace Committee, who would have the power of final decision in the event of disagreement between the others.[12] During the next six months the Commission, with the assistance of Pan American Union personnel, presided over the relocation of about 4,000 residents, made a detailed survey of the terrain establishing the exact boundary lines, and supervised the transference of the territory from Nicaraguan to Honduran jurisdiction, thus successfully completing the most extensive OAS executive action to date.[13]

Dictatorships vs. Democracies

In 1948 and again in 1955 conservative Costa Rican exiles based in Nicaragua and actively supported by the Nicaraguan government attacked moderately leftist and democratic Costa Rican governments. The action of the

OAS in these conflicts was almost as successful as its settlement of the Honduran-Nicaraguan dispute. Although the root cause of the hostilities—the ideological conflict between democracy and feudal despotism—was too deep to be solved by collective intervention, the OAS was able to preserve the peace.

The effectiveness of the OAS stemmed from a general compatibility between the objectives of the United States and of most Latin American states. The United States, motivated not so much by concern for Costa Rican democracy as by fear that Nicaraguan incursions would disrupt hemispheric stability, wanted vigorous action to restore the status quo. With varying degrees of enthusiasm, the Latin American states followed United States leadership. Although a few dictatorships, notably Argentina under Perón, were clearly uninterested in protecting Costa Rica and were able to force the OAS to move more slowly than the United States and several Latin American states considered desirable, the principle of collective security was too important to the Latin American majority for them to tolerate anything more than delaying tactics.

All of the major United States objectives were attained. First, the Investigating Committees of the Council brought about a quick end to the fighting. Nicaragua had clearly violated inter-American norms, and failure to protect Costa Rica could have endangered the independence of all small Latin American states. Moreover, in the 1955 case the Latin Americans were eager to demonstrate that the OAS, despite its embarrassing role in the Guatemalan affair, could in more traditional circumstances function effectively as an instrument of collective security.

Secondly, punitive action against Nicaragua was avoided. A few Latin American states insisted that Nicaraguan aggression required the imposition of sanctions, especially in 1955, but the United States argued that the primary role of the OAS after the fighting had been stopped should be to help establish a climate in which Costa Rica and Nicaragua could resume normal relations, an object for which sanctions were unsuitable.[14] Since this position was also consistent with the general Latin American predilection for limiting collective action to the minimum required to maintain the peace, it had majority support.

Finally, the United States was able to avoid the specter of Yankee intervention. This was particularly important to Washington in 1955, after the storm of Latin American criticism of the unsavory Guatemalan affair. Although the United States played a major role in both Costa Rican–Nicaraguan conflicts, operating both unilaterally and through the OAS, it went to great lengths to secure specific multilateral authorization for its most important actions, especially the supplying of crucial military assistance to Costa Rica in 1955.

The invasion of Costa Rica in 1948 was the first interstate conflict in the hemisphere after the signing of the Rio Treaty; and in the subsequent OAS action, a number of highly significant precedents for future collective action were established, including (1) the decision that exile invasions, a common occurrence in Latin America and especially in the Caribbean area, would be considered not primarily an internal matter but a threat to the peace of the hemisphere, therefore justifying OAS intervention under Article 6 of the Rio Treaty; (2) the use of the Council instead of meetings of foreign ministers to guide OAS action; (3) the establishment of an OAS presence at the scene of conflicts in the form of "investigating" committees; and (4) the implicit threat of sanctions to force acceptance of OAS peace terms.

The conflict stemmed from the victory in early 1948 of a Costa Rican rebellion led by the social democrat José Figueres, in which a rightist government attempting to annul recent presidential elections was overthrown. As the rebellion neared success, the Costa Rican government appealed for military assistance to the Nicaraguan dictator Anastasio Somoza, who, fearing or disliking the prospect of a successful popular uprising and the establishment of a progressive government on his southern border, sent Nicaraguan troops across the border. After a series of United States diplomatic representations, however, culminating in the "strongest possible protest" against continued Nicaraguan intervention, Somoza withdrew his troops, and the Costa Rican government collapsed.[15]

In the ensuing months, though, relations between Somoza and the new Costa Rican government continued to deteriorate, and on December 14, 1948, Costa Rica charged that it had been invaded by conservative supporters of the former government, now based in Nicaragua, with the active support of the Somoza regime. Nicaragua denied the charges, in turn accusing the Costa Rican government of harboring the "Caribbean Legion," a force supposedly made up of antidictatorial exiles from Nicaragua, Honduras, and the Dominican Republic.[16]

At the suggestion of the United States, the Council agreed to investigate the situation under its authority as "provisional" organ of consultation of the Rio Treaty. Ten days later the Investigating Committee (composed of representatives of the United States, Brazil, Colombia and Mexico), after interviewing government and military officials of both countries, Costa Rican exile leaders in Nicaragua, and captured members of the invading force, reported to the Council that the Nicaraguan government had sheltered, supported, and probably trained the invaders, although it found no evidence that Nicaraguan troops had joined the invasion. On the other hand, the Committee also confirmed Nicaragua's charges, reporting that "the Caribbean Legion, with material and moral help from the Costa Rican government, enjoyed official sympathy and facilities for carrying out its programs and activities [which] . . . were designed to overthrow certain governments, among them the present regime in Nicaragua."[17] No armed assistance to Costa Rica was recommended; there had been practically no armed encounters between the exile group and the Costa Rican forces, and the government clearly had the situation in hand.[18]

Upon receipt of the Committee's report, the Council unanimously approved a resolution chastising each government and calling on them to refrain from further hostile actions. More importantly, an "Inter-American Commission of Military Experts" (consisting of military officers of five countries, including the United States) was sent to Costa Rica and Nicaragua to insure that the border was closed and that rebels on both sides were disarmed and their illegal activities curtailed. No sanctions were mentioned, but the decision of the Council to continue its role as organ of consultation until the Military Commission reported its findings suggested that failure of compliance could result in punitive measures.[19]

Several months later the Military Commission reported to the Council that the Costa Rican government had disarmed the Caribbean Legion and deported its leaders, and that Nicaragua had closed its border with Costa Rica and was apprehending and interning remnants of the exile bands.[20] The OAS action ended when both nations signed a formal "Pact of Amity," drawn up by the Council, pledging themselves to prevent the repetition of border incidents and rebel activities and to settle peacefully any future disputes.[21]

The renewal of the conflict in 1955 was much more serious, and only the combination of sustained United States and OAS pressures averted full-scale warfare between Costa Rica and Nicaragua. Acting mainly through the OAS but supplementing its diplomacy by unilateral measures as well, the United States played the crucial diplomatic and military role in the settlement of the dispute.

The conflict probably would not have occurred but for the Nicaraguan government's miscalculation of United States policy. The Somoza regime apparently took the United States involvement in the Guatemalan anti-Communist coup as an indication that the United States would no longer oppose a move against Costa Rica. However, the government of José Figueres, though undoubtedly "leftist" by traditional Latin American oligarchical standards, was pro-American and vigorously anti-Communist. The United States had temporarily abandoned its support of collective security and the political status quo in the Guatemalan situation but only because of the presumed exigencies of the Communist threat. Although Nicaragua tried to pin the "Red" label on Figueres,[22] its transparent strategy did not convince Washington, and traditional policies remained in effect.

Throughout 1954, tensions between the Figueres and Somoza regimes mounted, Nicaragua accusing Costa Rica of complicity in plots to assassinate Somoza and Costa Rica accusing Nicaragua of renewed aid to Costa Rican exiles planning a new attack. A possible clash was averted in July, 1954, when, after Nicaragua had moved troops to the border, the United States signaled its displeasure by sending a large shipment of arms to Costa Rica, as well as dispatching six military planes on a "good will visit" to San José.

Nonetheless, on January 11, 1955, the anti-Figueres exile force crossed into Costa Rica. In an urgent telegram to the Council, Costa Rica requested OAS assistance, accusing Nicaragua of a "systematic campaign of . . . aggression," including a propaganda campaign by the government-controlled Nicaraguan press and radio, Nicaraguan troop movements along the border, the closing of the San Juan River to Costa Rican shipping, and direct support of the exile invasion.[23]

The ensuing role of the OAS represented the most far-reaching intervention of the inter-American system in a hemispheric conflict until that point. Moving cautiously to avoid the outright opposition of a number of dictatorships, the Council nevertheless progressed from an on-the-ground investigation of the facts to the establishment of a multilateral observation and patrol force, the explicit threat of sanctions to end the fighting, and, for the first time in the history of the inter-American system, the authorization of military assistance to the victim of aggression. Once hostilities had finally been ended, the Council established a military presence on the scene to maintain the ceasefire while bilateral negotiations under OAS mediation proceeded.

Shortly after the Investigating Committee (United States, Mexico, Brazil, Ecuador, and Paraguay) arrived in Costa Rica, the Figueres government requested OAS military assistance, paralleling an earlier request directly to the United States.[24] There was no majority for such drastic action at that time, however, perhaps because the Investigating Committee had not yet determined the extent to which the fighting involved more than a mere internal rebellion, as Nicaragua was contending. As a result, the Council limited its response to a request that the member states place aircraft at the disposal of the Investigating Committee for "observation" purposes, although it clearly hoped that an OAS presence in the air might also serve to deter further fighting.[25] The United States, later joined by Ecuador, Mexico, and Uruguay, quickly responded to the Council resolution, and the patrol was soon in operation.[26]

These measures proved inadequate, however. On January 13 and 14 the Investigating Committee reported that aircraft "proceeding from abroad" had bombed parts of Costa Rica, including the capital city of San José, and recommended that the Council warn Nicaragua that if it did not cease its intervention immediately further collective measures might be forthcoming.[27]

Although there was considerable sentiment in the Council for following this course, Argentina and most of the other dictatorships held out for more limited action. To preserve unanimity, the Council merely issued a plea to Nicaragua that it comply with its legal obligations, and requested the Investigating Committee to verify the origin of the material pouring into Costa Rica by stationing observers in airports and other key points "in the region involved in the situation."[28]

On January 15, Costa Rica charged that new and large-scale landings along its coast were imminent and urgently requested immediate OAS assistance in the form of coastal patrol boats, an OAS land patrol along the Costa Rican–Nicaraguan border, and combat planes to repel air attacks. At about the same time, the Investigating Committee confirmed that the situation was deteriorating and pointed out in strong terms that Costa Rica lacked aircraft to defend itself.[29]

Under heavy pressure from the United States as well as

the members of the Investigating Committee and several other Latin American states, the Council finally took forceful action. At the urgent request of Assistant Secretary of State Henry Holland, the Council authorized a United States "sale" (at $1.00 apiece) of four fighter planes, fueled and waiting to take off.[30]

The arrival of the aircraft in Costa Rica was the turning point of the conflict. Within several days the rebel planes had been destroyed or had surrendered to Costa Rican government forces. Meanwhile Nicaragua, although continuing to deny any role in the Costa Rican fighting, had acceded to an Investigating Committee plan in which under OAS supervision the Nicaraguan Army was to disarm and intern any rebels attempting to cross the border. Furthermore, a land and air buffer zone was established along the border and patrolled by an OAS force (consisting primarily of United States personnel and equipment)[31] under the direction of the Investigating Committee.[32]

One more major problem had to be surmounted in the peace-keeping phase of the OAS action. With Costa Rica regaining control of the air and with reinforcements to the rebels cut off by the buffer-zone plan, the fighting was quickly brought under control and the rebels were forced into a full-scale retreat toward the Nicaraguan border. Instead of crossing into Nicaragua, however, the rebels camped in the demilitarized zone, safe from Costa Rican pursuit. After several fruitless appeals to Somoza to order the rebels to continue into Nicaragua, the Investigating Committee finally threatened to return to the Council and demand sanctions against Nicaragua. Although Somoza denied he had the ability to comply, several hours before the Committee was to depart the rebels decamped, moved back into Nicaragua, and were interned by Nicaraguan forces.[33]

In the interest of a return to harmony, the Investigating

Committee in its public report to the Council stopped just short of charging official Nicaraguan participation in the invasion, merely stating, rather coyly, that there had been "foreign intervention" in the financing and arming of the rebels, who had entered Costa Rica "by way of the Costa Rican–Nicaraguan frontier."[34] There was no doubt, though, as the United States member of the Committee later admitted, that "Nicaraguan authorities were deeply involved in the whole operation,"[35] and even at the time the Ecuadoran Committee member protested the suppression of incriminating evidence.[36]

As was by now the normal procedure, hemispheric action continued even after the fighting had stopped and the rebellion had ended. A nine-man Council committee was appointed to mediate negotiations between Costa Rica and Nicaragua at the Pan American Union.[37] At the same time, the United States continued its unilateral diplomatic pressures, as Vice-President Nixon in a tour of Central America succeeded in exacting promises from Somoza and Figueres that they would act in a conciliatory manner.[38] The joint United States–OAS activities culminated in January, 1956, when Costa Rica and Nicaragua in a formal treaty agreed, once again, to curb the exiles and refrain from hostile activities against each other. This time, though, enforcement measures were included. Joint Costa Rican–Nicaraguan military patrols would guard the border and co-operate in preventing illegal crossings. Even more significantly, a new Commission of Investigation and Conciliation, consisting of representatives of the United States (Chairman), Uruguay, and Brazil, as well as Costa Rica and Nicaragua themselves, would be allowed free access to both countries and would have the authority to settle all further disputes.[39] With these steps, open conflict between the two nations ended.

Democracy vs. Dictatorship

In the Honduran-Nicaraguan and Costa Rican-Nicaraguan disputes the United States played an extremely important role, providing political leadership in the Council and serving as the major source of logistical services, military technical assistance, planes and ships for patrol and observation functions, and, in 1955, armaments authorized by the OAS for the victim of aggression. In fact, though, the majority in the OAS needed little prodding by the United States to take effective action, for the application of collective security created far less conflict of values and domestic political difficulties for the Latin American states than when dictatorships were the beneficiaries of collective action.

The Dominican Republic and Nicaragua, the main targets of numerous exile plots and invasions in 1949-50 and 1959, were the very symbol of totalitarian despotism in Latin America, and even the more conservative states were not eager to advertise their ideological affinities with Trujillo and the Somozas. As a result, when pro-democratic exiles attacked their homelands, OAS action was hesitant and half-hearted, and if it had not been for active United States leadership, there almost certainly would have been no action at all.

The crucial issue in the cases was whether the attainment of democracy, ostensibly a key principle of the inter-American system, justified bypassing the principle of collective security. Although there is no inherent contradiction in the two, in the prevailing circumstances it was evident that the one could be achieved only at the sacrifice of the other. Although the United States was motivated not by the desire as such to protect dictatorship but by its concern for stability, the effect of its action was clearly to stabilize an unjust status quo.

Seeking desperately to deny this, United States spokesmen in the decade from 1949-59 maintained that democracy could not be "imposed" on countries by force but could only be "achieved from within."[40] Moreover, the argument ran, collective security positively *contributed* to the cause of democracy, because it "assures each country the opportunity to develop its political life free from outside interference."[41] In the context of Caribbean realities, though, this was nonsense: Nicaragua, the Dominican Republic, and other local feudalisms were hardly likely to "develop" in any direction, let alone toward democracy, without outside intervention. And it was precisely the function of collective security, reinforced by the non-intervention principle, to prohibit such intervention.

The strategy of the United States, then, was to emphasize persistently the incompatibility of exile activities, no matter what their goals, with hallowed inter-American norms. The strategy was well-chosen, for when publicly forced to a choice, even the majority of democratic states had to give priority to non-intervention. And while OAS action, especially in 1959, was lackadaisical compared with its role in previously discussed situations, the action that was taken did help to inhibit the exile activities and thereby preserve the status quo.

The 1949–50 Conflicts

No sooner had the Costa Rican–Nicaraguan conflict of 1948 been brought under control than a rash of similar conflicts involving most of the Caribbean states broke out. Some of the friction was merely of the "outs" vs. "ins" variety, as in the campaign of Haitian exiles in the Dominican Republic against the government of Dumarsais Estimé, but most of it arose from genuine demands for economic development, social reform, and democracy. The Dominican Republic was the focal point of most of the tensions, for exiles from the brutal Trujillo regime had found asylum and support throughout the Caribbean, especially in the relatively liberal states of Cuba, Guatemala, and Costa Rica.

Throughout 1948 and the spring of 1949, the general Caribbean situation deteriorated as the Caribbean Legion reorganized and with the aid of the pro-democratic regimes in the area prepared to overthrow the dictatorships.[42] The reaction of the United States to these developments was made clear by Secretary of State Acheson in September, 1949:

> For more than two years the Caribbean area has been disturbed by plots and counterplots. These plots are . . . inconsistent with our common commitment not to intervene in each other's affairs. . . . This situation is repugnant to the entire fabric of the inter-American system. The United States could not be faithful to its international obligations if it did not condemn it in the strongest terms.[43]

Although Acheson went on to add that the United States would "continue to work for a world in which each citizen participates freely in determining periodically the identity of the members of his government," the exile activities, he implied, could not be supported or even tolerated. Not only was hemispheric stability being disrupted, but the failure of the OAS to take action would threaten the very existence of the collective security system itself, for which the United States had so vigorously fought at Rio only two years earlier.

Accordingly, after the breakdown of several informal Peace Committee attempts at mediation,[44] the United States moved to begin broader collective action. Although

Washington would have preferred Latin American leadership in the problem, as it generally does, no Latin American state was willing to take the initiative. Nor could the targets of the exile plots themselves do so, for in view of their widespread unpopularity they feared that collective action might backfire. As a result, if collective security was to remain an operative principle in the inter-American system, United States leadership was essential. Washington was forced to act literally as the spokesman for the Caribbean dictatorships.

The initial United States step was to introduce the Caribbean situation formally before the Peace Committee, of which it was a member, in the hope of deterring outright armed expeditions and obtaining a general statement condemning the exile activities, which could later be used, if necessary, as the basis for the application of Rio Treaty procedures. From the United States point of view it would have been preferable to have dealt with the problem under the Rio Treaty from the beginning, but the obvious lack of enthusiasm of most Latin American states made this impossible.[45]

In a detailed memorandum to the Peace Committee outlining the history of the Caribbean disturbances, the United States emphasized that it took a grave view of the situation. As far as the democracy issue was concerned, the memorandum argued:

> whatever may be the motivation of these individuals, some of whom declare that the cause of their exile is the absence of democratic practices in their home countries, the methods they have chosen may involve violations by established governments of their international obligations with the consequent disruption of friendly relations among the countries in the area.[46]

The Committee's subsequent report closely paralleled

the United States position. Although affirming that democracy was "a common denominator" of hemispheric political life, it placed far more emphasis on the principle of non-intervention and the duty of each state "to prevent its territory from being used for the preparation or initiation of aggression." To re-establish harmony, it was necessary that all states curb "systematic and hostile propaganda" attacks, as well as take "adequate measures to rid [their] . . . territory of groups of nationals or foreigners, organized on a military basis with the deliberate purpose of conspiring against . . . and preparing to fight against [other] . . . Governments."[47]

The Committee's statement of principles did not suffice to prevent further disturbances, however. Within a few months, the Council was forced to resort to the Rio Treaty, utilizing the procedures and precedents that had been established in the 1948 Costa Rica–Nicaragua clash. The Treaty was invoked in January, 1950, at the request of both Haiti and the Dominican Republic. Haiti charged that Dominical officials were aiding an exile plot to overthrow the Estimé government; the Trujillo regime denied this, and demanded OAS assistance to meet an allegedly imminent invasion by a reactivated and strengthened Caribbean Legion, aided by the governments of Haiti, Cuba, Costa Rica, and Guatemala.[48] Several months later, the Council's Investigating Committee (United States, Bolivia, Colombia, Ecuador, and Uruguay), in a highly detailed and well-documented report, substantiated both the Haitian and Dominican accusations, but clearly indicated that the Dominican Republic had been and continued to be the main target of the well-armed Caribbean Legion.[49] Trujillo's charge that the Cuban and Guatemalan governments had been heavily involved in an abortive invasion of the Dominican Republic in June, 1949, was confirmed, and the Committee concluded that the situation was worsening:

a. It is evident that there is a will on the part of various groups of exiles, not only to persist in their struggle, but also to seek surreptitious support from the Governments.

b. Moreover, certain authorities in some countries are failing to conceal their ideological sympathy with the . . . exiles, and even their willingness to give such groups, either openly or surreptitiously, official aid tending to facilitate the development of subversive activities in other nations.[50]

The Council decided to meet head-on the basic issue in the Caribbean conflicts: whether the overthrow of tyranny excused external pressures on non-democratic governments. In view of the priority given to collective security in the Rio and Bogotá conferences, there could be little doubt of how this question would be resolved, but the Council's strong restatement of policy was nonetheless significant. Admitting that "there exists some confusion of ideas concerning the means of harmonizing the effective execution and application of the basic principle of non-intervention and that of the exercise of representative democracy," the Council bluntly warned that the pursuit of democracy did not "in any way and under any concept authorize a Government or group of Governments to violate inter-American commitments relative to the principle of non-intervention."[51]

In terms of the maintenance of peace, the Council's action in the Caribbean conflicts proved successful. For the first time, sanctions were explicitly threatened, the Dominican Republic, Guatemala, and Cuba all being warned that continued violations of the non-intervention principle "would give occasion for application of the procedures of the Inter-American Treaty of Reciprocal Assistance."[52] A "new" committee (consisting of members of the original Investigating Committee) was appointed to insure compliance with the Council's demands and to mediate negotiations between the conflicting states. The committee subsequently reported that all the governments concerned had taken effective measures to reduce tensions between them, curb hostile propaganda, control and restrict subversive activities of exile groups, and re-establish normal diplomatic relations.[53] The "Caribbean Legion" was apparently broken up, and with the exception of the Costa Rican–Nicaraguan conflict of 1955, there were no further serious hostilities of a similar nature in the next decade.

The Caribbean Conflicts of 1959

In 1959 a series of exile conspiracies and invasions again created serious tensions in the Caribbean area. Most of the conflicts grew out of the democracy vs. dictatorship issue, as in 1949-50, but were further complicated by the intrusion of the "Communist issue."

The renewed tensions were related both directly and indirectly to the victory of the Castro movement in Cuba at the end of 1959. Indirectly, the overthrow of the Cuban dictator Batista encouraged the aspirations of opposition groups throughout the Caribbean, especially in Somoza's Nicaragua, Trujillo's Dominican Republic, and Duvalier's Haiti. Moreover, some of these groups received moral and perhaps some material assistance—though that is a matter of controversy—from Cuba, as well as from Costa Rica and Venezuela.

As a result, the traditional United States policy of support of peace and quiet was reinforced and made more urgent by growing concern with the Cuban revolution and the desire to prevent its export by means of "liberating" expeditions to neighboring Caribbean countries. It was not easy for the United States to get OAS action, though, for the Castro revolution had stimulated a wave of populist nationalism and antidictatorial sentiment throughout the hemisphere, and few Latin American governments were eager to appear as the defenders of Somoza and Trujillo. Yet the United States emphasis on collective security and non-intervention could not be ignored indefinitely, and although in the attacks on Nicaragua and the Dominican Republic the OAS delayed action as long as possible and moved with far less efficiency and force than in most previous cases, the mere fact of OAS involvement, however limited, helped deter further invasions and made it difficult for the pro-democratic governments to support or even tolerate the exile movements.

Panamanian Affair.—The initial 1959 conflict raised relatively few problems, for the Panamanian government, though hardly democratic, was not of the same ilk as the Somoza and Trujillo regimes. Moreover, it soon became clear that the whole affair grew more out of an internal squabble among politicians than ideological conflict, and as a result there was no opposition to OAS peacekeeping action.

In late April, 1959, a hundred men or so landed on the Caribbean coast of Panama. In a note to the Council requesting the urgent application of the Rio Treaty, Panama charged that the "invasion" had been mounted in Cuba.[54]

Panama's request met with the immediate support of the United States, which pointed out that the non-intervention principle was at stake. There was no opposition from Cuba. The Cuban delegate did not deny that the expedition had departed from Cuba, but he stressed his government's disapproval of the rebellion against the "democratic" government of Panama, reaffirmed Cuba's "absolute" commitment to the principle of non-intervention, and vowed to support the OAS completely in any action it took. Moreover, obviously anxious to disentangle itself from the affair, Cuba announced that it was offering the use of a frigate to patrol the Panamanian coast and was sending two army officers to Panama to contact the rebels and attempt to persuade them to surrender.[55]

In view of the Cuban statements, there was no obstacle blocking quick OAS action, and the Council unanimously agreed to apply the Rio Treaty. An Investigating Committee (composed of Brazil, Argentina, Costa Rica, Paraguay, and the United States) was appointed. Moreover, the member states were requested to supply the Committee with planes and ships for observation and patrol duties and to "view favorably Panamanian requests for military assistance." This request was met promptly by the United States, which placed naval ships and planes under the OAS and began shipping small arms to Panama.[56]

Soon after its arrival in Panama, the Investigating Committee, with the help of the two Cuban army officers, was able to induce the rebels (almost all of whom were Cuban) to surrender to the Panamanian National Guard. In view of Panama's concern that further invasions were imminent, the Council authorized the Investigating Committee to use the patrol craft under its jurisdiction to stop and investigate any suspicious craft approaching the Panamanian coast. As no new threats materialized, however, this rather strong measure was not instituted, and in early June the case was closed.[57]

The Investigating Committee found no evidence of Cuban government complicity in the invasion, and the Panamanian government had not accused Cuba of aggression.[58]

Although the invasion had been mounted in Cuba, it had been organized by the Panamanian politician Roberto Arias, who had managed to persuade a group of overly enthusiastic Cubans that they were extending the Cuban revolution to Panama,[59] when in fact they were merely acting as tools of a cynical attempt of the "outs" to replace the "ins." All this is of some historical significance, for although at the time the United States publicly praised Cuba for its co-operative attitude,[60] the State Department in its later campaign to demonstrate the existence of Cuban "aggression" baldly stated that official Cuban support of the expedition "has been established beyond a reasonable doubt."[61]

Nicaraguan Case.—The leadership of the United States in the Panama conflict, although important, had not been crucial, for there had been unanimous agreement that Panama should be helped. In the exile invasion of Nicaragua one month later, however, there was considerable reluctance in the Council to assist the Somoza regime, and there would have been no action at all but for the insistence of the United States.

Since there was no dispute that anti-Somoza exiles based in Costa Rica had invaded their homeland, the principle of collective security clearly required the support of Nicaragua. In 1948 and 1955, when the situation had been reversed, the OAS had quickly and effectively intervened. For the Latin American states actively concerned with democracy, though, the overthrow of Somoza justified a double standard.

The renewed clash between collective security and democracy was occasioned by Nicaragua's request for OAS assistance in meeting an air and sea invasion departing from Costa Rica and allegedly assisted by the forces of "international communism." Obviously aware of the general hostility in the Council, the Nicaraguan government made it clear that it was not accusing the Costa Rican government of aggression, or even of compliance with the exile cause; it merely wanted help in meeting the revolt.[62]

Nonetheless, the opposition was vigorous. According to Cuba, "Neither factually nor technically is there an invasion, such as occurred in the case of Panama, because it cannot be said in all good logic that a country can be invaded by its own nationals."[63] Venezuela went further, arguing that the attackers must be considered as "liberators" rather than invaders, and that oas action would constitute an intervention in the internal affairs of Nicaragua against the wishes of the Nicaraguan people themselves. Doubt that collective action was warranted was also expressed by Bolivia, Honduras, and Mexico.[64]

In its strong leadership on behalf of Nicaragua the United States may have been concerned as much with the "Communist" issue, so cleverly introduced by Nicaragua, as with the principle of collective security. Publicly, however, the United States based its case that the Rio Treaty was applicable solely on the latter, in which it was on much firmer ground. There could be no dispute over the United States argument that the oas had never before considered the nationality of an invading force to be a relevant factor in determining whether a conflict was international in scope.[65] In view of the powerful nature of the United States argument and because Costa Rica, anxious to avoid conflict with Nicaragua, firmly supported the Somozan government's request for an "investigation," the Council could scarcely avoid some kind of action.

Nonetheless the opposition was still strong enough to dictate a minimal role for the oas. The Council voted 17-2 (Venezuela and Cuba voting against) to apply the

Rio Treaty and appoint a committee to investigate the Nicaraguan charges; it was noteworthy, however, that the members were not called upon to lend assistance to the victim of the attack, as they had been in the recently concluded Panamanian case. Moreover, the resolution rather gratuitously noted that the action did "not imply, in any way, prejudgment of the nature of the facts, nor intervention in the affairs of a member state."[66]

In fact, however, the presence of the Investigating Committee, which by the nature of its role would be bound to work for peace and conciliation, would help deter further invasions and generally help support the Nicaraguan regime. It was perhaps for this reason that the Committee (composed of Uruguay, Mexico, Brazil, and the United States) delayed going to the scene of the conflict for almost two weeks, in flagrant contrast to its rapid action in most earlier cases. Ignoring repeated Nicaraguan requests that it proceed immediately to Nicaragua, the Committee remained in Washington, ostensibly "gathering information," until June 12, and did not arrive in Nicaragua until the sixteenth, twelve days after the Council resolution and four days after the rebels had surrendered to the Nicaraguan National Guard![67]

In its report to the Council, the Committee confirmed that a group of 110 armed men, all but three of whom were Nicaraguan, had been flown from Costa Rica to Nicaragua. Although the force was aided and given moral support by certain Costa Rican "elements,"[68] the group acted without the knowledge of the Costa Rican government. Furthermore, that government had broken up a later attempt of another exile force to cross into Nicaragua to reinforce the rebellion.[69] No armed assistance was recommended to Nicaragua nor were any warnings, let alone punitive action against any government, suggested. On July 28 the

Council accepted the Committee's report, thereby ending the affair.

The role of Cuba in the Panamanian and Nicaraguan invasions perhaps deserves further attention, especially in light of the controversy that still surrounds the general nature and foreign policy intentions of the Castro regime in its early stages. Evidence of Cuban involvement in the Nicaraguan invasion was mixed. During the crisis, Nicaragua had implied that the Castro government was behind the affair and on several occasions had asserted that seaborne invasions from Cuba were imminent.[70] Although no such invasions materialized, Mexico reported that it had captured a group of armed Cubans and Nicaraguans disembarking from a Cuban fishing boat on Mexican territory.[71] Also, the Investigating Committee found that most of the arms captured from the rebel groups based in Costa Rica were of Cuban manufacture.[72]

On the other hand, although refusing to allow first-hand investigation in Cuba on grounds that the matter was purely an internal Nicaraguan rebellion, the Castro government during the affair promised it would abide by its international commitments and asserted it had recently disarmed and interned Nicaraguan exiles living in Cuba and had broken up a number of plots directed against the Nicaraguan government.[73] Nicaraguan exiles themselves confirmed that they had been refused aid by the Cuban government.[74] As far as the arms were concerned, the Investigating Committee pointed out that they apparently had been obtained on the Costa Rican black market.[75] Finally, a follow-up report of the Investigating Committee, signed by the United States, concluded that

Although the revolutionary movement in Nicaragua is viewed with sympathy in Cuba, the Government of that country not only is not sponsoring any armed movement but it imposes penalties on any persons who are found to be engaged in such activities; and because of that attitude, the expedition . . . was prepared secretly.[76]

There is nothing on the public record, therefore, to substantiate *post hoc* United States assertions that Ché Guevara had a hand in the proceedings or that there was official Cuban support in the form of arms and money.[77]

It seems apparent that disgruntled exile groups had little trouble in recruiting enthusiastic Cuban revolutionaries for the invasions against Panama and Nicaragua, as well as the later ones against the Dominican Republic and Haiti. But in view of the chaotic conditions prevailing in Cuba in the spring of 1959, it was perfectly possible that these activities could have proceeded without the knowledge or support of the Cuban government; such an interpretation is lent credence by the actions the Castro regime took to help facilitate the largely bloodless termination of the Panamanian and Nicaraguan invasion.

Dominican Case.—Despite the failure of the invasions of Panama and Nicaragua, tensions in the Caribbean mounted in the spring of 1959. With the Somoza regime firmly in control, the exile groups turned their attention to Trujillo. In mid-June, Dominican forces crushed several small-scale invasions, apparently mounted in Cuba,[78] but several weeks later the Dominican government, perhaps encouraged by the action of the OAS in the Panamanian and Nicaraguan cases, requested collective assistance under the Rio Treaty to deal with alleged plans for larger-scale exile invasions supported by Venezuela as well as Cuba.[79]

The Dominican request put the collective security-or-democracy issue in the sharpest focus yet. If the charges were correct, and the evidence was impressive, the Trujillo regime was clearly entitled to OAS assistance. But with Trujillo under heavy internal as well as external pressures, and his rule challenged for the first time in almost three decades, inter-American action on his behalf would be not only ideologically repugnant to many states, but could lead to serious popular repercussions throughout the hemisphere.

As a result, the Council's reaction to the Dominican request was markedly cool, and it was clear from the debate that if a vote had been taken the Dominican Republic would have been denied OAS assistance.[80] But the United States, despite the unfavorable image it was creating, pressed for some kind of collective action.

To the traditional United States concern for stability was now added the Communist issue. The Caribbean disturbances were creating conditions conducive to communism, the United States feared, on the assumption that communism thrives on "internal conflict and international distrust and ill-will."[81] Moreover, the conflicts between democracies and dictatorships in the Caribbean were disrupting hemispheric unity, considered by the United States to be an essential element of its global anti-Communist strategy:

The United States is concerned over the Caribbean situation from the standpoint of the Americas in the world as a whole. The inter-American system and the Organization of American States constitute one of the bulwarks of freedom in a world that continues to be threatened by the aggressive and imperialistic designs of international communism. The maintenance of a strong inter-American system is therefore an integral part of the supreme effort in which all of us participate to preserve our liberties and the finer aspects of civilization itself.[82]

Added to this was the United States growing alarm over

the leftward, anti-American drift of the Castro regime, which was at least the inspiration for the exile movements. Thus the United States was anxious for some kind of multilateral action that would at once support the status quo in the Caribbean and contain the Cuban revolution.

Exercising strong leadership in informal consultation, the United States was able to gather majority support for a compromise plan, under which the Dominican Republic would cancel its request for Rio Treaty action in return for a meeting of foreign ministers to consider both the "general situation" in the Caribbean *and* the question of democracy. This was acceptable to the Latin Americans, for such a meeting would not have to consider the specific Dominican charges: the proposal specified that the purpose of the meeting was "to examine the present situation in the Caribbean on a broad front," but *not* "to air or judge charges by one country against another."[83] On July 13, the Council unanimously agreed to convoke the Fifth Meeting of Consultation of Ministers of Foreign Affairs (Santiago Conference).[84]

The United States had both positive and negative objectives at the conference. By focusing hemispheric attention on the Caribbean situation and dramatizing its own concern, it hoped to deter future conflicts. More specifically, a strengthening of inter-American machinery to make it possible to consider future Caribbean-type conflicts *before* they exploded into violence was sought. Initially the United States had in mind the creation of a permanent OAS committee under the Rio Treaty, a committee which would have the authority to threaten or impose sanctions to deter prospective conflict. Pre-conference consultations revealed, however, that there was a great deal of opposition to this proposal both from the democracies, who feared it would become an instrument to insulate the dictatorships from external pressures, and from the traditional Latin American opponents of an expanded political role for the OAS.[85] By the time the conference convened, therefore, the United States proposal was watered down to provide merely for the expansion of the powers of the Peace Committee "to consider problems of the sort that have plagued the Caribbean region before they reach the point of becoming threats to the peace."[86] This was a significant change, for the Peace Committee, not being associated with the Rio Treaty, would not have the means at its disposal to give teeth to its actions.

As far as the democracy question was concerned, the United States hoped to prevent the adoption of Venezuelan and Cuban proposals for a vigorous program of multilateral action to attain democracy and protect human rights. Such action would surely split the system and increase rather than dampen political instability throughout the hemisphere. Until that point the OAS had done nothing at all about democracy, and that was perfectly all right with Washington.

Before the conference began, the United States for the first time officially linked the Caribbean disturbances to communism:

In many cases [the] . . . exiles are motivated by high ideals of democracy and justice . . . However, it is equally clear that some of those responsible for these revolutionary movements organized in foreign countries have either knowingly or unknowingly become associated with political elements whose interests are far removed from those of any government represented around this table. To put it in simple terms, Communists have attempted, and with some success, to infiltrate some of these revolutionary movements in accordance with their well-established policy of taking advantage of any sort of disturbance and unrest to promote their own sinister designs.[87]

No evidence was offered to support this allegation, however, and at the conference this line was not pursued, at
least not publicly. Instead, the strategy of the United
States was to appeal to the traditional precepts of collective security and non-intervention. Never before, in fact,
had the United States spoken in such unqualified praise of
non-intervention:

> The most important foundation stone of the relationship
> which has been developed in this hemisphere is the principle
> of non-intervention. . . . The United States has accepted this
> principle and with the years has become increasingly con-
> vinced of its importance to the entire inter-American relation-
> ship. The non-intervention principle is essential to confidence
> among the 21 member governments of this Organization, and
> that confidence is, in turn, essential to creative effort and
> progress in the collective achievement of the great purposes
> set forth in the charter of our Organization.[88]

The non-intervention principle was clearly being violated in the Caribbean, Secretary of State Herter pointed
out, and the claims of the exile groups and their supporters
that they were striving for democracy was no defense:
the hemispheric states "cannot conduct . . . inter-American relations on the theory that the end justifies the means
and that the charter and other treaties may be flouted at
will."[89] In any event, he argued, in a vein reminiscent of
Acheson's "democracy can only come from within" theme,

> the basis for the soundest and most durable growth of demo-
> cratic institutions within a country stems from the people
> themselves. History has shown that attempts to impose
> democracy upon a country by force from without may easily
> result in the mere substitution of one form of tyranny for
> another.[90]

Moreover, Herter—no doubt stung by criticisms that the
United States non-interventionist stand was in reality a

device to shield dictatorships—went on to say that non-intervention and democracy were actually complementary rather than mutually conflicting:

> The principle of non-intervention and its companion principle of collective security are important to democracy because they assure to each country the opportunity to develop its political life free from outside interference. That opportunity and that freedom are the first necessary condition for the growth of democracy.[91]

Therefore, it was implied, measures to curb the exiles would not only strengthen the inter-American collective security system and enforce non-intervention, they would have a beneficial effect on democracy as well!

As for direct OAS action on behalf of democracy, the OAS could declare "its profound belief in the importance of democratic principles," and perhaps even go so far as to establish a committee, which could "gather the views of the American Governments and people" as to how the nature of democracy could be "clarified."[92]

Venezuela and Cuba led the opposition to the United States, arguing that since the root cause of the Caribbean problems, especially in the Dominican Republic, was dictatorial repression, the way to alleviate tensions was to apply multilateral pressures to secure democracy and respect for human rights. In the absence of such collective action, they implied, the efforts of the exile groups should not be blocked. As for the "democracy can only come from within" argument, Venezuela noted that the United States itself had successfully imposed democracy on Japan after World War II.[93]

Facing up to the implications of its position, Venezuela directly attacked the principle of non-intervention, the first time in the history of the OAS that a Latin American state had done so. Non-intervention, it (incorrectly) asserted, was designed to protect only popular and legitimate states, not dictatorships. Moreover, the non-intervention principle was an expression of the concept of the absolute sovereignty of all states, a concept that was outmoded and undesirable in the modern interdependent world.[94]

Whatever the objective merits of the Venezuelan arguments, the stategy was hardly well chosen. No support was forthcoming from other Latin American states; on the contrary, delegate after delegate strove to outdo one another in lyrical defenses of non-intervention and in warnings that the OAS should not attempt to act as a "superstate."[95]

Nonetheless, in accordance with the usual OAS procedures, some deference had to be given to minority views, so a good deal of lip service was paid to democracy in the final resolutions of the conference, mainly in the form of initial steps toward the creation of an Inter-American Commission on Human Rights and in the "Declaration of Santiago," a verbose collection of platitudes and pieties stating the "principles and attributes" of democracy, "so as to permit national and international public opinion to gauge the degree of identification of political regimes and governments with that system."[96] At the insistence of the United States and several Latin American governments, though, the Declaration contained no direct condemnation of any state, let alone provisions for enforcement.

Other than various reiterations of the non-intervention principle, the most important concrete result of the conference was the authorization to the Peace Committee, along the lines of the United States proposal, to examine "methods and procedures to prevent any activities from abroad designed to overthrow established governments."[97]

By the end of 1959, it was apparent that the combined United States–OAS pressures, culminating in the Santiago Conference, had been reasonably successful. After the abortive "invasion" of Haiti by thirty Cubans during the conference itself, there were no further exile invasions.[98] In October and November the Peace Committee toured most of the states of the Caribbean area and reported that although tensions were still high, the threat of interstate warfare had considerably diminished.[99]

Conclusion

Support for collective security has proved to be a useful tool for the attainment of United States objectives. A number of threats to hemispheric stability have been successfully met, and although the United States undoubtedly could have unilaterally maintained the peace throughout the hemisphere, it could have done so only at enormous material and moral costs. The primary function of the OAS has been to cloak and thereby legitimize the predominant role of the United States in the settlement of most hemispheric conflicts, thus avoiding potential opposition in the United States, in Latin America, and in the rest of the world.

Rarely has it been necessary for the United States to bring to bear more than the smallest fraction of its power. Normally, the very existence of overwhelming United States power, coupled with clear indications that this power was in fact at the disposal of the OAS, has made its actual application unnecessary. In part this has been the case because most serious hemispheric conflicts have occurred in the Caribbean area. The Caribbean has traditionally been within the "sphere of influence" of the United States, and it has always been a cardinal point of United States foreign policy to keep the area stable and friendly. Moreover, the means have been adequate to the end, for the smallness and weakness of the Caribbean states have made them especially vulnerable to United States pressures and therefore especially receptive to United States objectives.

Conversely, the OAS has been less effective in solving interstate problems in South America, both because the United States is generally less concerned about developments there and because the size and distance from the United States of most South American states makes them considerably less vulnerable to United States power. Thus, the OAS has been unable to settle the Peruvian–Ecuadoran border dispute;[100] it has been ineffectual in the present Bolivian–Chilean dispute;[101] and it played no role at all in the violent Argentine–Paraguayan conflicts of 1960.[102]

Not only have there been limitations in effectiveness,[103] there have also been important costs in the operation of the hemispheric collective security systm. The moral underpinning of collective security is often quite shaky, for collective security seeks to maximize only one value: interstate peace. Although theoretically neutral with regard to other values, such as democracy, in operation collective security may in fact impede their realization. This has certainly been the case in the Western Hemisphere, where the United States/OAS pursuit of stability has often served to set back the cause of democracy and human rights, especially by protecting dictatorships against the efforts of their own peoples to liberate their country. Although this was the by-product rather than the purpose of OAS action, the results were no less unfortunate.

Still, the success of the inter-American system in peacefully settling a number of disputes and in deterring major conflict throughout the hemisphere is of great significance. A collective security system is not a system of international government and by its very nature is concerned primarily with "the surface manifestations of tensions"—interstate conflict—rather than their underlying causes.[104] The prevention of war is no small blessing, though, and few would deny the value of a universal system of collective security that insured that all interstate conflicts were waged by relatively non-violent methods.

1. The terms "democratic" and "dictatorial," full of pitfalls in the Latin American context, are used relatively and only to indicate rough tendencies.

2. Cf. the role of the OAS in the 1965 Dominican Republic affair.

3. Official statement of the Department of State, *New York Times*, May 3, 1957.

4. Inter-American Peace Committee, *Report to the Eighth Meeting of Consultation of Ministers of Foreign Affairs* (Washington, D.C.: Pan American Union, 1962), Part I. (Cited hereinafter as *Peace Committee, Report to the Eighth Meeting*.)

5. *New York Times*, April 26, 1957.

6. Pan American Union, *Aplicaciones del Tratado Inter-Americano de Asistencia Recíproca, 1948-1960* (Washington, D.C.: Pan American Union, 1960), pp. 219-30 (Cited hereinafter as *Aplicaciones*); *Actas del Consejo*, May 1, 1957.

7. *Actas del Consejo*, May 2, 1957.

8. *Aplicaciones*, pp. 231-32, 262-63; *Actas del Consejo*, May 17, 1957. The seventeen-man Military Commission was composed of officers furnished by eight Latin American states and headed by a United States Colonel. (*Annals of the OAS*, No. 3, 1957, pp. 264-70.)

9. *Actas del Consejo*, May 17, May 24, 1957; quote from the Report of the Investigating Committee, *Aplicaciones*, pp. 276-77.

10. *Actas del Consejo*, July 5, 1957.

11. Peace Committee, *Report to the Eighth Meeting*, pp. 3-4; Appendixes to Part 1, pp. 1-7.

12. *Ibid.*, pp. 4-7; Appendixes, pp. 7-18.

13. *Ibid.*, pp. 8-17; Appendixes, pp. 19-56.

14. *Actas del Consejo,* December 24, 1948. The United States position is further recounted by John Dreier, former United States delegate to the Council, in his *The Organization of American States and the Hemisphere Crisis* (New York: Council on Foreign Relations, 1962), pp. 65-66. (Cited hereinafter as *Hemisphere Crisis.)*

15. Department of State announcement, *New York Times,* April 20, 1948.

16. Pan American Union, *Applications of the Inter-American Treaty of Reciprocal Assistance,* 1948-1956, (Washington, D.C.: Pan American Union, 1957), p. 19-21. (Cited hereinafter as *Applications.) The New York Times* placed the strength of the Legion at 200 to 500 men (November 2, 1948).

17. *Applications,* pp. 26-27.

18. Report of the Investigating Committee, *ibid.,* p. 26. On December 24, the Costa Rican government reported that the last invaders had fled back to Nicaragua. (*New York Times,* December 25, 1948.)

19. *Applications,* pp. 27-31; *Actas del Consejo,* December 24, 1948.

20. Report of the Military Commission, *Applications,* pp. 38-47.

21. The text of the Pact is in *Applications,* pp. 48-50.

22. Nicaraguan speech, *Actas del Consejo,* January 10, 1955.

23. Costa Rican note to the Council. *Applications,* pp. 159-60.

24. *Applications,* p. 164; *New York Times,* January 12, 13, 1954.

25. *Actas del Consejo,* January 12, 1955.

26. *Applications,* p. 165.

27. *Ibid., pp.* 166-67.

28. *Actas del Consejo,* January 14, 1955.

29. *Applications,* pp. 169-70.

30. *Actas del Consejo,* January 16, 1955.

31. Dreier, *Hemisphere Crisis,* p. 67.

32. *Applications,* pp. 171-77.

33. *Applications,* Report of the Investigating Committee, p. 185; *Hemisphere Crisis,* p. 66.

34. *Applications,* Report of the Investigating Committee, p. 188-90.

35. Dreier, *Hemisphere Crisis*, p. 65.

36. *Applications*, p. 190.

37. *Actas del Consejo*, February 24, 1955.

38. *New York Times*, February 22, 1955.

39. The text of the treaties is in *Applications*, pp. 203-14.

40. Secretary of State Dean Acheson, *Department of State Bulletin*, September 26, 1949 (Vol. 21, No. 534), p. 463.

41. Secretary of State Christian Herter, *Department of State Bulletin*, August 31, 1959 (Vol. 41, No. 1053), p. 303.

42. United States memorandum to the Inter-American Peace Committee, in the *Department of State Bulletin*, September 26, 1949, pp. 450-54; See also a summary article on the Caribbean situation, *New York Times*, August 20, 1949.

43. *Department of State Bulletin*, September 26, 1949 (Vol. 21, No. 534), p. 463.

44. Peace Committee, *Report to the Fifth Meeting of Consultation*, pp. 13-14, pp. 32-64; *Applications*, pp. 59-68.

45. Personal interviews. See also the book by the former Argentine delegate to the Council and Chairman of the Council during this period, Enrique Corominas, *In the Caribbean Political Areas* (Cambridge, Mass.; University Press of Cambridge, 1954), pp. 51-52.

46. *Department of State Bulletin*, September 26, 1949, p. 451.

47. Conclusions of the Peace Committee in the Situation in the Caribbean, *Report to the Fifth Meeting of Consultation*, pp. 35-38.

48. *Actas del Consejo*, January 6, 1950; *Applications*, pp. 71-80.

49. According to the Committee, the Legion consisted in part of "sincere and idealistic individuals who, being deprived of democratic guarantees in their native lands, inevitably strive to return to democracy," but in part of "adventurers, professional revolutionaries, and mercenaries whose primary objective appears to be the promotion of illegal traffic in arms and revolutionary expeditions against countries with which they have no ties whatever." (Report of the Investigating Committee, *Applications*, p. 121.)

50. *Ibid.,* p. 120. The entire report is reprinted, pp. 87-123.

51. Resolution IV, *Actas del Consejo,* April 8, 1950.

52. Resolutions I and II, *ibid.*

53. The committee submitted three reports, in June and October, 1950, and May, 1951. The text of the reports is in *Applicaciones,* pp. 135-48.

54. *Aplicaciones,* p. 295

55. *Actas del Consejo,* April 28, 1959. The Cuban offer was rejected by Panama, which urged the Cuban government to use the frigate to patrol its own coast and prevent further expeditions.

56. *Actas del Consejo,* April 28, 1959; Aplicaciones, pp. 310-11. Besides Colombia and Ecuador, the only other OAS state to offer patrol craft was Cuba itself, an offer which the investigating committee declined as "unnecessary." (*Aplicaciones,* p. 312.)

57. Report of the Investigating Committee, *Aplicaciones,* pp. 303-15.

58. *Ibid.*

59. Panamanian statements, *Actas del Consejo,* April 28, 1959; Statement of the rebels to the Investigating Committee, *Aplicaciones,* p. 309.

60. Statement of the United States delegate, *Actas del Consejo,* April 28, 1959.

61. Department of State memorandum, "Responsibilities of the Cuban Government for Increased International Tensions in the Hemisphere," in *Castro-Communist Subversion in the Western Hemisphere,* Hearings before the Subcommittee on Inter-American Affairs of the Committee on Foreign Affairs, House of Representatives, 88th Cong., 1st. sess., 1963, p. 285. (Cited hereinafter as *Castro-Communist Subversion.*)

62. *Actas del Consejo,* June 3, June 4, 1959; Department of State, *Inter-American Efforts to Relieve International Tensions in the Western Hemisphere, 1959-1960* (Washington, D.C.: U.S. Government Printing Office, 1962), p. 123. (Cited hereinafter as *Efforts.*)

63. *Actas del Consejo,* June 3, 1959.

64. *Actas del Consejo,* June 3, June 4, 1959.

65. *Actas del Consejo,* June 4, 1959.

66. *Aplicaciones,* p. 346

67. Report of the Investigating Committee, *Ibid.,* pp. 347-81.

68. Nicaragua had charged that followers of former president Figueres, some of whom were in the Costa Rican legislature, had helped the exiles. (*Actas del Consejo,* June 4, 1959.)

69. Report of the Committee, *Aplicaciones,* pp. 352-61.

70. *Ibid.*

71. *Efforts,* pp. 14-15.

72. Report of the Committee, *Aplicaciones,* pp. 360-61.

73. *Actas del Consejo,* July 27, 1959.

74. Report of the Investigating Committee, *Aplicaciones,* pp. 360-61.

75. *Ibid.*

76. *Efforts,* p. 143.

77. *Efforts,* p. 14; *Castro-Communist Subversion,* p. 286.

78. No investigation was made, but it is generally accepted that the invasions did take place and that Cuba was involved. The United States later charged that the June invasions had been organized in Cuba "with the undoubted assistance of Cuban officials," and that "the Cuban Navy escorted the three landing crafts used by the invading force on their voyage to the Dominican Republic." (*Castro-Communist Subversion,* p. 286.)

79. The Dominican note is reprinted in *Inter-American Efforts,* pp. 132-35.

80. *Actas del Consejo,* July 2, 6, 1959.

81. Meeting of Consultation of Ministers of Foreign Affairs, Fifth, Santiago, Chile, 1959, *Actas y Documentos* (Washington, D.C.: Pan American Union, 1961), Secretary of State Christian Herter's speech to the Second Plenary Session, Document 36. (Cited hereinafter as *Fifth Meeting, Document.*)

82. *Ibid.*

83. *Actas del Consejo,* July 10, 1959.

84. *Actas del Consejo,* July 13, 1959.

85. *Interviews.*

86. Herter's speech, *Fifth Meeting, Document* 36.

87. *Actas del Consejo,* July 10, 1959.

88. Speech of Secretary of State Herter, *Fifth Meeting, Document* 36.

89. *Ibid.*

90. *Ibid.*

91. *Ibid.*

92. *Ibid.*

93. Speeches of the Venezuelan and Cuban foreign ministers, *Fifth Meeting, Documents* 67, 93.

94. *Ibid. Document* 67.

95. See the summary of speeches in *Efforts,* pp. 28-30.

96. See Chapter VII below for a discussion of the Human Rights Commission. The Declaration of Santiago is Resolution I of the Final Act of the conference *(Fifth Meeting, Documents).*

97. Resolution IV, Final Act, *Fifth Meeting, Documents.* The Peace Committee was also authorized to study "the relationship between violations of human rights or the non-exercise of representative democracy, on the one hand, and the political tensions that affect the peace of the hemisphere, on the other," and this eventually proved to be of much greater significance. (See Chapter V.)

98. The Castro government admitteed the invasion had originated in Cuba, but without its consent or foreknowledge. (Speech of Cuban foreign minister, *Fifth Meeting, Document* 93.)

99. Inter-American Peace Committee, *Report to the Seventh Meeting of Consultation of Ministers of Foreign Affairs* (Washington, D.C.: Pan American Union, 1960), p. 10. (Cited hereinafter as "Report to the Seventh Meeting.")

100. Since the early nineteenth century, Peru and Ecuador have each claimed jurisdiction over an area consisting of about 120,000 square miles of unexplored jungle lying along their border. In 1942, after hostilities broke out, international pressures were brought to bear to force Ecuador to accept a settlement in which most of the area was ceded to Peru. Along with Argentina, Brazil, and Chile, the United States was named a "guarantor" of the settlement, responsible for any future problems concerning its interpretation and enforcement. (Mecham, *op. cit.,* pp. 166-70.)

The border dispute has continued to be a major issue in Ecuadoran domestic politics, however, and recent Ecuadoran governments have been forced to press for a new treaty and generally to keep the issue alive. Beginning in 1953, incidents involving Peruvian and Ecuadoran armed forces along the border increased in number and severity, and relations between the two countries progressively deteriorated. In September, 1955, Ecuador charged that Peru was preparing to invade and asked for OAS assistance under the Rio Treaty. (*Applications,* pp. 227-28.) Acting in effect as the Council's Investigating Committee, the United States and the other guarantor powers sent a military team to the area to examine the situation, and soon reported to the Council that they found no evidence to support the Ecuadoran charges. Shortly afterward Ecuador withdrew its OAS requests, citing the effectiveness of the guarantors in "preventing military action" by Peru. (*Actas del Consejo,* September 8, 1955; *Applications,* pp. 230-37.)

The dispute was resumed in late 1960, however, when Ecuador unilaterally denounced the 1942 pact. As incidents along the border increased and nationalistic sentiments in Ecuador threatened to precipitate a major clash, the guarantors again intervened. The issue was too intertwined with Ecuadoran domestic politics for a settlement to be attained, though, and a mediation attempt ended with a joint statement of the guarantors denouncing Ecuador's abrogation of the 1942 agreement and reaffirming its validity. The guarantor's stand was given teeth by a United States announcement that in the event any country used force in the dispute the United States would "comply with its obligations under the Rio Treaty," even including the application of unilateral force if necessary to prevent aggression. (*New York Times,* December 14, 1960.) Although the issue is still very much alive, there have been no other threatened outbreaks of violence.

101. In April, 1962, Bolivia complained to the Council that Chile was guilty of "aggression" because of its plans to divert the Lauca River, which flows through both Chile and Bolivia, for irrigation purposes. Bolivia requested the invocation of the Rio Treaty, but Chile produced a complex legal argument defending its right to utilize the waters of the Lauca and warned that the application of the Rio Treaty would "produce the collapse of our system of collective security." In view of the Chilean threat and the complexities of the case the Council refused to apply the Rio Treaty. Instead, it merely offered to provide its good offices to facilitate direct negotiations. In subsequent informal negotiations, the United States joined with Brazil, Honduras, Mexico, and Venezuela to attempt mediation of the dispute.

The issue was further complicated, however, when Bolivia tied the Lauca River dispute to its traditional demands for access to Chilean ports on the Pacific Ocean, and the whole matter became an inflammatory nationalistic issue in the domestic politics of each country, precluding meaningful negotiations. As a result, the mediatory efforts of the OAS broke down, and in June, 1963, Bolivia withdrew from participation in the political (but not economic) activities of the Council. The unwillingness of the United States to apply real pressures on the disputants left the OAS without the necessary leverage to impose a settlement.

102. Throughout 1959 and 1960 Paraguayan exiles living in Argentina crossed into their homeland and engaged the armed forces of the Stroessner government. Paraguay officially charged Argentina with assisting the exiles but refrained from requesting OAS assistance, perhaps because it feared a rebuff. The United States, unlike its reaction to similar situations involving exile attacks on Nicaragua and the Dominican Republic, did not take the lead in pressing for OAS action, and nothing was done.

103. See the concluding chapter.

104. Senate Committee on Foreign Relations, *United States–Latin American Relations, Study No. 3, The Organization of American States* (by Northwestern University), 86th Cong., 2d sess., 1960, p. 217.

CHAPTER **3**

The OAS as an Anti-Communist Alliance (I):

The Korean War and the Guatemalan Crisis

THE AUTHOR'S DECISION to treat United States policy and the role of the OAS in the Korean War, the Guatemalan crisis of 1954, and the Cuban situation since 1959 as alliance rather than collective security action is somewhat arbitrary, for the differences between these two kinds of systems are often quite difficult to determine. The problem arises from the inherent fuzziness of the concept of "aggression," particularly when it is defined as broadly as it is in the OAS. Article 6 of the Rio Treaty, it will be recalled, authorizes collective action in the event of any "fact or situation that might endanger the peace of America." The vagueness of this language has on several occasions lent itself to political—i.e., alliance—usages.

For collective action to be properly considered collective

107

security, two essential requirements must be met: violent challenges to the international status quo must be collectively resisted, and impartial criteria must be applied in determining when to activate the system. Both these criteria have been violated by the OAS in dealing with the Guatemalan and Cuban situations.

The case for OAS action against Guatemala and Cuba under the Rio Treaty has been based not so much on impartial criteria as on arguments conditioned by the cold war. The first is that "international communism" is inherently aggressive and that therefore any defensive action by the inter-American system, even including the overthrow of Communist governments, is perfectly consistent with collective security. As policy-makers were no doubt aware, however, the historical evidence does not support this contention. In an era of polycentric national communism, the notion that all local Communist movements are mere pawns in a highly co-ordinated, centrally directed "plot" does not bear serious analysis. Nor can it be persuasively shown that all Communist governments invariably seek to expand by the use of armed force; Yugoslavia alone demonstrates the contrary, and even Soviet foreign policy cannot adequately be so characterized today.

More importantly, the United States has sought to demonstrate that in any event Guatemala and Cuba were in fact guilty of aggression against their neighbors, in the form of subversion. "Subversion," however, is a highly imprecise and emotional concept, closely bound up with ideological conflict and the cold war. The evidence of Guatemalan aggression in Central America was flimsy, and certainly not sufficient to justify the actions of the United States and the OAS under a reasonable interpretation of "collective security." The Cuban case has been somewhat more complex. The importation of Soviet missiles in 1962 was a clear threat to the hemisphere, to which the missile blockade was a legitimate collective security response. Moreover, there is no question that the Cuban government has been exporting arms, training revolutionaries, and financing the efforts of dissident Latin American groups to overthrow hemispheric governments, justifying defensive efforts on the part of the OAS. On the other hand, though, non-Communist Central American and Caribbean governments have been waging political warfare—"subverting" each other—for decades, and the OAS has not reacted to these activities as it did to the cases involving the Communist issue.

Not only has the OAS taken action against Guatemala and Cuba beyond that required by collective security, but in a negative sense it has failed to protect them from or, more realistically, at least condemn United States–sponsored exile invasions. The Castillo Armas "rebellion" of 1954 and the Bay of Pigs expedition were as flagrant violations of inter-American norms as Communist subversion, but in the latter case the OAS remained silent and in the former it acted as a foil for the United States. When similar actions have been directed against non-Communist states, regardless of the initial provocations, the OAS has assisted the victim, not the attacker.

United States policies in the OAS with regard to Guatemala and Cuba have reflected a concern with the establishment in the Western Hemisphere of Communist-dominated governments per se, that is, with the *domestic* ideologies and political structure of the two nations at least as much as with their international activities. A collective security system, though, is not concerned with internal policies; Cuba's removal from the OAS because its government and policies were "incompatible" with the inter-America system was itself an action incompatible with the requirements of collective security. Thus, to the extent that the United States has been able to gain OAS support for its cold war policies, the OAS has ignored its responsibilities as a collective security system and acted instead as an anti-Communist alliance.

The OAS and the Korean War

The first of a series of steps by which the United States and a number of Latin American states have given the inter-American system an anti-Communist character was taken at the Bogotá Conference of 1948. Although the United States had opposed the introduction of the Communist question at the Rio Conference, it changed its position under the impact of the Czechoslovakian coup and a general intensification of the cold war, and now firmly supported a Latin American initiative for a strong statement condemning the subversive activities of "international communism."[1]

At the Bogotá Conference, initial opposition to the resolution by a number of democratic states, which feared that it would sanction repressive measures against all antidictatorial movements, was modified after the conference was disrupted by allegedly Communist-led riots. When the Conference reconvened, the democratic bloc, led by Romulo Betancourt of Venezuela, agreed to support the resolution provided it condemned *all* totalitarian doctrines,[2] and unanimous agreement was obtained for a statement declaring that "by its anti-democratic nature and its interventionist tendency, the political activity of international communism or any other totalitarian doctrine is incompatible with the concept of American freedom."[3]

The first real test of how the OAS would respond to United States anti-Communist leadership came during the Korean War. In December, 1950, shortly after Communist China entered the war, the Council agreed to a United States request to convoke the Fourth Meeting of Consultation of Ministers of Foreign Affairs (Washington Conference) to consider "coordination of the common effort required to meet . . . the aggressive policy of international communism."[4]

The Washington Conference foreshadowed the difficulties that Guatemala and Cuba would cause the United States in the inter-American system. The agenda contained three subjects: (1) "political and military cooperation for the defense of the Americas; (2) strengthening of the internal security of the American Republics; (3) emergency economic cooperation."[5]

The United States sought several objectives. First, it was hoped that the Latin Americans might make a substantial contribution to the Korean War effort, in part through the actual provision of combat forces to the United Nations command, but principally through an economic "mobilization," especially in the production of strategic raw materials, similar to that of World War II. Within the hemisphere, the Conference might pave the way for a strengthening of the armed forces of the Latin American states under the aegis of the new United States military assistance program, partially in preparation for a possible Soviet armed attack on the hemisphere,[6] partially to combat internal Communist subversion. Finally, at a minimum, a verbal show of hemispheric unity would serve symbolically to bolster the United States role in the Korean War and in the world-wide anti-Communist struggle in general.[7]

The Latin Americans, despite their unanimous consent to the holding of a conference, had different ideas. A large group, led by Mexico, Argentina (under Perón) , and Guatemala (under José Arévalo) was not convinced that the security of the hemisphere required Latin American participation in the Korean War and was very cool toward involvement in United States overseas activities. Moreover, almost all Latin American states were unhappy about the United States emphasis on economic "mobilization." The conference was held in an atmosphere of increasing bitterness over the failure of the United States to provide a "Marshall Plan" for Latin America. The Latin Americans had gone along with the United States economic mobilization plans in World War II, and in return they had expected massive United States assistance in postwar economic development, an expectation that had proved false. Furthermore, prices on Latin American exports—primarily to the United States—were falling, while import prices were rising, and rightly or wrongly, the United States was held responsible.

In his opening address to the conference, President Truman emphasized the threat of "Communist imperialism" to the Western Hemisphere and made it quite clear to the Latin Americans that any hopes that the United States might reverse its economic policies were ill-founded. On the contrary, the President bluntly stated, "defense production must have prior claim upon our economic reserves. We shall have to increase the production of strategic materials. We shall have to divert the manufacturing capacity to defense purposes."[8] Throughout the conference the United States followed this line, rejecting Latin American pleas to give economic development priority as the best means of fighting communism in the hemisphere, and emphasizing "the seriousness of the existing emergency and the need of subordinating economic development plans to the requirements of the common defense."[9]

In brief, then, conference debate centered around one major issue: to what extent, militarily and economically, should Latin America support the overseas security efforts of the United Nations"? Verbally, the outcome was a victory for the United States. Although partially modified in order to gain unanimity, the United States proposals formed the basis of the Final Act of the conference. The Ministers agreed that

> the present world situation requires positive support by the American Republics for: (1) achievement of the collective defense of the continent through the Organization of American States, and (2) cooperation, within the United Nations organization, to prevent and suppress aggression in other parts of the world.[10]

Pursuant to these ends, four major politico-military steps were recommended, all of them very close to the original United States proposals. First, each American Republic should

> give particular attention to the development and maintenance of elements within its national armed forces trained, organized, and equipped so that, in accordance with its constitutional norms and to the full extent that, in its judgment, its capabilities permit, they may be promptly available, (1) for the defense of the Continent, and (2) for service as United Nations unit or units.[11]

Second, the American Republics were to "increase . . . their resources and strengthen . . . their armed forces . . . [so] that they can be promptly available for the defense of the Continent."[12]

Third, the Inter-American Defense Board was charged "with preparing, as vigorously as possible . . . the military planning of the common defense."[13]

Fourth, it was recommended that each American Republic enact and strengthen its national laws "to assure that the subversive activities of the agents of international communism . . . may be adequately prevented and punished," and especially to restrict the travel of persons "who there is reason to expect will attempt to carry out subversive acts."[14]

The success of the conference, despite the unanimous approval of the United States proposals, was dubious. The subsequent failure of the Latin Americans to put the recommended steps into practice made it apparent that they had gone along very reluctantly, perhaps in the hope of eventually acquiring United States economic assistance; even the State Department was to admit that the follow-up was "disappointing."[15]

Only Colombia sent a large enough combat force to Korea to be acceptable to the UN command. (Bolivia, Costa Rica, Panama, El Salvador, and Cuba offered small units.) Within the hemisphere, the Inter-American Defense Board remained insignificant, and "to all intents and purposes, inter-American military cooperation continued within the familiar confines set by bilateral agreements."[16]

Economically, there is no evidence that the Latin American states made any special efforts to repeat their World War II co-operation. On the contrary, Truman's plea for economic sacrifices was bluntly answered by the Brazilian foreign minister in a statement taken to be representative of the feelings of all Latin America: "We could not repeat past practices without ruining ourselves with no benefit accruing to the world therefrom. . . ."[17]

About the most that can be said for the conference was that the United States could claim to have verbal hemispheric support for its Korean policies and a multilateral authorization for its military assistance program. But the price was high. The conference had conclusively demonstrated that *operational* hemispheric solidarity did not include meaningful support for United States overseas policies and actions. Within the hemisphere, bitterness against the United States increased because of its refusal to send large-scale development aid to Latin America. Still another cost was the blow dealt to the cause of freedom in Latin America. To avoid the introduction of "extraneous" issues, the United States joined forces with the dictators to prevent consideration of the creation of an inter-American court for the protection of human rights[18]—predictably, the dictators had been the most vigorous supporters of the United States and of the "defense of the free world." Even more significantly the United States emphasis on military buildups and antisubversive measures fostered militarism in Latin America. Finally, the conference reflected the growing tendency of the United States to view Latin American political instability as a function of "Communist subversion," thus obscuring far more basic factors and paving the way for Washington's misunderstanding of the Guatemalan and Cuban revolutions.

The Guatemalan Crisis

The Guatemalan counter-revolution of 1954 capped a decade of United States blunders in that country. Throughout most of its history as an independent republic, Guatemala had been ruled by a series of authoritarian, quasi-feudalistic regimes, typical of Central America. In 1944, however, the despotic Jorgé Ubico was overthrown and replaced by a reformist regime headed by José Arévalo, who considered himself a nationalist and democratic socialist.

Had the United States succeeded in grasping the significance of the 1944 revolution, instead of treating it as merely another palace coup, it might have helped to guide Guatemalan affairs into moderate channels by sympathetic encouragement and material assistance to the Arévalo regime. Almost from the start, however, relations between the United States and the Arévalo regime were bad. In contrast to his predecessors, who had worked closely with United States fruit and electrical power interests, Arévalo proposed agrarian reform and controls over foreign investment. This brought him into sharp conflict with the United Fruit Company, which had extensive plantation holdings in Guatemala, and with the United States Ambassador, who firmly supported that Company. As a result, the United States not only failed to assist in Arévalo's attempt to introduce social and economic reforms but hindered it in a number of ways.[19]

In 1951, Arévalo was succeeded by Jacobo Arbenz, an army officer. Although Arbenz was not a Communist, at least not initially, he was willing to co-operate with the local Communist party, and in the next two years the Communists became increasingly powerful in his regime. By the end of 1953, the Communists, having gained control of the police and infiltrated the army, were the dominant force in Guatemala. The antireform attitudes of the State Department had helped to create a climate of extremism and anti-Americanism that made it possible for the Communists to gain control of the state.

In any event, the point of no return in United States–Guatemalan relations had been reached. The Arbenz regime was anathema to the Untied States on a number of counts. The very existence of a Communist state in Latin America was a blow to United States prestige abroad and to the Eisenhower administration at home. Moreover, it was feared that Guatemala might stimulate further Communist gains in Latin America, both by its example and more directly by assistance to dissident groups. Even if Guatemala should fail to export its revolution, at a very minimum its virulent attacks on United States "imperialism" would certainly increase the already widespread anti-Americanism in Latin America. Finally, it was even conceivable that the Arbenz regime might consent to become a Soviet military base, thereby breaching the Monroe Doctrine and posing a direct threat to United States strategic interests.[20]

Therefore, the administration decided, the Arbenz regime had to be removed. If this could be done through the OAS, so much the better; if not, then other measures were available. Initially, then, a multilateral approach was adopted and the administration decided to seek an OAS statement of policy clearly prohibiting the establishment of Communist regimes in the Western Hemisphere. Optimally, such a declaration would encourage the anti-Communist forces inside Guatemala and bring about the internal collapse of the Arbenz regime. That failing, the way would be paved for later, more substantive multilateral actions. And if worse came to worse, an OAS statement could at least help legitimize unilateral United States measures.

The first step in this strategy was taken at the Tenth Inter-American Conference, held at Caracas in March, 1954, when the United States proposed that the OAS declare "that the domination or control of the political institutions of any American State by the international Communist movement . . . would constitute a threat to the sovereignty and political independence of the American States endangering the peace of America, and would call for appropriate action in accordance with existing treaties."[21]

The U.S. proposal went considerably beyond the Bogotá

anti-Communist declaration, for by invoking the language of Article 6 of the Rio Treaty it implied that the adoption of communism as an *internal* form of government anywhere in the hemisphere was an act of aggression per se, irrespective of the *international* policies of the state concerned.

Not surprisingly, this renewed attempt to transform the OAS into an anti-Communist alliance met with a cold Latin American reaction. If adopted, the door would be wide open for OAS—i.e., United States—intervention in the internal affairs of Latin American states. Beyond the non-intervention problem, the conference was meeting at a time when United States–Latin American relations were at their lowest point since the pre-Good Neighbor days. Bitter over the subordination of Latin American economic development and social progress to the demands of private enterprise and to what the United States considered to be the exigencies of the cold war, many Latin American states were in no mood to co-operate. Moreover, the Latin American democracies were increasingly unhappy over United States co-operation with dictatorships; the very site of the conference—the Venezuela of Peréz Jiménez—seemed to symbolize the indifference of the OAS to democracy.[22]

Guatemala played upon these resentments with great effectiveness. Guatemalan Foreign Minister Guillermo Toriello denied his country was dominated by communism and charged that those who made this accusation were in reality reactionaries motivated by concern over Guatemalan economic reforms, which had "affected the privileges of foreign firms." Specifically, he accused the United States of supporting "plots" against his government because of its recent expropriation of United Fruit Company land. The United States anti-Communist proposal he warned, was designed to serve as a pretext for intervention in Guatemala's internal affairs and, more generally, would insure that any Latin American government attempting to institute a national development program that offended the interests of the United States would be accused of being "Communist." If the United States proposal were adopted, he went on, "Pan Americanism would become an instrument exclusively in the service of monopolistic interests and a weapon of coercion to strangle any attempt at political and economic liberation of the oppressed peoples of Latin America."[23] At the conclusion of his speech, Toriello received the warmest ovation of the conference, one delegate remarking that he had said "many things some of the rest of us would like to say if we dared."[24]

Put on the defensive by the Guatemalan attack and the sympathy it aroused in a number of Latin American countries, Secretary of State Dulles found it necessary to promise that in exchange for solid support of the anti-Communist resolution the United States would agree to a special conference to consider Latin American economic problems.[25] But beyond that Dulles was forced to agree to a number of extremely damaging amendments to the original United States proposal and to assure the Latin Americans that the purpose of the resolution was merely "preventive," since the United States did not consider any existing Latin American government to be under Communist domination.[26]

Even with these concessions, the approval of the United States proposal, though by a 17-1-2 vote (Guatemala against, Mexico and Argentina abstaining), was, to say the least, unenthusiastic.[27] With the exception of the reactionary dictatorships of Nicaragua, the Dominican Republic, El Salvador, Peru, and Venezuela, delegation after delegation specified that their approval was based on the understanding that the resolution would not be used to justify unilateral or collective intervention in the internal affairs of any state, that all states have the right to govern themselves as they see fit, and that the best way to fight communism is to raise the living standards of the Latin American peoples.[28]

In short, the Latin Americans had approved the anti-Communist declaration with the understanding that it meant nothing. On its face the resolution was either inconsistent or meaningless. Although it began with the declaration that "the domination or control of the political institutions of any American state by the international communist movement . . . would [endanger] . . . the peace of America and would call for a Meeting of Consultation to consider the adoption of appropriate action in accordance with existing treaties," it added, as the price for Latin American approval, that the declaration did *not* "impair the inalienable right of each American state freely to choose its own form of government and economic system." Thus, it was implied, Communist regimes coming to power without overt Soviet intervention were not prohibited; at any rate, this was the interpretation of the majority of Latin American states. In this sense, the resolution added nothing to past anti-Communist declarations or, for that matter, to the Rio Treaty itself, and it amounted to little more than a face-saving device for the United States.

Seen in this light, Dulles' claim that the Caracas Conference had "multilateralized" that part of the Monroe Doctrine that "prohibits" the extension of "European" political systems to the Western Hemisphere is extremely dubious.[29] There was even less validity in the United States argument that the resolution laid the basis for the later Castillo Armas rebellion; as has been indicated, the affirmative votes of many Latin American states were gained only after Dulles' explicit assurances that the resolution would not be used as a weapon against Guatemala.

Despite, then, numerical victory for the United States resolution, gained at the cost of openly expressed anti-Americanism and a barely papered-over hemispheric split, the Caracas Conference had actually demonstrated that there was little Latin American support for the United States pressures against Guatemala, and it foreshadowed the difficulties the United States was to have in the OAS over its role in the Castillo Armas rebellion.[30]

The Castillo Armas Rebellion

With multilateral efforts coming to naught and the strength of the Communist forces in Guatemala continuing to grow, the Eisenhower administration decided to resort to unilateral methods to remove the Arbenz regime. Matters came to a head in mid-May, 1954, when a 2,000 ton arms shipment from Soviet-bloc countries arrived in Guatemala. The armaments gave Guatemala a more powerful military capability than all of the rest of the Central American states combined, and although they may well have been intended purely for defensive purposes—the emergence of an active opposition movement inside Guatemala and mounting friction with Honduras and Nicaragua had brought heavy pressure on the Arbenz government—the State Department interpreted them as a prelude to Guatemalan aggression in Central America and decided to take direct action.[31]

A two-front strategy was adopted. Clandestinely, the United States would join forces with a group of Honduran-based anti-Communist Guatemalan exiles under the leadership of former Guatemalan army officer Carlos Castillo Armas in an attempt to overthrow the Arbenz regime.[32] Meanwhile, on the diplomatic level, the United States would go through the motions of seeking another OAS conference, ostensibly to review the Guatemalan situation in the light of the arms shipment, but primarily as a smoke screen to obscure preparations for the impending Castillo Armas attack. Moreover, if the exiles should fail, an OAS conference might after all be of some use; in that event the fallback United States position would be that the arms shipment constituted a threat to the peace under Article 6 of the Rio Treaty, justifying an OAS naval blockade (or an OAS-authorized United States blockade), presumably to prevent further arms shipments, but also to generally harass the Guatemalan government and disrupt its overseas trade.[33]

Accordingly, one week after the Guatemalan arms shipment, the United States began airlifting large quantities of arms to Honduras and Nicaragua, supposedly for "hemispheric defense" tasks but in reality for use by Castillo Armas. Simultaneously, consultations were begun with Latin American governments to gain support for a foreign ministers' conference, and when, on June 10, Mexico, the most vigorous opponent of anti-Guatemalan action, announced that in view of "general Latin American sentiment" it would agree to a formal multilateral gathering, the way was cleared for an OAS meeting.[34]

On June 18, however, before the United States officially requested a conference, the Castillo Armas forces crossed into Guatemala. The strategy of the United States in the period immediately following the invasion was to give the attacking forces sufficient time to overthrow the Arbenz government, while preventing that regime from obtaining assistance from either the UN or the OAS. To this end it was necessary for the OAS to take just enough action to justify the exclusion of the UN, but not so much as to endanger the success of the Castillo Armas coup.

This delicate United States strategy was aided by a tactical error of the Guatemalan government. On June 19, Guatemala appealed to both the Security Council and the Peace Committee for help, charging that Nicaragua and Honduras were guilty of aggression and requesting an immediate Peace Committee investigation at the scene of the fighting.[35] This was an error, for the presence of the United States on the Peace Committee made it very unlikely that the Committee would be of much help to Guatemala, even assuming the sympathy of the other members (Mexico, Brazil, Argentina, and Cuba). At the same time, it would allow the United States to argue in the UN that Security Council action was unnecessary because the OAS had assumed jurisdiction over the case.

Apparently in realization of this, Guatemala the following day hastily withdrew its request for Peace Committee intervention, officially on the grounds that a Security Council resolution calling for a cease fire had made the Committee's assistance unnecessary.[36] To counter this and reinvolve the OAS, however, Honduras and Nicaragua promptly requested the Peace Committee to continue its role in the "dispute" and investigate Guatemala's "calumnious" charges.[37] Although Guatemala now refused to co-operate with an investigation, the Peace Committee accepted the Honduran-Nicaraguan request and reassumed jurisdiction in the matter, prompting a bitter protest from the Arbenz regime:

The Government of Guatemala is greatly displeased to see a body as high and useful as the Inter-American Peace Committee shown disrespect to the extent of taking advantage of its exalted mission and its generous concern with continental peace and solidarity to cover a maneuver of aggressors endeavoring to neutralize the action brought by the Government of Guatemala before the Security Council of the United Nations [sic].[38]

The Guatemalan charges were perfectly accurate, for while the fighting was continuing in Guatemala the United States was exerting great efforts in the Security Council to prevent UN intervention. On June 22, Guatemala had protested that the Council's cease fire call was being ignored and had requested further action. Taking advantage of his position as President of the Security Council, United States Ambassador Henry Cabot Lodge delayed calling the Council into session for nearly three days, charging that the rebellion was merely a "civil war" and that Guatemala was acting as a tool of the Soviet Union in bringing its case to the UN instead of to the OAS.[39]

In the ensuing debates, Lodge warned that Security Council intervention might doom the UN:

Let us not delude ourselves. If it is not now possible to make a living reality of the formula [regional arrangements] which made possible the adoption of the charter, then the United Nations will have destroyed itself in 1954 as it would have been destroyed still-born in 1945, had not the present formula been devised.[40]

Perhaps partially as a result of this threat, the Council by a 5-4 vote acceded to the United States insistence that the Peace Committee be permitted to complete its "investigation" before further UN action was undertaken.[41]

Meanwhile, the Castillo Armas forces, numbering no

more than a few hundred men, were making great progress, primarily because of the refusal of the Guatemalan army to engage them. With internal pressures thus increasing and no help available from outside, the Arbenz regime collapsed. On June 27, Arbenz resigned at the "request" of the army and turned over power to a military junta. In ensuing negotiations, "assisted" by the United States Ambassador in Guatemala, John E. Peurifoy, the junta agreed to a ceasefire, a leading role for Castilla Armas in a new government, and the eradication of communism in Guatemala.

Just one day before Arbenz' fall, the United States and nine Latin American countries had finally officially requested a foreign ministers' meeting to consider "the demonstrated intervention of the international Communist movement in the Republic of Guatemala and the danger which this involves for the peace and security of the Continent."[42] The belated timing of this move, coming as it did two weeks after nearly unanimous Latin American consent for a conference had been obtained and with an anti-Communist victory in Guatemala imminent, suggests that it was designed only to provide a mantle of legitimacy for a *fait accompli*.

This United States decision to delay calling for OAS action until the last minute and to rely instead on the exile invasion was quite understandable, for the OAS Council debates over the United States/nine-nation request clearly demonstrated that not only would it have been unlikely that a two-thirds majority for effective action against Guatemala could have been obtained, but that the United States itself might well have been on trial at an OAS meeting. The main issue in the debates was whether the proposed conference should consider only the "intervention of the international communist movement" in Guatemala, or "the *general* situation" (emphasis added) there. Under the broader mandate, of course, the foreign ministers could consider the illegal actions of the United States and Honduras. Uruguay and Argentina led the group favoring this latter course, explicitly arguing that not only Communist interventions but *all* interventions that "may interfere with the political, economic, or military sovereignty of any state" should be considered. In the ensuing vote, the more general wording was rejected, but only by the narrowest of margins: five in favor, seven opposed, and eight abstentions. Only Cuba, El Salvador, Honduras, Paraguay, Peru, and Venezuela, all right-wing military dictatorships, joined the United States in voting no. In view of the split, compromise was necessary, and the final wording specified that the conference could consider "all aspects" of the dangers "resulting from the penetration of the political institutions of Guatemala by the international communist movement."[43] In any event, the fall of the Arbenz regime made the issue academic, and on July 2, the conference was canceled.[44]

Conclusion

The OAS had played hardly any role in the Guatemalan affair. The Peace Committee never did get to Guatemala, and it canceled its jurisdiction over the case when Guatemala, Honduras, and Nicaragua jointly informed it "that the controversy between them, which was the occasion for the Committee's [proposed] trip, has ceased to exist."[45] It had not had anything to do with the overthrow of communism in Guatemala, nor, conversely, had it done anything about the flagrantly illegal activities of the United States and Honduras. It had not even helped in the post-hostilities negotiations, which were dominated by the United States. As Arthur Whitaker put it:

> The situation in Guatemala and the neighboring countries unfolded in the traditional Central American way, almost as if neither the OAS nor the United Nations had ever come into existence.[46]

The results of the Guatemalan affair were mixed. Had it not been for the errors of the United States in the decade after 1944 the crisis might never have occurred. But that was in the past and the alternatives available to the United States in 1954 were limited. In terms of its immediate objective, the elimination of the Communists as a serious political force in Guatemala, the United States strategy was obviously successful.

Moreover, the inter-American system had managed to withstand the strain. The Latin American reaction, at least at the governmental level, had been reasonably mild, considering the gross nature of the United States violations of inter-American norms.[47] Certainly in the UN the Latin American states had closed ranks behind the United States, and even in the OAS, although a good deal of Latin American unhappiness was manifest, most states at least tacitly went along with the United States intervention.

But the Guatemalan affair had a number of costs. First of all, the UN had been weakened, its jurisdiction in effect excluded from the Western Hemisphere. The cynicism of the United States position in the UN was striking. In 1947 the United States had asserted that the Rio Treaty "does not, of course, impair the right of states to bring a dispute to the attention of the United Nations,"[48] but now the United States had warned that the exercise of that right would destroy the United Nations.

The OAS, too, was brought into disrepute. No doubt there was widespread amusement in Latin America over Dulles' statement that "we can be grateful that the OAS showed that it could act quickly and vigorously in aid of peace . . . [and that] there was proof that our American organization is not just a paper organization, but that it has vigor and vitality to act."[49]

Naturally the image of the United States was also badly tarnished. The downfall of the Arbenz government unleashed a widespread and often violent wave of anti-Americanism in Latin America. It was universally assumed that Castillo Armas was merely a puppet of the United States, an assumption given credence by Peurifoy's boast that "people are complaining that I was forty-five minutes off schedule."[50] Moreover, the timing of the invasion, shortly after the expropriation of United Fruit Company land, inevitably raised the specter of "dollar diplomacy."[51] It is impossible to calculate how important or permanent was the damage done to the United States, but it is clear that the perspectives of the emerging nationalistic and leftist Latin American groups were significantly influenced.

But perhaps the most disastrous consequence of the whole affair was its very success. Instead of understanding communism in Guatemala as primarily an indigenous movement growing out of backward social and economic conditions, the United States saw it as a conspiracy imposed externally by the forces of "international communism." Any future Communist threats in Latin America, it was assumed, could be met by techniques similar to those employed in Guatemala. In the meantime, the whole affair—like Latin America itself—could safely be forgotten.

And that is precisely what the United States did in

Guatemala. Instead of recognizing its special responsibilities for insuring that the abortive Guatemalan social revolution went forward under non-Communist leadership and with large-scale aid, the United States abandoned Guatemala to the incompetent, corrupt, and increasingly reactionary rule of Castillo Armas and his equally dreary successors.

Thus, the failure of the United States in Guatemala was merely a microcosm of its failure in all of Latin America. The magnitude of this failure was not perceived nor its lessons understood until after the Castro revolution and the catastrophe at the Bay of Pigs.

1. The struggle to gain support for the resolution was led by Chile, Brazil, and Peru, all of whom had been having internal difficulties with allegedly Communist movements.

2. See especially Bogotá Conference, Speech of Romulo Betancourt, *Diario,* pp. 527-28.

3. Bogotá Conference, *Final Act,* Resolution XXXII.

4. United States note to the Council, December 20, 1950. Reprinted in Fourth Meeting of Consultation of Ministers of Foreign Affairs, *Proceedings* (Washington, D.C.: Pan American Union, 1951), pp. 2-3. (Cited hereinafter as *Proceedings.)*

5. *Proceedings,* p. 6.

6. It will be recalled that there was widespread fear that the Korean War was only a prelude to a much more massive Soviet offensive.

7. Interviews.

8. *Proceedings,* p. 131.

9. Fourth Meeting of Consultation of Ministers of Foreign Affairs, *Report of the Secretary of State of the United States* (Washington, D.C.: Department of State Publication 4928, U.S. Government Printing Office, 1953), p. 33.

10. Resolution II, Final Act, *Proceedings,* p. 238.

11. *Ibid.* Mexican and Argentine attempts to emasculate this resolution were vigorously opposed by the United States, which agreed only to accept the addition of the tortured phrases bowing to "sovereignty." Argentina was still openly unhappy about the prospective involvement in the Korean War, but agreed to go along—verbally—"for the sake of inter-American solidarity." (*Proceedings,* pp. 190-92.)

12. Resolution III, Final Act, *Proceedings,* p. 239.

13. *Ibid.*

14. Resolution VIII, Final Act, *Proceedings,* p. 244.

15. Assistant Secretary of State Edward Miller, Senate Committee on Foreign Relations, *Mutual Security Act of 1951, Hearings,* 82d Cong., 1st sess., 1951, p. 395.

16. Richard P. Stebbins (ed.), *The United States in World Affairs, 1951* (New York: Harper & Bros., 1952), p. 304.

17. *Proceedings,* p. 136.

18. See the Fourth Meeting of Consultation of Ministers of Foreign Affairs, *Documents* (Washington, D.C.: Pan American Union, 1951), Document 159, Minutes of the 7th meeting of Committee II, in which an El Salvadoran motion proposing discussion of the court was defeated by a 10-9-2 vote.

19. Arévalo later charged that the United States had promoted internal revolts against his government. (*New York Times,* July 9, 1951.)

20. For discussions of the events in Guatemela from 1944 to 1954 see Frederick B. Pike, "Guatemala, the United States, and Communism in the Americas," *Review of Politics,* April, 1955; Ronald M. Schneider, *Communism in Guatemala* (New York: Frederick A. Praeger, 1958), pp. 188-93; Daniel M. James, *Red Design for America: Guatemalan Prelude* (New York: John Day Co., 1954); H. Bradford Westerfield, *The Instruments of America's Foreign Policy* (New York: Thomas Y. Crowell, 1963), Chapter 21.

21. Tenth Inter-American Conference, *Chronological Collection of Documents* (3 vols.) (Washington, D. C.: Pan American Union, 1954), Document 110, United States Declaration on Solidarity for the Preservation of the Political Integrity of the American States against International Communist Intervention. (Cited hereinafter as *Caracas Conference, Documents.*)

22. For this reason, Costa Rica refused to attend the conference. (*New York Times,* February 19, 1954.)

23. *Caracas Conference, Documents,* Document 95, Speech to Third Plenary Session.

24. Quoted in Mecham, *op. cit.,* p. 442.

25. *New York Times,* March 14, 1954. One Latin American delegate commented bitterly that "if the United States wanted to badly enough, it could have a resolution passed declaring two and two are five." (*New York Times,* March 8, 1954.)

26. Dulles' Statement to the March 11 meeting of the Politico-Juridical Committee, reprinted in the *Department of State Bulletin,* March 22, 1954, p. 424.

27. As the Uruguayan foreign minister later put it, "We contributed our approval without enthusiasm, without optimism, without joy and without the feeling that we were contributing to the adoption of a constructive measure." (*New York Times,* March 16, 1954.)

28. *Caracas Conference, Documents, Minutes of the Politico-Juridical Committee,* Documents 368-81.

29. *Department of State Bulletin,* March 22, 1954, p. 429.

30. In fact, in Washington's subsequent maneuvers in the rebellion, the United States invoked the Rio Treaty, not the Caracas resolution, rather than try to prove that Guatemala was dominated by "international communism" (Dreier, *Hemisphere Crisis,* p. 53).

31. State Department release, *New York Times,* May 23, 1954.

32. Recent information has confirmed the widely reported heavy United States involvement in the Castillo Armas attack. Most observers at the time noted numerous signs of CIA activity in the Castillo camp (cf. numerous reports in *New York Times* in June, 1954, and Donald Grant, "Guatemala and United States Foreign Policy," *Journal of International Affairs,* No. 1, 1955), and President Eisenhower has admitted that the Castillo forces were supplied with United States aircraft. (*New York Times,* November 1, 1963.) But of most significance was Senator Thruston Morton's description of the United States role: "When the plans were laid to overthrow the Communist government of Guatemala . . . [President Eisenhower said] 'Are you sure this is going to succeed?'—he was reassured it would, and said 'I'm prepared to take any steps that are necessary to see that it succeeds. For if it succeeds it's the people of Guatemala throwing off the yoke of communism. If it fails, the Flag of the United States has failed.'" (*Washington Post,* February 18, 1963.)

33. Interviews.

34. *New York Times,* June 11, 1954.

35. Report of the Inter-American Peace Committee on the Controversy Between Guatemala, Honduras, and Nicaragua, Appendix D of the *Report of the Committee to the Fifth Meeting of Consultation,* pp. 57-58. (Cited hereinafter as *Guatemalan Report.*)

36. *Guatemalan Report,* pp. 58-59.

37. *Ibid.,* pp. 60-61.

38. *Ibid.,* p. 62.

39. *United Nations Security Council Official Records,* 676th Meeting, June 25, 1954. Earlier Lodge had suggested that "many persons will wonder whether the whole imbroglio in Guatemala was not cooked up precisely for the purpose of making Communist propaganda here in the United Nations." Statement of Ambassador Lodge, June 22, 1954, in *Intervention of International Communism in Guatemala* (Department of State Publication, Inter-American Series 48, August, 1954), p. 18. (Cited hereinafter as *Intervention.*)

40. *United Nations Security Council Official Records,* 676th Meeting, June 25, 1954, paragraph 168.

41. *New York Times,* June 26, 1954. The lineup was significant: Chile, Brazil, Colombia, and Turkey joined the United States; Denmark, Lebanon, New Zealand, and the Soviet Union voted no; Britain and France abstained.

42. *Applications,* p. 151.

43. *Actas del Consejo,* June 28, 1954.

44. *Actas del Consejo,* July 2, 1954.

45. *Guatemalan Report,* pp. 69-70.

46. Arthur Whitaker, "The Organization of American States," in London Institute of World Affairs, *The Yearbook of World Affairs, 1959* (London: Stevens & Sons, 1959), p. 131.

47. No doubt many states, especially in Central America, were privately pleased with the overthrow of Arbenz.

48. Rio Conference, *Report of the Delegation of the United States,* p. 14. To add to the irony, shortly before the affair Lodge had commented, in another context, that he hoped "he would never see the day when a small nation would be asked 'what's

the hurry' in response to a call for assistance." (Quoted in John A. Houston, *Latin America in the United Nations* [New York: Carnegie Endowment for International Peace, 1956], p. 111).

49. Speech to the nation, June 30, 1954, reprinted in *Intervention*, p. 33.

50. Quoted in *New York Times*, July 18, 1954.

51. Perhaps in response to these sentiments, the Department of Justice instituted an antitrust suit against the United Fruit Company during the Guatemalan crisis. (*New York Times*, July 3, 1954.)

CHAPTER 4

The OAS as an Anti-Communist Alliance (II):

Cuba

UNITED STATES POLICY TOWARD CUBA since the Castro
revolution has been troubled by a number of cross-
pressures. The Eisenhower, Kennedy, and Johnson administrations have sought to isolate, contain, and if
possible destroy communism in Cuba. Yet all three
administrations were well aware of the danger of on
the one hand proceeding so vigorously as to alienate
large numbers of Latin Americans and risk a confrontation with the Soviet Union, or on the other hand, so
cautiously as to risk repudiation at home and the spread
of Communist movements in the rest of the hemisphere.

As a result, United States policy in the OAS has been

135

somewhat different from what it is widely assumed to be. The United States has generally *not* been the most active champion of multilateral anti-Cuban measures but rather has been in the middle, seeking to balance the demands of domestic public opinion and the majority of Central American and Caribbean states for strong action against the firm resistance of Mexico and a number of South American states to any effective action at all. Thus, the United States has sought not only the positive objective of anti-Cuban action but also the negative objectives of avoiding as much as possible major hemispheric splits and domestic upheavals in Latin American nations with large pro-Castro minorities.

More specifically, United States policy toward Castro has gone through three phases. The first, beginning with the collapse of the Batista regime and lasting until the end of 1959, was initially a period of "watchful waiting," gradually crystallizing into the decision to oppose the Castro regime actively.

Although relations between the Eisenhower administration and Castro were bad to begin with and became continually worse throughout 1959, the administration was unwilling to take the sort of drastic action that would have been necessary to overthrow Castro—action that was demanded in an increasingly strident manner in the United States and by a number of Latin American governments. On the contrary, for about a year Washington's reaction to Cuban propaganda and the seizure of American private property was surprisingly mild and confined primarily to verbal protests and perhaps a toleration of minor anti-Castro exile activities. There is even evidence that the United States sought to gain Castro's friendship by offering him substantial economic assistance.[1]

By the end of 1959, however, United States–Cuban relations were hopelessly bad, and after the signing of the Cuban-Soviet trade pact in February, 1960, the Eisenhower administration began to cast about for measures that would increase pressures on Cuba but at the same time obviate the need for harsh United States actions. The strategy adopted was to stress the multilateral nature of the Cuban problem. The purposes of this approach were two-fold. By convincing the dubious Latin American states that Cuba represented an increasing threat to their security, the administration hoped to lay the foundations for possible inter-American action in the future. Perhaps even more important, by emphasizing its multilateral obligations and commitments, the administration hoped to reduce domestic pressures for unilateral action. Castro was at the height of his popularity in Latin America, and anti-Cuban measures would severely strain inter-American relations.

In the Spring of 1960, for example, the administration opposed passage in the House of Representatives of a belligerent resolution implying that the United States should take unilateral action against Cuba. Assistant Secretary of State Roy Rubottom told the Foreign Affairs Committee that

> [the Soviet] objective is to provoke the United States into actions and attitudes inconsistent with the spirit of partnership which regulates inter-American relations and thus not only permanently to damage our relations with Latin America but also to offset the image of Hungary and Tibet by portraying the United States before the world as an "aggressor" intervening in the internal affairs of its neighbors.[2]

It was the policy of the administration, therefore,

that the problem of international Communist intervention in the Americas . . . should be approached on a multilateral basis in conformity with the international instruments available for that purpose.[3]

During this period, then, the primary function of the OAS in United States policy was to justify the Eisenhower administration's unwillingness to take strong unilateral anti-Castro action.

The second phase of United States policy began in mid-1960 and lasted until the missile crisis. Increasingly alarmed by the domestic policies of the Castro regime; its strident anti-Americanism; and, most of all, its growing ideological, economic, and military ties with the Soviet Union, the Eisenhower (and later the Kennedy) administration concluded that the continued existence of the Castro regime was intolerable. As a result, the United States attempted to destroy Castro by all methods short of outright invasion by United States armed forces. The primary role of the OAS during this period was to support symbolically, and thereby help legitimize, essentially unilateral United States actions, such as the trade embargo.

Since the missile crisis, however, which was settled on the basis of a tacit United States commitment not to invade Cuba so long as offensive weapons were not reintroduced and Cuba refrained from direct aggression against other Latin American states, the United States has been forced to abandon its hopes of overthrowing Castro. Instead, the main thrust of United States policy now is to prevent the spread of "Castro-communism" elsewhere in Latin America. The United States posture toward Cuba, in fact, bears a striking resemblance to its posture toward the Soviet Union in the 1950's: containment of the Cuban (Soviet) revolution within its present borders and an unacknowledged, belligerent co-existence with Castro's Cuba (the Soviet Union) itself.

Present policy consists of three major elements: (1) measures to insure that Cuba does not again become a direct threat to United States security; (2) the maintenance of external pressures against the Castro regime, but at a level below that which might provoke a direct Soviet–United States confrontation; (3) measures designed to control Cuban-inspired subversion in Latin America.[4]

Only in the unlikely event that offensive missiles and bombers were reintroduced into Cuba, it is felt, would the Castro regime constitute a direct threat to the U. S. Aerial surveillance is maintained to guard against surprise, and should new Soviet adventures develop, United States policy is clear: "Under no circumstances can the United States accept or tolerate the reintroduction of offensive weapons into Cuba . . . if that should occur, the crisis of . . . October [1962] would look relatively trivial compared to the crisis that would be engendered."[5]

Pressure is maintained on Cuba primarily through diplomatic isolation and the trade embargo, exile harassments of Cuban and Soviet shipping having been halted by the Kennedy administration in the spring of 1963. The purpose of the embargo, according to the Johnson and Kennedy administrations, is to increase internal unrest in Cuba, diminish Cuba's capacity for subversion in the hemisphere, reduce Cuba's "showcase" appeal to Latin America, and so burden the Communist nations that they will be persuaded that "they are backing a losing and expensive horse."[6] The success of the embargo is dubious. Although the Cuban economy has been hurt, Western Europe is increasing its trade with Cuba, the Castro regime remains internally strong, and the Soviet Union shows no signs of cracking under the strain.

As time passes it becomes increasingly unlikely that these pressures will suffice to bring down Castro or precipitate a rupture in Cuban-Soviet economic and military ties. Only an outright invasion would get rid of Castro, and the Soviet Union's commitment to defend Cuba "with all the means at its disposal"[7] makes that impossible. As a result, the maintenance of economic and diplomatic pressures are at least as much a response to domestic political requirements as they are to international realities. The main focus of United States policy is now the prevention of *further* Communist gains in Latin America.

The United States maintains a constant air and sea patrol around Cuba and has indicated that any Cuban attempts to invade neighboring countries, or even to supply arms to dissident elements, will be resisted by military force. In April, 1963, Secretary of State Rusk made this explicit:

> It has been made very clear that the armed forces of the hemisphere, including our own, are . . . available to insure that arms that are now in Cuba not be used outside of Cuba, either in terms of organized effort or through piecemeal infiltration.[8]

Even more significant is the United States commitment to intervene with military force if necessary to prevent even purely internal Communist movements in Latin America from overthrowing existing governments.[9] In effect, the United States has guaranteed the maintenance of a non-Communist status quo in Latin America, outside of Cuba. In all essentials this is a unilateral policy, although an attempt has been made to ground it in multilateral commitments. Resolution II of the Punta del Este Conference "urged" the member states "to cooperate . . . to strengthen their capacity to counteract threats or acts of aggression, subversion, or other dangers to peace and security resulting from the continued intervention in this hemisphere of Sino-Soviet powers."[10] The administration interprets this language to cover the furnishing of material assistance and training in "internal security defense" and also "the provision, upon request, of military forces to maintain surveillance against threatened aggression from abroad or otherwise to help a government threatened by a Communist takeover."[11]

Since the missile crisis, the role of the OAS in the Cuban problem has been minimal. In part this is a reflection of continued division among the Latin American nations, but it is equally important that the United States has not only ceased to exercise "leadership" over Cuba but on the contrary in this matter has become a force for *restraint* within the inter-American system. For example, shortly before the missile crisis Costa Rica proposed the formation of a "NATO-type" military alliance, to include the United States, Colombia, Venezuela, and the Central American and Caribbean states. The object of such an organization would be to bypass the OAS while retaining a multilateral façade for military action against Cuba. Initially, the plan was strongly supported by the United States, and it was discussed favorably at an informal meeting of foreign ministers in Washington in early October, 1962.[12] After the missile crisis, however, the plan was dropped. As President Kennedy explained to the Central Americans, the Cuban problem had to be seen in its cold war context, with all the inherent risks of nuclear war.[13] Thus, while in the early Castro years the United States had sought to impress the Latin Americans that the Cuban situation was not a United States problem but a hemispheric one, the United States was now saying, in effect, that the situation was no longer a hemispheric problem, but a United States–Soviet one. The result has been that except for a marginal and mostly symbolic antisubversion role, the OAS to all intents and purposes has ceased to be concerned with the Cuban problem.

The OAS and Cuba: The Early Phase

The Cuban situation was first brought to the OAS in the summer of 1960. By late June, the deterioration of United States–Cuban relations had reached crisis proportions. On June 29, the Cuban government seized the Texaco and Esso oil refineries, allegedly because of their refusal to refine Soviet crude oil. A week later, in its first really severe anti-Castro action, the Eisenhower administration cut 700,000 tons from Cuba's 1960 sugar quota. Cuba immediately retaliated by nationalizing all remaining United States private property.

The breaking point was reached in early July, when Castro welcomed Khrushchev's threat to support Cuba with "rocket firepower" against any United States aggression and requested a Security Council meeting to consider his charges of United States "economic aggression" and intervention in Cuba's internal affairs.[14]

Two days after the Cuban request, Peru called for an OAS foreign ministers' conference to consider "the exigencies of hemispheric solidarity" in light of the recent "events."[15] In supporting the Peruvian move, which had undoubtedly been cleared first in Washington, the United States had several objectives. There could be no question of sanctions; reflecting sparse Latin

American support for really meaningful collective action against Cuba, the Peruvian request had not accused Cuba of aggression or even mentioned it by name and had invoked Article 39 of the Charter (providing for foreign ministers' meetings to consider problems "of an urgent nature") rather than the Rio Treaty. But some sort of OAS action was necessary in order to keep the Cuban problem out of the UN,[16] and beyond that the administration had hopes that the foreign ministers would agree to a verbal condemnation of Cuba, thereby raising the issue above a bilateral United States—Cuban conflict and laying the foundation for later, more significant collective action if that should prove necessary. Optimally, the United States hoped to obtain a condemnation of the growing strength of communism in Cuba. At a minimum, though, the Eisenhower administration would settle for a strong statement censuring Cuba's expanding ties with the Soviet Union, particularly its acceptance of Soviet military support. Finally, multilateral action might pacify domestic critics of the administration's policy of "patience."[17]

Two weeks before the conference the United States submitted a long memorandum to the Peace Committee, designed to build support for its anti-Cuban policies and perhaps to construct a case for future sanctions under the Rio Treaty. Carefully avoiding statements that could be construed as opposition to economic and social reforms inside Cuba, the memo charged that the Castro revolution had degenerated into despotism and repression under the growing influence of the Cuban Communist party. In its external policies the Cuban government, by its frequent public attacks on the United States and the OAS, its expanding economic and military ties with the Soviet bloc, and its support of subversive movements throughout Latin America, was "undermining hemispheric solidarity" and becoming an "instrument" of the "Sino-Soviet powers."[18]

By the time the foreign ministers convened in San José, Costa Rica, in mid-August, however, the United States had been forced to modify its objectives, modest as they had been. Consultations had revealed that there was still a great deal of Latin American resistance even to a verbal condemnation of Cuba. Although the Khrushchev threats had alarmed some Latin American governments, traditional hostility to United States intervention in Latin American internal affairs remained strong and Castro was still very popular with Latin American populist groups.

As a result, Secretary of State Herter chose to play down the Communist threat in Cuba itself and focus on the danger to the hemisphere posed by Cuba's foreign policy. To be sure, Herter did note that "the trends and the general pattern we see developing in Cuba would indicate to any reasonable person that it is in the Communist direction that the present Cuban leadership . . . is leading the country,"[19] but it was significant that he stopped short of charging that Cuba was actually "dominated" by communism, for in that case the Caracas resolution would have been "violated" and a call for collective action required, a course the Latin Americans were clearly not prepared to consider.

As modified, the United States proposals focused on Cuba's external policies—"the intervention by the Sino-Soviet bloc, the threat of armed attack by the Sino-Soviet bloc, the export of communism from Cuba to other countries in this hemisphere"[20]—and called merely for the "vigorous condemnation" of Communist intervention in the hemisphere and an expression of "grave concern" over Cuba's encouragement of this intervention.[21]

Cuba's strategy was to portray itself as a victim of United States unilateral intervention, an appeal designed to remind the Latin Americans of the Guatemalan affair and other instances of North American intervention in Latin America: "The gravest, most urgent matter facing our America . . . [is] not a hypothetical extracontinental threat, but the actual threat to continental security and peace resulting from repeated acts of harassment, reprisal, and aggression by the Government of the United States against Cuba." Washington's aim, Cuban Foreign Minister Raúl Roa charged, was to destroy the progressive and anticapitalist Cuban revolution and return Cuba to the "political, diplomatic, and military orbit" of the United States. The purpose of the memo to the Peace Committee and of the conference itself was "to establish, by guile, calumny, and falsehood the basis for a unilateral or collective aggression."[22]

In view of the United States actions, the Cuban delegate went on, Cuba's acceptance of the Khrushchev declaration was essential. What would the OAS do to help Cuba, he asked sardonically, if it were invaded by the United States, and what will it do if the United States continues its "economic aggression"? Since "the aggressions Cuba has suffered [thus far] . . . have not been criticized in the slightest" by the OAS, Cuba has no choice but to find help where it can.[23] Thus, it was implied, Cuba was prepared to defy not only the United States but the inter-American system itself. If Foreign Minister Roa had not made that clear enough, Castro did. In an emotional Havana speech during the San José deliberations, the Cuban leader explicitly flaunted the

OAS and reaffirmed that "we are friends of the Soviet Union and of the Chinese People's Republic."[24]

Quite obviously the conference had demonstrated that United States–Cuban relations had reached the point of no return. Still, the strategy of the major Latin American states was to attempt to bridge the gap and bring Cuba back into the inter-American system.[25] Thus, although almost all the Latin Americans dutifully defended the OAS against Cuba's sardonic attack and all called upon Cuba to refrain from accepting Soviet intervention in hemispheric affairs and from attempting to export its revolution by force to the rest of Latin America, the tone of their speeches was in most cases conciliatory and often quite critical of the United States.

Moreover, the Latin Americans were not only extremely reluctant to support a direct condemnation of Cuba's ties with the Soviet Union—even Peru, the initiator of the meeting, declared that there was no question of "determining or fixing responsibilities and sanctions"[26]—but they positively vied with each other in their expressions of sympathy with the Cuban revolution itself. For example, Mexico pointed to parallels between the Mexican and Cuban revolutions and exhorted the foreign ministers to "remember that a revolution necessarily involves transitory disturbances and profound change"; Costa Rica added that "insofar as the Cuban Revolution manifests itself as a purely national phenomenon . . . that revolution cannot be judged by any people except the Cuban people"; and Venezuela bluntly warned that it "considers it necessary to ratify unreservedly the principle of the self-determination of peoples, and, consequently, Cuba's unquestionable right to carry out freely its spontaneous cultural, political, and economic revolution."[27]

Clearly, then, the Cuban attack on United States interventionism had struck a responsive chord in Latin America. Even the rightist states, ruled by oligarchies that undoubtedly would have been elated to see Castro overthrown, found it politic to wax rhetorical over the Cuban revolution and stress the principle of "non-intervention," meaning the non-intervention by the Soviet Union in hemispheric affairs, the non-intervention by Cuba in Latin American affairs, and the non-intervention by the United States in Cuban affairs. In short, there was practically no support for the United States position that Cuban domestic policy per se represented a potential threat to the peace of the hemisphere.

The conference ended with the unanimous approval (except Cuba's) of the "Declaration of San José," which the United States claimed as a victory for its viewpoint.[28] This interpretation was based primarily on the first and fourth clauses of the Declaration. The former "condemns energetically the intervention or the threat of intervention . . . by an extracontinental power in the affairs of the American Republics and declares that the acceptance of a threat of extracontinental intervention by any American state endangers American solidarity and security." The latter "reaffirms that the inter-American system is incompatible with any form of totalitarianism and that democracy will achieve the full scope of its objectives in the hemisphere only when all the American republics conduct themselves in accordance with . . . [its] principles."

Actually, read carefully and in the context of the conference debates, the Declaration constitutes as much of a repudiation of the United States position as the Latin Americans felt it prudent to administer.[29] The *minimum* United States objective, it will be recalled, was a specific condemnation of Cuba, but the Declaration neither singled out Cuba nor threatened sanctions in the event Cuba continued its ties with the Soviet Union. Moreover, the fourth clause merely restated past "condemnations" of "totalitarianism," which could mean right-wing as well as left-wing totalitarianism. Communism was not specifically mentioned and the effect was further diluted by the exhortation to *all* the American states to live up to democracy.

Finally, the third clause of the Declaration, conveniently ignored by State Department propagandists, was clearly designed to apply at least as much to the United States as to Cuba, for it reaffirms "the principle of non-intervention by any American state in the internal or external affairs of the other American states, and reiterates that each state has the right to develop its cultural, political, and economic life freely and naturally."

The Latin Americans were clearly unhappy about the Declaration, even in its diluted form. The Peruvian and Venezuelan Foreign Ministers, in fact, at first refused to sign it and had to be ordered to do so by their governments.[30] A number of other countries, especially Uruguay, Brazil, Panama, and Bolivia, stressed that the Declaration should be regarded as an appeal to Cuba to return to the fold, not as a condemnation.[31] Finally, Mexico insisted on adding to the official record its view that the Declaration "is a resolution of a general character for all the member states of the Organization, and that in no way is it a condemnation or a threat against Cuba, whose aspirations for economic improvement and social justice have the fullest support of the Government and the people of Mexico."[32] Only Guatemala, Nicaragua, and Paraguay, all under right-wing dictatorships, had joined the United States in pressing for stronger action.

In short, the San José Conference was a defeat for the United States. Not only was no collective action taken, but the United States had been denied even symbolic Latin American support for its own increasingly severe anti-Cuban actions. Even the administration's more limited hope that by going through the motions of a conference it might appease its domestic critics was not fulfilled; on the contrary, the tepidness of the OAS response only increased the clamor for drastic United States action.

The Imposition of Sanctions

Unilateral measures proved no more effective, however, and after the disaster at the Bay of Pigs in April, 1961, the United States renewed its efforts for multilateral action against Cuba. Latin American attitudes had shifted considerably since the San José Conference, for leftist political groups, encouraged and assisted by Cuba, had increased their militancy throughout Latin America, especially in Central America and northern South America. As a result, Costa Rica, Honduras, Venezuela, and Colombia had joined the rightist states in pressing for anti-Castro action.

No doubt, too, President Kennedy achieved his intended effect in his post–Bay of Pigs warning that "if the nations of this hemisphere should fail to meet their commitments against outside Communist penetration then this government will not hesitate in meeting its primary obligations, which are the security of this nation."

Put on notice that the United States was prepared to

go it alone, the Latin Americans had to demonstrate a willingness to take collective action if they hoped to retain influence over United States policy.

Meaningful action was now defined by the Kennedy administration as requiring a collective severance of diplomatic and commercial relations with Cuba and establishing OAS mechanisms to combat Cuban subversion. Although resistance to subversion was primarily the responsiblity of the individual states, the OAS could help co-ordinate national efforts and bring pressures to bear on states indifferent to the alleged danger. Diplomatic and economic sanctions, though adding little to measures already taken by the United States,[33] would at least to some degree increase the psychological pressures on Castro.

In any case the Kennedy administration did not have a free hand, for it was the focus of repeated demands, both international and domestic, that it maintain heavy pressure on Castro. Cries from the Central American and Caribbean states for strong anti-Cuban action, even including an open invasion, were becoming increasingly insistent and were not limited to the usual rightist sources. At home, Cuba was still a highly emotional political issue and Congress was clearly restless; on May 17, 1961, for example, the House of Representatives approved by 404-2 a resolution calling on the administration to initiate steps in the OAS to impose sanctions on Cuba.[34] It was feared that the necessary appropriations for the very foundation of the administration's Latin American policy, the Alliance for Progress, would be endangered without a multilateral show of support for a hard Cuban line.[35]

At the same time, however, the major Latin American states were still adamantly opposed to anti-Cuban action. Mexico was traditionally dedicated to non-intervention was to some degree ideologically sympathetic with the Cuban revolution, and had qualms about the legality of collective action. Argentina, also traditionally non-interventionist, was in the throes of a revival of pro-Castro Peronism. Brazil under Quadros had adopted a generally "independent" foreign policy and was sympathetic to Castro; the Brazilian foreign minister had recently declared that "the Brazilian government . . . defends the determination of the Cuban people [and] . . . is opposed to any foreign intervention, be it direct or indirect . . . and considers that economic measures . . . constitute indirect intervention."[36] Bolivia, Ecuador, and Chile all had strong domestic leftist groups that they feared to antagonize by supporting anti-Castro action.

The Kennedy administration, then, was faced with a painful dilemma. A conference on Cuba would, at a minimum, dramatize the deep split in the hemisphere and, at worst, result in a total defeat for the anti-Castro forces. On the other hand, failure to press for hemispheric action soon could result in serious damage to the administration both at home and abroad. Much to the administration's surprise and unhappiness, though, this dilemma was prematurely resolved by Peruvian and Colombian moves to force OAS consideration of the Cuban problem. In mid-October, 1961, without prior notification to the United States, Peru requested that the Rio Treaty be invoked and an investigation held into "violations of civil rights" in Cuba and Cuban subversion in Latin America.[37]

The Peruvian move was doubly unwelcome, for it focused on Cuban internal policies as well as the subversion issue and so invited the certain resistance of the non-interventionist bloc. With some difficulty, the issue was temporarily buried when the Council agreed to refer the request to a committee for "additional study."[38]

One month later, however, Colombia requested a foreign ministers' meeting under Article 6 of the Rio Treaty "to consider the threats to the peace and to the political independence of the American states that might arise from the intervention of extracontinental powers directed toward breaking American solidarity."[39] This time, Cuba was not specifically cited; moreover, Colombia was careful to emphasize that it was proposing only an examination of "situations of an international character," not of the internal affairs of any state.[40]

Once again the United States had not been consulted. The State Department was still reluctant to agree to a conference for which no advance agreement on the action to be taken had been obtained, but the administration felt that it could no longer politically afford to stall a Latin American initiative for anti-Cuban measures.[41] Thus, on December 4 the Council approved the Colombian request, but only by the bare two-thirds majority required by the Rio Treaty, 14-2-5 (Cuba and Mexico against; Argentina, Bolivia, Brazil, Chile, and Ecuador abstaining).[42]

The conference was scheduled for late January at Punta del Este, Uruguay. In the time remaining, the State Department initiated intensive consultations. The prospect for effective anti-Cuban action was even gloomier than the vote on the Colombian proposal had indicated, for Haiti was considered to be unreliable and the Uruguayan National Council was known to be internally divided. The loss of either of these two would make action impossible.

As consultations revealed the depth of the hemispheric split and the uncertain nature of the outcome, a number of State Department officials pressed for a delay, or at least for a "soft" United States line designed to gain as much unanimity as possible—perhaps a "last call" to Cuba to break its military ties with the Soviet Union.[43] But under heavy pressure from Congress and the Caribbean area countries, the administration decided to proceed with the conference and to press for diplomatic and economic sanctions, although leaving a good deal of latitude to the United States delegation to work out a final position at the conference itself.[44]

The main objecive of the United States at the conference was the moderate one of attaining as much unanimity as possible for some sort of anti-Cuban action beyond another mere paper condemnation. Its strategy was to act as a broker between the "outer six" on the left and the Central American-Caribbean countries on the right. Its freedom of maneuver in this role, however, was highly circumscribed, for both blocs were willing to sacrifice inter-American unity, normally so important a criterion in any multilateral action, rather than depart significantly from their positions.[45] The "outer six" were willing to verbally condemn Cuban subversive activities and ties with Communist nations, but would not support punitive actions and were primarily interested in trying once again to reintegrate Cuba into the inter-American system.[46] The Central American-Caribbean bloc was still holding out for a collective break in diplomatic relations and an economic boycott.[47]

As a result, the United States was in an extraordinarily delicate position. If it asked for too much, it risked a damaging bifurcation of the system, an intensification of internal unrest in the large South American states, and even a possible defeat. On the other hand, if it asked for too little it risked a revolt of the Central American-Caribbean bloc, even including a walk-out,[48] internal complications in the anti-Communist states,[49] and harsh criticism at home.

Faced with these conflicting pressures, the United States dropped its demands for full economic sanctions and a collective break in diplomatic relations. Secretary of State Rusk outlined the new United States position in a carefully worded speech to the conference. The United States, he emphasized, had "no quarrel" with the purposes of the Cuban revolution or with the economic organization of Cuba. It was not even unduly concerned about Cuban dictatorship and repression, he candidly implied, since dictatorships, "if kept within the confines of one unhappy country, . . . [do] not constitute a direct threat to the peace and independence of other American states." Having thus tried to anticipate and so avoid the charge of intervention in Cuban internal affairs, Rusk attempted to place the Cuban problem in the context of collective security: "What we cannot accept . . . is the use of Cuba as the means through which extracontinental powers seek to break up the inter-American system, to overthrow the governments of other countries and to destroy the autonomous democratic evolution of the Hemisphere."

To meet the Cuban threat, Rusk proposed that the foreign ministers "move in four major directions": (1) the oas should proclaim that Cuba's ties with the Sino-Soviet bloc are "an ever present and common danger" to hemispheric peace and security and are "incompatible" with the inter-American system; (2) the Castro regime should, as a result, be excluded from participation in the oas and the Inter-American Defense Board; (3) all hemispheric states should "interrupt the limited but significant flow of trade between Cuba and the rest of the hemisphere, especially the traffic in arms"; (4) a Special Security Committee should be established to recommend individual and collective measures to the governments to protect them against subversion.[50]

The crucial battle came over the question of excluding Cuba from the oas. Argentina was the key state.[51] The "incompatibility" formula had actually been developed by the Argentine foreign minister, and in the expectation of gaining Argentine support the United States had dropped its proposal for a mandatory break in diplomatic relations in its favor. Moreover, it was expected that if Argentina came over, so would Bolivia and Ecuador. But just prior to the Conference, President Frondizi ordered the Argentine delegation to abstain, and the "outer six" held firm.[52]

Nonetheless, the United States continued to strive for unanimity. A last minute effort in fact almost succeeded, when Rusk agreed to a proposal under which the exclusion resolution would be modified to read that Cuba's tie with Communism "makes impossible" her participation in the inter-American system, but leaving it to the Council to take the appropriate action at an unspecified later date. Although this plan was agreeable to all of the "outer six" but Brazil, it fell through when the Central American–Caribbean bloc rejected it and insisted on the immediate suspension of Cuba.[53]

The willingness of Rusk to accept the watered-down version was significant, for far more than a mere semantic issue was at stake. Had the actual decision to suspend Cuba been left to the Council, it is all but certain that the "outer six" would have continued to oppose it and sought by the usual tactics to delay it indefinitely. Thus, unless Rusk had simply underestimated the capacity of the oas to "study" a problem to death, the United States had been willing to go to remarkable lengths to attain consensus.

The final stumbling block on the exclusion action was

overcome when Haiti, which earlier in the conference had joined with the "outer six" in a statement opposing sanctions of any kind against Cuba, at the last minute joined the hard-liners, apparently as a result of a deal with the United States under which it would later receive a $13,000,000 loan.[54] Thus, a resolution declaring that Cuba's demonstrated "incompatibility" with the inter-American system excluded her from participation in the OAS was passed by the bare two-thirds majority required, 14-1-6 (Cuba opposing, Brazil, Mexico, Chile, Argentina, Bolivia, and Ecuador abstaining).[55]

Officially, the abstentions were based on "juridical" considerations. Exclusion was illegal, it was argued, on two counts. First, Article 6 of the Rio Treaty, the juridical basis for the convoking of the conference, was designed to deal only with immediate and urgent threats to the peace, whereas the conference had been called ostensibly to deal with threats that *might* arise. Thus, since the Conference itself was "illegal," any action taken at it would also, per force, be illegal. Second, the ouster of Cuba was in itself illegal, since neither the Charter nor Article 8 of the Rio Treaty contains provisions for such action.[56]

It is not necessary to get involved in an extensive exegesis of the "juridical" arguments, primarily because they were undoubtedly not taken very seriously by the proponents themselves, possibly excepting Mexico, but were designed to cover the far more important political conflicts and thereby avoid public confirmation of the deep hemispheric split. Nonetheless, counterarguments were made; in brief, they were (1) that the Cuban danger already *was* urgent and that there was no juridical prohibition on protective measures, and (2) that the sanctions listed in Article 8 were not meant to be exclusive.[57] The most telling point, though, was that the OAS in the past had taken many actions that stretched the Charter and the Rio Treaty, or for which no specific authorization existed—Uruguay reminded the dissenters, for example, that they had all supported the establishment of armed OAS patrols in past conflicts, a measure not provided for by Article 8 of the Rio Treaty.[58]

Two other important measures were taken at Punta del Este. After the hard-liners had dropped their demands for an immediate total economic embargo, Argentina and Bolivia joined the majority in approving 16-1-4 a collective embargo on armaments trade with Cuba, and the Council was charged with "studying the feasibility and desirability of extending the suspension of trade to other items, with special attention to items of strategic importance."[59] Finally, the Council was directed "to establish a Special Consultative Committee on Security, composed of experts on security matters, for the purpose of advising the member states that may desire and request such assistance."[60] Although the details of the structure and procedures of the SCCS were left to be worked out by the Council, the basic decision that it would be only an advisory body with no sanctions at its command insured that the new body would be considerably less than the full-fledged collective mechanism for controlling subversion that the United States had hoped would emerge from the conference.

The Punta del Este Conference had been designed to achieve a multiplicity of objectives, some of them conflicting. The Kennedy administration's view, expressed both officially and off the record, was that the conference had been a success. A plausible case could indeed be made for this evaluation, especially if a short-run perspective is adopted.

After the United States had been pushed into the conference by the precipitate action of Peru and Colombia, its objectives had been progressively modified, at first to insure the support of at least two-thirds of the OAS membership, and later in a largely unsuccessful attempt to win over the "outer six." But once the United States position had been solidified, all of its immediate objectives had in fact been attained. As outlined by Rusk, they were the exclusion of Cuba from the OAS, a hemispheric arms embargo against Cuba, and the creation of an antisubversion OAS committee.

Nonetheless, insofar as these measures were designed to tighten the pressures against Castro and thereby hasten the day of his downfall, they amounted to precious little indeed. The value of the exclusion resolution was at best symbolic, although the official United States line was that exclusion was even better than a collective break in diplomatic relations since all but seven of the Latin American states had already broken relations with Cuba and the remaining embassies in Havana were useful as "listening posts," channels of communication with the Castro government, and places for refuge for exiles; on the other hand, the ouster of Cuba from the OAS removed opportunities for Cuban propaganda and disruptive tactics.[61] Moreover, it was unofficially pointed out, with Cuba out a multilateral cover had been provided for any actions a country might wish to take unilaterally.[62] For example, immediately after the conference President Kennedy announced that the United States, "in accordance with" the Punta del Este decisions, was imposing a nearly total trade embargo on Cuba;[63] this move had been held up for several months, precisely in anticipation of the legitimacy the OAS could provide.[64]

In fact, these by-products of the exclusion action were of minimal significance. Cuba hardly needed the OAS as a forum for propaganda; the supposed advantages of maintaining embassies in Cuba did not prevent the United States from joining Venezuela in pressing for a complete diplomatic break in 1964,[65] and in light of the wide variety of unilateral measures the United States had already taken against Cuba, the importance of symbolic OAS approval could hardly have been very great. As far as the arms embargo was concerned, Cuba was getting all the arms it needed from the Soviet Union and in any event hemispheric arms trade with the Castro regime was already nonexistent.[66] The creation of the Special Consultative Committee on Security (SCCS) was largely a face-saving device to cover the fact that a good many of the Latin American states strongly opposed a really effective mechanism for combating subversion, either because they considered the danger exaggerated or because they feared the remedy ("super-statism") more.[67] Since the conference, the SCCS has done more harm as a source of inter-American friction than it has accomplished as a tool for co-ordinating antisubversion activities.

Finally, as has been discussed, the missile crisis completely changed the nature of the Cuban problem, rendering anachronistic the Punta del Este Conference and all other previous United States efforts to involve the OAS in its struggle against Castro.

But there were other United States objectives at the conference, objectives that had little to do with combating Cuba. One was the appeasement of domestic groups clamoring for a more aggressive Cuban policy. Here there was some success, for Senators Wayne Morse and Bourke

B. Hickenlooper, the chairman and ranking minority member of the Subcommittee on American Republic Affairs of the Senate Committee on Foreign Relations, had been included on the United States delegation, and they returned full of praise for the administration and for the results of the conference.[68]

The administration also had sought to avoid unduly antagonizing the major Latin American states and precipitating a lasting hemispheric split. To this end, the diplomacy of the United States at the conference was conciliatory and low-pressure, especially in contrast to the Dulles days. Prior to the conference there had been some indications that the administration might attempt to use the Alliance for Progress to extract political concessions; Rusk had seemingly hinted at this in remarking that the success of the Alliance would depend on the security of the Western Hemisphere from outside interference,[69] and the very presence of Congressional leaders on the delegation might in part have been designed to remind the Latin Americans that the Alliance depended on the approval of Congress. Nonetheless, there apparently were no economic pressures employed at the conference, for the Brazilian foreign minister later praised the United States for not using the Alliance as a political weapon,[70] and soon after the conference the State Department made commitments of almost half a billion dollars to Brazil and Argentina. Still, no amount of skilful diplomacy was capable of concealing the continued indifference of the major Latin American states to the Cuban problem and their concern over United States interventionism in Latin American internal affairs.

Finally, the effort to avoid disruptive effects on politically unstable Latin American states, which in large part accounted for the conciliatory position of the United States at the conference,[71] came to naught, although some of the repercussions have in fact been welcomed in Washington. Most dramatically, since the conference four of the dissenting governments—Argentina, Ecuador, Brazil, and Bolivia—have been overthrown by military coups and replaced with regimes committed to a hard line on communism in general and Cuba in particular.

The Missile Crisis

For all practical purposes, the United States chose to act alone during the missile crisis. Although the OAS participated in the actual implementation of the Cuban blockade, the crucial decision to force the withdrawal of Soviet missiles and offensive bombers from Cuba was made solely by the Kennedy administration, without even informing, let alone consulting, the members of the OAS. [72]

In the months following the Punta del Este conference, Cuba's ties with the Soviet Union grew stronger, and during the summer of 1962, as evidence became available of massive Soviet military assistance to Cuba, domestic and Central American pressures for radical United States action again mounted. Although the administration resisted these pressures, President Kennedy did spell out conditions under which the United States would take action:

If at any time the Communist build-up in Cuba were to endanger or interfere with our security in any way, including our base at Guantanamo, our passage to the Panama Canal, our missile and space activities in Cape Canaveral or the lives of American citizens in this country, or if Cuba should ever attempt to export its aggressive purposes by force or the threat of force against any nation in this hemisphere or become an offensive military base of significant capacity for the Soviet Union, then this country will do whatever must be done to protect its own security and that of its allies.[73]

Under such circumstances, it was clear, the United States would attempt to gain multilateral support for its action, but it would not allow the absence of such support to influence its decision: "we ought, *if possible,* to deal with this [possible threat to United States security] on a hemispheric basis, but we did not renounce at the very bottom, at the very essence of our own national commitments, we did not renounce a national unilateral interest in those problems if they could not be handled on a hemispheric basis."[74]

When the crisis came, the oas was regarded by the Kennedy administration as more or less superfluous. In his famous speech to the nation, disclosing the United States discovery of Soviet offensive missiles and bombers in Cuba, President Kennedy announced that "acting . . . in the defense of our own security and of the entire Western Hemisphere . . . I have directed that the following initial steps be taken *immediately.* First . . . a strict quarantine on all offensive military equipment inside Cuba is being initiated."[75] Although the actual signing of the official blockade proclamation was delayed twenty-four hours until after the oas Council had met, it was perfectly clear that the blockade in no way depended on the outcome of that meeting.[76]

Nonetheless, great efforts were made to obtain consensus. The United States proposal to the Council, based on the argument that the missile emplacements in Cuba were a threat to the peace justifying collective action under Article 6 of the Rio Treaty, called for "the immediate dismantling and withdrawal from Cuba of all missiles and other weapons with any offensive capability," and "recommended" that

> the member states . . . take all measures, individually and collectively including the use of armed force, *which they may deem necessary* to ensure that the Government of Cuba cannot continue to receive from the Sino-Soviet powers military material and related supplies which may threaten the peace and security of the continent and to prevent the missiles in Cuba with offensive capability from ever becoming an active threat to the peace and security of the Continent.[77]

Since the United States was far more interested in moral and symbolic support than actual Latin American participation, the wording was designed to obtain the broadest possible verbal unanimity while leaving considerable latitude to the individual states to determine the degree of their compliance.

Still, there were some qualms. The last clause of the second part of the resolution seemed to authorize the destruction of missiles already in Cuba—this in fact was the interpretation the United States later adopted[78]—and Brazil, Mexico, and Bolivia apparently preferred to limit OAS involvement to the prevention of further missile shipments.[79] Nonetheless, although they abstained in the vote on this section, they did vote for the resolution as a whole, and thus for the record there was complete unanimity.[80]

Undoubtedly two factors were responsible for this show of inter-American unity, easily the greatest since the halcyon days of 1945-47. For the first time many Latin American states were apparently convinced that Cuba really did represent a threat to their own security. But in any event, since the United States was obviously determined to force withdrawal of the missiles regardless of what the oas did or did not do, the Latin Americans had no hope of exerting leverage over United States policy and therefore had nothing to gain and perhaps much to lose by opposing it.

Although the administration was to claim that the invocation of the Rio Treaty added "legality" to the blockade and that "unanimity in the oas . . . had some bearing on what Moscow's decision turned out to be,"[81] it was clear that the successful outcome was conditioned solely by the military power and skilful diplomacy of the United States.

The Subversion Issue

Since the end of 1962, the primary role of the oas in the Cuban problem ostensibly has been to control and punish Cuban subversion in Latin America. In fact, however, the subversion issue has served periodically to highlight the division in the hemisphere that reappeared after the missile crisis. Despite all of Castro's threats to turn Latin America into "a vast Sierra Maestra," the very existence of Cuban subversion, let alone what to do about it, has been a matter of much controversy—the first really hard evidence linking Cuba with dissident groups in Latin America was the discovery of a Cuban arms cache in Venezuela in late 1963. In any event, the majority of Latin American states have resisted the centralization of real antisubversion authority in the oas, in part because of fears that such a role for the oas might facilitate repression of the democratic left in Latin America,[82] and in part because the very nature of the problem directly involves the domestic politics of the member states and thus raises the intervention issue.

The United States has not pushed the subversion issue very hard, not only because of the Latin American resistance but also because the extent of Cuban subversion in Latin America has not reached serious proportions, except perhaps in Venezuela in 1963-64. The standard State Department line is that Cuba has engaged in subversion in Latin America since the early days of 1959, at first "sponsoring" armed expeditions against Caribbean countries, then switching to the more indirect tactics of propaganda campaigns, covert material support of subversive organizations, and indoctrination and training of Latin Americans in sabotage and terrorism.[83] Privately, though, United States officials freely admit that Cuba is really allocating little effort and money to "export its revolution," and that most guerrilla movements in Latin America are basically indigenous; in early 1963, in fact, Secretary of Defense McNamara embarrassed the State Department when he admitted that Cuba was not being "used as a base for the export of Communism in any substantial degree today" and that there was no "extensive propaganda" campaign from Cuba.[84]

In general, both the Kennedy and Johnson administrations have resisted demands by the Central American–Caribbean countries for a more aggressive policy, while at the same time exhorting Mexico and the major South American states to join in periodic symbolic anti-Cuban gestures, hoping thereby to avoid a new crisis with the Soviet Union, demonstrate a continuing concern with the Cuban problem to United States public opinion, and maintain at least some pressure on Cuba.

The difficulties inherent in the subversion question

have been reflected in the controversy that has surrounded the Special Consultative Committee on Security,
which has been a dead letter from the start. At Punta
del Este the OAS unanimously agreed to establish the
SCCS, but the apparent consensus was misleading, for
the troublesome problems of the actual composition,
scope, and authority of the SCCS were mostly bypassed
and left for later solution to the Council. The statutes
of the SCCS, approved by the Council in April, 1963, provided that it would be a purely advisory body, composed
of seven members acting in a private capacity rather
than as representatives of their countries. Thus the
SCCS was established as a non-governmental body, with
no powers of enforcement and no authority to bring
pressures to bear on recalcitrant states. Most of the
Latin American states, it was clear, did not want a
revival of a body similar to the World War II Emergency Committee for Political Defense, a relatively powerful intergovernmental agency that had exposed Nazi subversion in several Latin American countries.

Even these important concessions were not enough
to gain the support of a number of Latin American
states, however. A major split developed over whether
the SCCS should provide advice only to member states
so requesting, or to the Council of the OAS as well.
Under the latter, broader mandate, the Council could
theoretically ask the SCCS to investigate subversion in
any Latin American state, even without the consent
of the state in question.[85] A number of Latin American
states insisted that this was a step on the road to "super-
statism" and attempted to deny the Council this authority. A Venezuelan amendment to the statutes embodying
this restriction was defeated, but by the close vote of
7-11-2, Venezuela, Brazil, Mexico, Haiti, Bolivia, Chile,
and Uruguay voting in its favor.[86] Nonetheless, although

the broader mandate was retained, the opposition to it had been so severe that the sccs has so far limited its "assistance" to those countries that have requested it.

Since the establishment of the sccs only one country, in fact, the Dominican Republic in 1963, has bothered to ask for assistance in combating subversion. No doubt this is in part due to nationalistic pride; as the former United States Ambassador to the oas conceded, "implicit in an appeal by a government for assistance . . . is an admission of its own inability to handle the danger."[87]

As a result, the sccs has been limited to the preparation of "general reports" on Communist subversion in the hemisphere.[88] These reports have been little more than simplistic primers on "how to fight communism," reflecting the military backgrounds of most of the sccs members. Warning direly of the progress of the "Sino-Soviet" offensive in Latin America and of the ineffectiveness of existing measures to resist it, the reports have called for the co-ordination of hemispheric security and intelligence services "especially trained in anti-Communist action,"[89] and for various restrictive measures to control the movement of arms, money, and personnel to and from Cuba. Other than understandably to frighten democratic forces in Latin America, the results of the reports have been nil; the sccs itself frequently complains bitterly that it is ignored by most hemispheric governments. The United States, although lending half-hearted verbal support to the sccs recommendations, has not actively sought their implementation.

The subversion issue has been kept before the oas primarily by Venezuela. In November, 1962, Venezuela told the Council that it had "documentary proof" of Cuban participation in recent acts of sabotage and subversion in Venezuela and charged that the OAS had failed to fulfil the mandate of the Punta del Este Conference to take strong action against such subversion. No OAS action was requested, however, until a year later, when Venezuela asserted that it had found a large cache of Cuban arms on its coast, destined for the use of pro-Castro terrorist groups attempting to prevent the 1963 Venezuelan elections.[90] Several months later an investigating committee of the Council, appointed at Venezuela's behest, confirmed that the arms were of Cuban origin and concluded that Venezuela had been "the target of actions sponsored and directed by the Government of Cuba, openly intended to subvert Venezuelan institutions and to overthrow the democratic Government of Venezuela through terrorism, sabotage, assault and guerrilla warfare."[91] In view of this report, the OAS had little choice but to accede to Venezuela's demand for a foreign ministers' conference under the Rio Treaty.

Although the United States supported Venezuela's insistence that Cuba be punished, it is unlikely that it did so with much enthusiasm. The hemisphere was still badly split; Brazil, Mexico, Chile, Bolivia, and Uruguay were firmly opposed to further anti-Cuban action; and Haiti, Peru, and Argentina were dubious. Only a few months earlier, the Johnson administration had dropped its own tentative plans to ask the OAS for a trade embargo against Cuba,[92] deciding in effect that the political advantages of a new move against Cuba did not outweigh the prospect of a renewed demonstration of the hemispheric division. But with the Central American–Caribbean countries again pressing for strong action, Venezuela direly warning that the continued functioning of the OAS itself was at stake, and a presidential election in the offing, the administration could hardly afford to block action. Still, there was a considerable amount of foot-dragging in actually convoking the meeting, for until the April, 1964, military coup brought Brazil into the anti-Cuban camp, efforts to find a formula that could get at least the minimum two-thirds support had been unsuccessful.[93]

The conference finally met in Washington in late July, although Venezuela's refusal to consider major concessions had prevented the reaching of full consensus. Venezuela wanted all the sanctions provided by Article 8 of the Rio Treaty, except the use of armed force—the suspension of diplomatic and consular relations by all OAS members, a hemispheric trade embargo, and the interruption of all air and sea transportation to Cuba.[94] Mexico, Bolivia, Uruguay, and Chile, the only states still maintaining contact with Cuba, were opposed to the sanctions. Another group, led by Argentina, was willing to go along with some action, but it argued that sanctions should be merely "recommended" to the members rather than made mandatory.

The states maintaining relations with Cuba all did so primarily because they feared the domestic consequences of a break. In particular, Chile was faced with a presidential election in a few months in which a pro-Communist coalition was thought to have an excellent chance to win, and the incumbent Alessandri regime did not want to appear to be yielding to alleged pressures from Washington. Therefore, asked Argentina with some logic, why insist on measures that can add little to the existing pressures on Cuba but could have serious disruptive effects on other nations?[95]

There were two other important issues at the conference. Although there was widespread agreement that

Cuba should be warned against further aggression in Latin America, there was disagreement over whether the use of armed force should be threatened. Secondly, there was disagreement over whether subversion should be specifically labeled an act of aggression, thereby, perhaps, making future action under the Rio Treaty more certain.

The United States took a cautious position on all questions. It agreed that Cuba should be warned in strong terms against further aggression; and it wanted sanctions, for the failure of the foreign ministers to act could turn Congressional and public opinion in the United States against the OAS and revive demands for unilateral action. On the other hand, it shared Chile's concern about its forthcoming elections. More generally, since it was well aware that sanctions could have only a symbolic and political impact, it wanted the largest possible majority, not merely the minimum two-thirds.

As a result, the United States followed a middle-of-the road strategy, as it had at Punta del Este,[96] supporting Venezuela in its refusal to accept non-obligatory sanctions, but persuading the hard-liners not to insist on immediate compliance and tacitly consenting not to push Chile to break diplomatic relations with Cuba until after its elections.[97] Moreover, it agreed to Mexico's request, opposed by a number of Latin American states, that the proposed suspension of air transportation to Cuba be dropped.[98] It called for a warning to the Castro regime "that if it persists in acts of subversion in other American Republics the full weight of the regional security system will be applied," but it did not explicitly threaten the use of armed force, in contrast to a Central American proposal.[99] It suggested that the OAS "urge non-OAS states to "examine the possibility" of suspending trade with Cuba as an act of solidarity with the OAS, but it refused to threaten retaliation against European nations trading with Cuba, as a number of Latin Americans demanded.[100] Finally, since there was considerable Latin American opposition to a specific statement characterizing subversion as aggression, probably stemming from a fear of playing into the hands of antireformist forces, Secretary of State Rusk argued (correctly) that the OAS already possessed enough authority under Article 6 of the Rio Treaty to take action against subversion.[101]

The outcome of the conference deliberations closely paralleled the United States position, with the significant exception that the warning to Cuba went *further* than the original United States proposal, specifying that in the event of continuing Cuban "aggression and intervention" in the hemisphere, "individual or collective self-defense . . . could go so far as resort to armed force."[102] By 14–4–1 (Mexico, Chile, Bolivia, and Uruguay opposing; Argentina abstaining), the foreign ministers also imposed a mandatory collective break in diplomatic and consular relations, a suspension of all trade except in foodstuffs and medicine, and a suspension of all sea transport except that necessary for "humanitarian" purposes.[103]

The "sanctions" hardly amounted to very much. The closing of the Cuban embassies in Chile, Bolivia, and Uruguay (Mexico has refused to comply with the resolution) may have had some marginal utility in making it more difficult for Cuba to funnel propaganda and material support to Castroist groups in Latin America, as the State Department claims, but its effect is primarily symbolic. As for trade, Cuba's 1963 trade with the hemisphere had dropped to $18,000,000, almost all in food and therefore exempt from the "embargo."[104]

As indicated, from the point of view of the United States the primary value of a continued role for the OAS in the Cuban situation was that it helped defray domestic pressures for more aggressive United States policies. The success of this strategy depended, however, on keeping OAS action confined to periodic reports and recommendations and other harmless activities. Full-scale conferences inevitably could produce only division, recriminations, and possible domestic upheavals in unstable Latin American states, without adding anything of much value to the United States policy of "isolation." A conference was considered a success if, on balance, the resulting damage was not too serious. In short, the value of the OAS to the United States depended on its continuing to do *something* about Cuba, but not much.

Conclusion

Insofar as they have urged anti-Communist action in the OAS, U.S. policy-makers have been motivated by several considerations. To some extent substantive Latin American participation in multilateral programs has been sought, as in the economic embargo of the Castro regime and in co-operative programs to control the movement of arms, funds, and people to and from Cuba. More importantly, symbolic participation in essentially unilateral United States measures and advance legitimization of projected United States actions have been the goals, as in the efforts to obtain token Latin American participation in the Korean War, to get a strong anti-Communist resolution at the Caracas Conference of 1954 prior to the Castillo Armas operation, and to obtain "authorization" for the Cuban missile blockade in 1962. By taking advantage of the provisions of Article 52 of the UN Charter, which specify that regional agencies shall be used for "pacific settlement" of local conflicts before they are referred to the Security Council, the United States has used the OAS as a shield to fend off the United Nations while it was unilaterally disposing of troublesome hemispheric problems, as in the Guatemalan affair. Finally, by providing an excuse for inaction when United States policy-makers were unwilling to take drastic unilateral action against Castro in the earliest and most recent stages of the Cuban problem, the OAS has served the United States domestic purposes.

But it has been far from easy for the United States to draw the Latin Americans into the cold war, and although a number of Latin American states have been privately quite pleased at strong United States anti-Communist action, multilateral support has generally been tepid and grudging. As a group, the Latin Americans have not shared Washington's anxiety over the threat of "international communism." On the contrary, they have been fearful that if used as an anti-Communist alliance the inter-American system, far from *insulating* the hemisphere from global conflict, as it had been designed to do, would increase the dangers to Latin American security. Moreover, the OAS was supposed to keep the United States out of the internal affairs of Latin American states, not facilitate intervention under the guise of "collective security." Beyond that, there has been a considerable amount of ideological sympathy with the targets of United States measures, particularly with the Castro regime in its early years. Also, the democratic states have feared that an excessive preoccupation with "communism" might legitimize repressive measures against *all* leftist movements in Latin America. Finally, a few countries, especially Mexico, have had genuine qualms about the legality of some anti-Communist measures.

As a result, even when the United States has been able to obtain multilateral backing, it has generally been at a very high price. United States policies have fed anti-Americanism in Latin America, especially among the increasingly important populist groups. The unanimity tradition in the OAS has been another casualty of the cold war; on a number of occasions paper victories have been attained at the cost of a bad hemispheric split, the most dramatic instance being the Punta del Este Conference of 1962, when all the "banana republics" sided with the United States, but the four largest, most populous, and most important Latin American states were in the opposition. Moreover, OAS action has exacerbated militarism and endemic political instability in Latin America: states that oppose OAS anti-Communist measures risk military coups from the right, and states that go along risk popular indignation from the left. More indirectly but perhaps even more importantly, the emphasis on antisubversion and counterguerrilla activities has increased the power and political role of the Latin American armed forces and encouraged them to block the growing forces of reform in the name of "anti-Communism." Whether the symbolic legitimacy the OAS has added to United States anti-Communist policies is worth these costs is indeed dubious.

1. Personal interviews; see also Daniel James, *Cuba: The First Soviet Satellite in the Americas* (New York: Avon Books, 1961), pp. 119-20.

2. House Committee on Foreign Affairs, *The Communist Threat in Latin America, Hearings,* Subcommittee on Inter-American Affairs, 86th Cong., 2d sess., 1960, p. 57.

3. *Ibid.,* p. 60.

4. For an authoritative statement on this policy see the speech by Undersecretary of State George Ball, *Department of State Bulletin,* May 11, pp. 738-44.

5. Secretary of State Dean Rusk, *Department of State Bulletin,* April 1, 1963, p. 470.

6. Assistant Secretary of State Edwin Martin, *Department of State Bulletin,* June 24, 1962; see also Ball, *op. cit.*

7. Official Soviet statement, quoted in *New York Times,* May 25, 1963.

8. *Department of State Bulletin,* April 1, 1963, p. 470.

9. Cf. the Dominican Republic, 1965.

10. The Punta del Este Conference is discussed on pp. 152 ff.

11. Edwin Martin, *Department of State Bulletin,* May 6, 1963, p. 712; Martin, testifying before the Subcommittee on Inter-American Affairs of the House Committee on Foreign Affairs, *Castro-Communist Subversion in the Western Hemisphere, Hearings,* 88th Cong., 1st sess., 1963, p. 48. Cf. also President Johnson's statement: "I now today assure you that the full power of the United States is ready to assist any country whose freedom is threatened by forces dictated to from beyond the shores of this continent." *(Actas del Consejo,* March 16, 1965.)

12. Interviews.

13. *New York Times,* March 25, 1963.

14. *UN Security Council Official Records,* 874th Meeting, July 18, 1960, paragraph 22.

15. *Efforts,* p. 221.

16. On July 19 the Security Council voted 9-0 (the Soviet Union and Poland abstaining) in favor of an Argentine-Ecualoran resolution "adjourning" debate on the Cuban charges "pending the receipt of a report" from the OAS. The usual jurisdictional debate was avoided by an informal compromise

plan worked out between the United States, Cuba, and the Soviet Union, under which the Cuban request was inscribed on the agenda of the Security Council and briefly debated before being returned to the OAS. (*New York Times,* July 20, 1960.)

17. Interviews.

18. The memorandum is in the Inter-American Peace Committee, Report to the Seventh Meeting of Consultation, Appendix J, pp. 5-34. An official summary of the memo can be found in *Efforts,* pp. 57-61.

19. Herter's speech to the third session of the General Committee, *Document 37,* Meeting of Consultation of Ministers of Foreign Affairs, Seventh, San José, 1960, *Documents.* (Washington, D.C.: Pan American Union, 1960). (Cited hereinafter as San José Conference, *Documents.*)

20. Herter's speech to the seventh session of the General Committee, in *Efforts,* p. 348.

21. San José Conference, *Document 37.*

22. Raúl Roa's speech to the sixth session of the General Committee, San José Conference, *Document 60.*

23. *Ibid.*

24. *New York Times,* August 25, 1960.

25. For example, a typical Latin American approach was the Colombian foreign minister's "formal invitation" to Cuba "to conform . . . to the discipline of the inter-American system" and abandon "all aims that may endanger hemispheric security and inter-American unity," or Mexico's admonition that the foreign ministers avoid "impatience" with the Cuban revolution and "show the Cuban Government and people that their 'natural sphere' is in the Americas." (*San José Conference, Documents 15* and *16.*)

26. *Ibid., Document 20.*

27. San José Conference, *Documents 15, 55, 59.*

28. Secretary of State Herter, *Bulletin,* September 12, 1960, p. 408.

29. Shortly before the Conference, the Eisenhower administration had reversed its policy on public aid to Latin America, asking Congress for $500 million for assistance to Latin American "social development and economic growth." (*Efforts,* pp. 261-62.)

Although there is no evidence the United States attempted to use the projected program as a means of leverage at San José, the significance of the timing of the announcement was surely not lost on the Latin Americans.

30. *New York Times*, August 30, 1960.

31. Minutes of the 8th sess. of the General Committee, San José Conference, *Document 79*.

32. Final Act, San José Conference, *Documents*.

33. The United States had broken diplomatic relations with Cuba in January, 1961, and most of its trade with Cuba had been disrupted.

34. *Congressional Record*, May 17, 1961, p. 8231.

35. Interviews.

36. Quoted in Edwin Lieuwen, *Arms and Politics in Latin America* (New York: Frederick A. Praeger, 1961), p. 286.

37. *Actas del Consejo*, October 16, 1961; interviews.

38. *Actas del Consejo*, October 25, 1961. From there, the matter was eventually turned over to the Peace Committee, whose subsequent report, charging that Cuba's ties with communism and its subversive activities in Latin America were "incompatible with the principles and standards" of the OAS, was used as the basis of the Punta del Este decision to exclude Cuba from the OAS. (Inter-American Peace Committee, *Report to the Eighth Meeting of Consultation of Ministers of Foreign Affairs* [Washington, D.C.: Pan American Union, 1962], pp. 22-48.)

39. *Actas del Consejo*, November 14, 1961.

40. *Ibid.*

41. Interviews.

42. *Actas del Consejo*, December 4, 1961. A positive majority is required; abstentions have the same effect as "no" votes.

43. Interviews.

44. Interviews.

45. For example, the Colombian foreign minister told the conference that the risk of a split had to be taken, "for if the system is capable of acting only when threats are not serious, when both parties to a conflict have equal respect for the organization . . . (and) if it can endure only by remaining idle . . . then there is neither rhyme nor reason for its continued exist-

ence." (Meeting of Consultation of Ministers of Foreign Affairs, Eighth, Punta del Este, 1962, *Documentos de la* Reunion [Washington, D.C.: Pan American Union, 1962], *Documento 19.* Cited hereinafter as *Documentos.*)

46. See especially the speeches of the Brazilian and Mexican foreign ministers, *Documentos 25* and *32.*

47. See *Documentos 29* and *45.*

48. Adolph A. Berle, *Latin America—Diplomacy and Reality* (New York: Council on Foreign Relations, 1962), pp. 100-105.

49. The El Salvadoran foreign minister was reported to have warned that his government would face a rightist coup if strong anti-Castro action was not taken. (Douglass Cater, "The Lesson of Punta del Este," *Reporter,* March 1, 1962.)

50. See *Documento 35.*

51. The Uruguayan National Council had finally decided to support a moderately hard line. (Interview.)

52. Interviews.

53. C. Neale Ronning, *Punta del Este: The Limits of Collective Security in a Troubled Hemisphere* (New York: Carnegie Endowment for International Peace, 1963), p. 20.

54. This transaction has been reported by a number of observers of the conference and has been indirectly confirmed by this writer in several interviews. If true, it is the only time the United States has *specifically* used its economic assistance program to gain political *quid pro quos* at Inter-American conferences, as far as this writer has been able to determine.

55. Final Act, *Documentos.* The six abstainers all voted in **favor of** the first two clauses of the resolution, declaring Cuba's incompatibility with the Inter-American system. The split was only over whether this incompatibility thereby "excluded" Cuba from participation in the OAS.

56. *Actas del Consejo,* November 14, 1961; Minutes of the 9th sess. of the General Committee, *Documento 72;* Minutes of the 2d Plenary sess., *Documento 74.*

57. In 1948, though, the official United States interpretation of the Charter had been that membership in the OAS was a right, conferred by location in the Western Hemisphere, "no provision [being made] for suspension or expulsion." (Ninth Inter-American Conference, Bogotá, 1948, *Report of the United States Delegation,* 1950, p. 15.)

58. *Documento 74.*

59. Resolution VIII, Final Act, *Documentos.*

60. Resolution II, Final Act, *Documentos.*

61. Interviews; see also Senate Committee on Foreign Relations, *Report of Senators Wayne Morse and Bourke B. Hickenlooper on the Punta del Este Conference,* 87th Cong., 2d sess., 1962.

62. Interviews.

63. *Department of State Bulletin,* February 19, 1962, pp. 283-84.

64. Interviews.

65. See below, pp. 167 ff.

66. *Cater,* p. 21.

67. See *Documento* 72.

68. *Morse-Hickenlooper Report; Congressional Record,* February 2, 1962, p. 1334.

69. *New York Times,* January 22, 1962.

70. *New York Times,* February 8, 1962. The Haitian affair was an exception, but it was a special case, in that the Haitian delegation apparently quite explicitly demanded a reward for its vote. (Interviews.)

71. Secretary of State Rusk, *Department of State Bulletin,* February 19, 1962, p. 288.

72. Some time later, Secretary of State Rusk revealed that the administration had reached its decision by Friday, October 19, and only *then* began "consulting"—i.e., informing—its allies. *(Department of State Bulletin,* December 17, 1962, p. 910.) Moreover, the Latin Americans were apparently given a very low priority, for they were not informed until Monday, October 22, just a few hours before the President's dramatic speech to the nation. (Interview.)

73. *New York Times,* September 14, 1962.

74. Secretary of State Rusk, U.S. Senate Committees on Foreign Relations and Armed Forces, *Situation in Cuba, Hearings,* 87th Cong., 2d sess. 1962, p. 55. (Emphasis added.)

75. *Department of State Bulletin,* November 12, 1962, p. 716. (Emphasis added.)

76. The delay was also designed to give the Soviets time to consider the situation and so preclude a "spasm response." (Roger Hilsman, "The Cuban Crisis: How Close We Were to War," *Look,* August 25, 1964.)

77. *Actas del Consejo,* October 23, 1962. (Emphasis added.)

78. Interview.

79. The abstentions were ostensibly based on "constitutional" factors. The next day, however, Brazil said explicitly that it would not support the use of armed force "for measures that imply intervention in Cuban territory." *(New York Times,* October 25, 1962.)

80. *Actas del Consejo,* October 23, 1962. In the ensuing week, Argentina and Venezuela contributed two destroyers each to the blockade, and eight other nations offered the use of seaport and airfield facilities for logistics purposes. (OAS Document OEA/ Ser G/V, C-d-1026 and addendums, October 24–November 23, 1962.)

81. Secretary of State Rusk, *Department of State Bulletin,* December 17, 1962, p. 911.

82. For example, a 1963 report of a committee of the Council was bitterly and publicly resisted by Chile, Mexico, Brazil, and Venezuela, in part because of a statement admitting that anti-Communist restrictions might involve some "sacrifice of civil and political liberties and of human rights." *(Actas del Consejo,* June 5, July 3, 1963.)

83. See the testimony of Assistant Secretary of State Edwin Martin, in *Castro-Communist Subversion in the Western Hemisphere,* p. 5 ff.

84. *New York Times,* March 30, 1963.

85. In no case, however, could the SCCS actually investigate *within* the territory of any country without its express authorization.

86. The debates, statute, and votes are contained in *Actas del Consejo,* April 3, April 23, 1963.

87. Testimony of the late deLessups Morrison, in *Castro-Communist Subversion in the Western Hemisphere,* p. 196.

88. Report of the SCCS to the Council, February 20, 1963, reprinted as Appendix I, *Castro-Communist Subversion in the Wes-*

tern Hemisphere; First General Report of the SCCS, in *Actas del Consejo,* May 2, 1962; Third Report of the SCCS, OEA/Ser. L/X/11.7, December 11, 1964.

89. Third Report, p. 3.

90. *Actas del Consejo,* December 3, 1963.

91. The text of the Committee's report is contained in Annex A, Meeting of Consultation of Ministers of Foreign Affairs, *Ninth,* Washington, D.C., 1964, *Actas y Documentos* (Washington, D.C.: Pan American Union, 1965). (Cited hereinafter as *Ninth Meeting, Actas y Documentos.*)

92. Interviews.

93. See the remarks of the Chilean delegate, *Actas del Consejo,* June 26, 1964.

94. Venezuelan speech, 2d sess., General Committee, *Ninth Meeting, Actas y Documentos.*

95. Argentine speech, 3d sess., General Committee, *ibid.*

96. In an unusual move, Mexico publicly complimented the United States for its conciliatory attitude and disassociated it from Latin American "extremists" who were demanding stronger action. (Mexican speech, 7th sess., General Committee, *Ninth Meeting, Actas y Documentos.*)

97. Interviews.

98. Interviews. Mexico maintained, uniquely, that since it would be the only state affected by the suspension, being the only hemispheric state still having air service to Cuba, a suspension would be inconsistent with the principle of the "juridical equality" of all states. (Mexican speech, 7th sess., General Committee, *Ninth Meeting, Actas y Documentos.*)

99. The quote is from the statement of Secretary of State Rusk to the 2d session of the General Committee, reprinted in the Department of State Bulletin, August 10, 1964, p. 174 ff; the United States proposal on the warning to Cuba is *Document 37* of the conference, the Central American proposal is *Document 12,* both found in *Ninth Meeting, Actas y Documentos.*

100. Interviews; *Document 36,* Ninth Meeting, *Actas y Documentos.*

101. Rusk's statement, *op. cit.*

102. Cuban Resolution, Final Act, *Ninth Meeting, Actas y Documentos.*

103. The vote is in the minutes of the 9th sess., General Committee, *ibid.* Non-OAS members were asked "to examine the possibility of effectively demonstrating their solidarity in achieving the purpose of this resolution."

104. *New York Times,* July 23, 1964.

CHAPTER **5**

The OAS as an Antidictatorial Alliance (I):

The Dominican Republic, 1960–1963

For a very short period after World War II the United States took seriously the democratic rhetoric in its inter-American policy and brought heavy pressures to bear on Latin American dictatorships. The failure of its most ambitious effort, however—Spruille Braden's 1946 attempt to destroy Juan Perón in Argentina—induced a return to the traditional policies of de facto recognition of, and normal relations with, all existing governments. The primary objective of United States policy became the maintenance of "maximum tranquility"[1] or of an anti Communist stability, defined to mean the preservation of the status quo. Since under this definition of stability the nature of the internal political organization of Latin America was irrelevant, democracy ceased to be of concern to the United States.[2]

In the OAS the requirements of this policy led the United States to join the majority of the Latin American states in rejecting attempts to include antidictatorial provisions in the Rio Treaty and the OAS Charter and subsequently to become one of the leading advocates of the doctrine of non-intervention, particularly in response to the numerous attempts in the Caribbean to overthrow dictatorial regimes.

Beginning in 1960, in response to the Cuban revolution, United States policy shifted abruptly. The new policy was based in part on the assumption that rightist dictatorships in Latin America, by blocking political change, were inadvertently fostering "Castro-Communist" movements. As a result, the United States began actively to press for democracy and economic and social reform in Latin America.

To the new pro-democratic policy was added a growing concern over the course of the Cuban revolution, resulting in a radical shift in the United States position in the OAS on the doctrine of non-intervention. As late as the 1959 Santiago Conference, it will be recalled, the United States had invoked non-intervention in an attempt to inhibit antidictatorial exile expeditions thought to be supported by Cuba. By mid-1960, however, the growing influence of communism inside Cuba had caused the United States to become increasingly concerned not only to prevent the exportation of the Cuban revolution but to destroy that revolution in Cuba itself. Clearly then, the doctrine of non-intervention was no longer very convenient. In order to gain Latin American support for a possible interventionist policy against

Cuba, though, the United States, it was felt, would have to demonstrate its willingness to support strong action against the right as well as the left.

Specifically, the new United States posture toward dictatorship was manifested in a shift in policy toward the Dominican Republic. For nearly three decades the Trujillo dictatorship had been one of the most stable regimes in Latin America; it had also been one of the most loudly anti-Communist. As long as Trujillo was firmly in power, then, the United States had found it convenient to work with him. Toward the end of 1959 and the beginning of 1960, however, the Dominican situation suddenly became more fluid. Internal opposition grew rapidly, and it became apparent that Trujillo was at long last losing his iron grip on the country. The departure of Trujillo from the Dominican scene, it was feared, might lead to chaos and the emergence of a new Castro. As a result, the United States began to cast about for a means to get rid of Trujillo but at the same time insure a "responsible" successor.

Thus, beginning in mid-1960, in response both to internal developments in Cuba and the Dominican Republic and the requirements of its new long-range strategy for combating communism in Latin America, the United States dropped its ardent support of the doctrine of non-intervention.

In the next two years the United States in the Dominican Republic engaged in its most massive intervention in the internal affairs of a Latin American state since the inauguration of the Good Neighbor policy. A wide variety of the instruments of power and influence available to the United States—ranging from multilateral diplomacy and pressures to unilateral economic rewards and sanctions and even the threat of military intervention—were brought to bear to assure the attainment of two related, but distinct, objectives: (1) to set the precedent and create the machinery for collective inter-American action against dictatorships, which could later be used against the Castro regime, and (2) to induce a liberalization in the internal Dominican political structure in order to forestall a Castro-type revolution.

The shift in United States policy was foreshadowed in two reports of the United States–chaired Inter-American Peace Committee, released in April and June of 1960.[3] The April report was based on a "study" of "the relationship between violations of human rights or the non-exercise of representative democracy, on the one hand, and the political tensions that affect the peace of the hemisphere, on the other," carried out in accordance with the expanded authority granted the Peace Committee at the Santiago Conference of 1959. The Committee concluded that there was indeed such a relationship, much as Larreta had argued fourteen years earlier:

> The existence of dictatorial governments inevitably results in numerous persons fleeing from their countries and taking refuge in other American States. There, because of the deeply held beliefs [in democracy and human rights] . . . they find sympathy and moral support. There they can organize movements against anti-democratic regimes which it is not feasible for them to launch in their own countries. These efforts often reach the stage of activities which impinge upon the obligations assumed by the American States under various inter-American instruments for the purpose of preventing the organization of military expeditions against other governments.
>
> When citizens are unable, because of the existence of a dictatorial regime, to effect political change legally and by the ballot, they often resort to force. Threats and actual attempts of invasion of their home lands give rise, in turn, to

countermeasures on the part of the antidemocratic regimes. These countermeasures are often directed at the governments of countries which have extended hospitality or political asylum to exiles. Thus, so long as a general sympathy with democratic aspirations exists, the moral support enjoyed by the exiles will continue to be an additional factor in creating or intensifying international tensions.[4]

The significance of this report and the reasoning that underlay it cannot be exaggerated. Heretofore, in similar cases, the OAS had followed traditional collective security precepts. Collective security requires that all regimes are entitled to protection against external opponents, regardless of considerations of moral justice. Now, however, the Peace Committee, though hastily adding that it was not suggesting

any formula that would violate the nonintervention principle or the solemn inter-American commitments which have as their aim the preservation of the right of each state to work out its own political destiny,[5]

had spoken with obvious sympathy for antidictatorial exiles and had come close to implying that since the cause of such exiles was just, the *real* culprit was the regime giving rise to their grievances, regardless of which side actually initiated armed hostilities.

It must be assumed that the rather atypical reasoning of the Peace Committee was at least partially a cloak for other considerations. Neither the United States nor the Latin American members were really very concerned with international tensions arising out of the dictatorship problem per se. The United States was concerned with the potential for communism inherent in a continuation of repression and reaction in Latin America and, thus, was anxious to find a way of creating a more active role for the OAS in the internal affairs of Latin American states. The Latin Americans, some of them at least, were concerned with the Dominican case because of their normative commitment to democracy.

A direct approach toward either objective, however, would necessarily require collective action based on the internal political structures of states and, consequently, would require the explicit jettisoning of the non-intervention principle. Since this would be unacceptable to the Latin American majority, a way had to be found to tie the dictatorship issue to collective security, the only role considered legitimate for the OAS. The April report of the Peace Committee accomplished this objective, opening the door to collective action against dictatorships on the assumption that they were inherently a threat to international peace.

A second Peace Committee report went even further. During the spring of 1960, at the instigation of Venezuela, the Peace Committee undertook an extensive investigation of violations of human rights in the Dominican Republic.[6] In June the Committee issued a public report confirming Venezuelan charges that there had been widespread violations, including "the denial of free assembly and of free speech, arbitrary arrests, cruel and inhuman treatment of political prisoners, and the use of intimidation and terror as a political weapon."[7] Because of this, in recent months the numbers of Dominican exiles finding refuge in sympathetic countries had increased, and their activities, "directed towards effecting a change in the government of their native country," had intensified, leading in turn to illegal and violent countermeasures by the Dominican government. As a result, the Committee concluded,

international tensions in the Caribbean region have been
aggravated by flagrant and widespread violations of human
rights which have been committed and continue to be committed in the Dominican Republic.[8]

It was the first time that an OAS body had so clearly
ignored the non-intervention principle and had bluntly
and vigorously condemned the internal policies of a
non-Communist American state. In similar cases in the
past the OAS had lent lip-service to democracy and
human rights but had placed the onus for international
tensions on the exiles and the regimes aiding them. The
cause of democracy did not excuse violations of the
principle of non-intervention, it had repeatedly asserted.
Now, it implied, democracy was a very good excuse
indeed. Taken together, the two reports of the Peace
Committee supplied the rationale for a possible transformation of the OAS into an antidictatorial alliance.

The new United States policy was made even more
explicit at the Sixth Meeting of Consultation of the OAS
foreign ministers in August, 1960, at San José, Costa
Rica. In early July, Venezuela had requested the urgent
invocation of Article 6 of the Rio Treaty to consider
"acts of intervention and aggression" by the Dominican
Republic against the Romulo Betancourt government.
After the fall of Pérez Jiménez in 1958, Venezuela
charged, the Dominican Republic flooded Venezuela
with propaganda urging revolution and sheltered reactionary followers of the former dictator. But more seriously, the Trujillo regime had become involved in direct
action against Betancourt, assisting in several attempts to
overthrow his regime, the most recent of which was an
assassination plot that had just missed success.[9]
The Venezuelan request for an investigation was

strongly supported by the United States, which had publicly eulogized the Betancourt government as the very model of a modern Latin American regime. One month later, the Council's Investigating Committee (the United States, Argentina, Mexico, Panama, and Uruguay) reported it had verified that the assassination attempt, part of a plot intended to overthrow the Venezuelan government, had been assisted by "high officials" of the Dominican government.[10]

When the foreign ministers convened at San José in mid-August, 1960, Venezuela demanded a collective interruption of diplomatic relations and an economic embargo against the Dominican Republic.[11] The United States, however, proposed an alternative course. The real task of the conference, Secretary of State Herter asserted, was not merely to punish the Dominican Republic for its past aggressions,

> but also to create a situation within the Dominican Republic whereby that country can be brought back into respected membership in the American community and its citizens permitted to enjoy the benefits of representative democracy.[12]

Quoting approvingly the Peace Committee's conclusion that international tensions in the Caribbean were directly related to the "flagrant and wide spread violations of human rights in the Dominican Republic," Herter argued that the Dominican Republic would be bound to continue its "aggressive and interventionist policy" as long as it was ruled by a dictatorship.[13] In order to get at "the root of the matter," then, the foreign ministers had to go beyond the imposition of "merely punitive" sanctions. This could be done by the establishment of a special committee to go to the Dominican Republic to assure that, within a specific and reasonable period of time, free elections by a people, who in fact shall have had the right of free expression and free assembly, be held under the supervision of the committee itself.[14]

To this end the committee should be endowed with powers sufficient "to forestall any attempt to obstruct or water down the creation of the necessary conditions for genuinely free elections."[15] If the Dominicans should refuse to agree, the OAS "should *then* consider what measures under Article 8 of the Rio Treaty might be most effectively applied in order to bring about acceptance of this proposal by the Dominican Government."[16] And as for the traditional United States position, reiterated as recently as the Santiago Conference a year earlier, that democracy can come only from within:

these goals [democracy, human rights] must, of course, be achieved primarily by the action of the peoples of each country. *When, however, a flagrant and notorious situation develops . . . [it] calls for action by the Organization.*[17]

The lesson of the Cuban revolution had not been lost. Herter's Dominican policy was based on a simple relation: "Batista is to Castro as Trujillo is to ———," and the United States wanted to insure that it could help fill in the blank. Thus, Washington hoped to seize upon the opportunity presented by the Dominican indiscretion in Venezuela to find an "orderly" way to get rid of Trujillo before the Dominican people did. Seen in this light, the Herter proposal was clearly an attempt to use the sanctions provided for by the Rio Treaty as a means of leverage to guide the coming political change in the Dominican Republic into non-Communist channels; any OAS committee would almost certainly have included the United States and would have provided a convenient collective umbrella under which the United States could operate to achieve its ends.

The Herter proposal, however, was clearly radically interventionist and was rejected as such, undoubtedly by an overwhelming margin.[18] In addition, some of the Latin American states might have felt that it was designed to serve as a precedent for similar action against Cuba—immediately after the Dominican question was disposed of the ministers took up the Cuban issue—and, as will be recalled, the great majority of the Latin American states were not at that time prepared to take any action against the Castro revolution.

Nevertheless, the action subsequently taken against the Dominican Republic at the meeting was to lay the basis for future United States–OAS maneuverings that, in effect, accomplished precisely the same objectives as those of the short-lived Herter proposal. For the first time since the creation of the OAS, sanctions were imposed (unanimously). Ostensibly based solely on the aggressive actions of the Dominican Republic against Venezuela, the sanctions included the interruption by all hemispheric states of diplomatic relations with the Dominican Republic and the cessation of arms shipments to the Trujillo regime.[19] In addition, the Council was authorized to "study the feasibility and desirability" of extending these sanctions and, if extended, discontinuing them when the Dominican Republic ceased "to constitute a danger to the peace and security . . . of the hemisphere."[20] Although the initial sanctions were primarily symbolic—the United States, the only important supplier of arms to the Dominican Republic, had previously unilaterally discontinued its arms shipments—the additional mandate granted the

Council allowed the oas to later play a crucial although unforeseen role in internal Dominican political developments.

In the ensuing months, the United States took the lead in the oas in pressing for even stiffer action and instituted unilateral action that went far beyond the San José resolution. A few days after the Conference, President Eisenhower asked Congress for authority to exclude 321,000 tons of Dominican sugar from United States markets. Although Congress refused to take action, the President promptly imposed a fee of two cents per pound on the sugar, thereby depriving the Trujillo regime of the usual United States margin above world market prices.[21]

In the next few months the Council, under United States and Venezuelan urging, moved toward increasing the pressures on the Dominican Republic. In December, 1960, a Council committee (the United States, Panama, Honduras, Mexico, Ecuador, Chile, and Brazil) reported that there had been no change in the attitude of the Dominican Republic toward the fundamental principles of the inter-American system and that therefore it would be desirable to impose more substantial economic sanctions.[22]

Opponents of further action, led by Brazil, pointed out that no new Dominican acts of aggression had been committed and argued that further sanctions were therefore unwarranted and would in fact be based on the *internal* nature of the Dominican regime, violating the non-intervention principle. In response, the United States argued that according to the formula of the Peace Committee, as long as the Dominican Republic continued to violate human rights it would constitute a threat to the peace; since the initial sanctions had failed to produce any changes in this respect, further measures were required.

The earlier consensus had disappeared, however, and the tougher new measures were supported by only the bare two-thirds majority required by the Rio Treaty. By a 14-1-6 vote (the Dominican Republic opposing; Brazil, Argentina, Guatemala, Haiti, Paraguay, and Uruguay abstaining), the Council voted that

> it is feasible and desirable that the [OAS members] . . . extend the suspension of their trade with the Dominican Republic to the exportation of petroleum and petroleum products, trucks and spare parts.[23]

The vote was of particular significance in indicating the firmness of United States leadership, for the State Department generally refrains from pushing highly controversial measures to a vote, especially when such major Latin American states as Brazil and Argentina are in the opposition, doing so only when it deems the issue of such importance as to make acceptable an open split in the hemisphere.

United States Policy after the Assassination of Trujillo

Thus, beginning in mid-1960, the United States attempted to force major changes in the Trujillo regime, if not actually to bring it down. It is not evident whether the actions taken were in fact achieving that objective when the situation was brought to an abrupt head with the assassination of Trujillo on May 30, 1961.[24] The subsequent United States role in the Dominican Republic sheds a great deal of light on four highly important areas: the changing nature of United States policy toward Latin America, the uses of the OAS as an instrument of United States policy, the possibilities for outside assistance in the democratization process in politically underdeveloped countries, and the changing nature in both theory and practice of the principle of non-intervention.

Immediately after the assassination, Trujillo's puppet President, Joaquin Balaguer, assumed control, supported by the armed forces under Rafael ("Ramfis") Trujillo but to "Trujilloism"—administration sources "constitutional" and in control of the country, normal diplomatic relations were not re-established, and the State Department quickly made it clear that its concern in the Dominican Republic had not been limited to Trujillo but to "Trujilloism"—administration sources were said to feel that the new Dominican government was just as "reprehensible" as its predecessor.[25]

On June 2, the Sanctions Committee met at the request of the United States and agreed to its proposal that the Committee appoint a subcommittee to go immediately to the Dominican Republic to "observe" the general situation "and particularly the character of the Government and its policies."[26] Officially the mission of the subcommittee was to determine whether the new Dominican government had ceased to constitute a threat to the peace and security of the hemisphere and whether, therefore, the sanctions should be lifted.[27] Clearly, however, the United States was primarily interested in establishing an OAS–United States "presence" in the Dominican Republic to deter repression by the new government and, in general, to exert leverage over a situation that might, it was feared, degenerate into chaos and invite an extreme left-wing take-over. When, then, the OAS subcommittee, composed of representatives of the United States, Panama, Colombia, and Uruguay, returned to Washington after only one week, the State Department publicly expressed its dissatisfaction. Although the United States representative on the subcommittee had favored an indefinite stay in the Dominican Republic, he had been overruled. At least some of the Latin Americans on the subcommittee were personally in sympathy with both the tactics and the objectives of the United States, but they felt that their involvement had to remain limited in order to avoid an OAS split. Mexico and Argentina had refused to serve on the subcommittee,[28] and had that body attempted to prolong its stay in the Dominican Republic, an open battle might have ensued.[29]

Nonetheless, the subcommittee decided to maintain its role in Dominican affairs. After speaking with Dominican exiles, opposition leaders, and political prisoners, it concluded that despite the Balaguer government's promises of reform, it was

> too early to determine the degree of change that may have occurred in the character and policies of the Dominican Government. Therefore, the subcommittee considers it necessary that the course of developments in this respect continue to be observed.[30]

As a result, the sanctions, which by this time included in fact, although not formally, United States restrictions on the importation of Dominican sugar,[31] were maintained. Whereas even the additional sanctions voted in January had been largely symbolic—Trujillo had been able to get oil and trucks from outside the hemisphere—the sugar boycott hurt, particularly since the Trujillo family owned most of the Dominican sugar plantations.

During the summer of 1961, the Balaguer regime, anxious to regain its sugar market and to ease United States pressures, took some small steps toward liberalization. The subcommittee, again at the request of the United States, returned to the Dominican Republic in early September to see whether the latest developments warranted the lifting of sanctions. The Dominican government promised the OAS group that it would observe in its foreign policy the principle of non-intervention (meaning it would refrain from active intervention in the internal affairs of other nations), would continue the democratization process, and would start negotiations to form a coalition government with opposition leaders. Blaming the increasing unemployment on the economic effects of the sanctions, it urgently requested that they be lifted. The opposition leaders, however, arguing that the democratization process was largely a sham and that the present regime was a continuation of Trujilloism, unanimously opposed the removal of the sanctions, which, they told the subcommittee, were hurting the government and the Trujillo family but not the Dominican people. The subcommittee concluded that while the government had made "a limited amount of progress" toward democracy, repressive measures were continuing, particularly on the part of the armed forces which were not under the effective control of the civil authorities. Therefore the subcommittee recommended that the sanctions be maintained until greater progress had been made.[32]

The subcommittee, it will be remembered, was acting under a resolution of the San José foreign ministers' meeting, in which the Council was authorized to lift the sanctions when the Dominican Republic ceased to constitute a threat to the peace and security of the hemisphere. Theoretically, then, the mandate of the Sanctions Committee authorized it to examine only the *foreign* policies of the Dominican Republic. In fact, however, the Committee was mainly concerned with the *domestic* character of the Balaguer regime, as the report of the subcommittee on its September investigation made clear:

Taking into account the existing relationship between the violation of human rights and the lack of effective exercise of representative democracy on the one hand, and the political tensions that affect the peace of the hemisphere on the other, the Subcommittee considers that there must be evidence of more progress [toward democracy] than has thus far been attained before it can be concluded that the Dominican government has ceased to be a threat to the peace and security of the hemisphere.[33]

Under a less far-reaching interpretation of "threats to the peace," the subcommittee would have had to recommend the lifting of sanctions, for the Balaguer regime had committed no external acts of aggression and, given its anxiety over the sanctions, would hardly have been likely to do so in the foreseeable future. Thus the subcommittee had passed through the door originally opened by the Peace Committee, for it was clearly implying that it would consider the existence of dictatorship in the Dominican Republic as per se a cause of international tensions and therefore a legitimate object of continued collective action. This was a sweeping extension of the basis for the initial sanctions, and thereby set a precedent under which the OAS might involve itself in what had heretofore been considered the purely internal affairs of the member states.

A turning point in the hesitant movement toward democracy in the Dominican Republic was reached in mid-November, 1961. In early November, after a good deal of "persuasion" on the part of the United States consulate in Ciudad Trujillo, a large number of the Trujillo family had been induced to leave the country.[34] In response to this and other indications of progress, the United States proposed to the Sanctions Committee on Novembr 14 that the sanctions on oil and trucks be lifted.[35] This proposal was part of the over-all United States carrot-and-stick policy toward the Balaguer regime. The partial lifting of sanctions was designed to appease the *Trujillistas* who were increasing their pressure on Balaguer to show some results from his policy of co-operation with the OAS and the United States, and at the same time to encourage them to permit continued liberalization so that they might win the real prize, the resumption of sugar purchases. It was, in effect, a bribe.

This was a highly risky proposal, for it did not have the support of the Dominican opposition leaders, and it left the United States open to charges—justifiable or not—that it was satisfied with the Dominican status quo and was preparing to resume normal relations with its representatives. Furthermore, the proposal did not attain its objectives, since only two days after it had been made two of the most notorious of the Trujillo brothers, apparently intending to attempt a return to power, came back to the Dominican Republic.

The vigor of the United States response, however, underscored the depth of the Kennedy administration's commitment to a democratic Dominican Republic. On November 18, as fears of a right-wing coup mounted, Secretary of State Rusk warned that the United States would not "remain idle" if the Trujillos tried to "reassert dictatorial domination."[36] A United States Navy task force was sent to the scene and patrolled just outside Dominican waters in plain sight of Santo Domingo. It was reported that the administration had decided to land Marines in the event of an attempt against the Balaguer regime.[37] In face of this show of force, the Trujillo brothers left the country on November 20.

In view of this development, the State Department felt freer to step up its pressures for further democratization. Postponed during the mid-November events, the United States request for a partial lifting of sanctions was not renewed. Administration sources let it be known that the Navy would remain in Dominican waters to "protect" Balaguer until he was able to form a temporary government with the participation of the democratic opposition, which at that time consisted primarily of the Union Civica Nacional (UCN) under the leadership of Dr. Viriato Fiallo. In the ensuing negotiations the United States acted, in effect, as the third party, ostensibly playing a mediating role between Balaguer and the armed forces on the one hand and the UCN on the other, but in fact using its influence, buttressed by its control over the Dominican sugar quota, to support the UCN.[38]

The major difficulty in reaching an accord was the resistance of the armed forces, then led by General Pedro Rodriguez Echevarria, but the insistence by the United States on an agreement before the lifting of sanctions helped break down their opposition. The compromise agreement specified the formation of a coalition Council of State with Balaguer to remain President, but only until the removal of sanctions, at which time he would resign.[39]

The role of the OAS in the crucial events of November and December had been minimal. On November 21, 1961, the sanctions subcommittee had returned to the Dominican Republic for its third and last investigating mission. The timing of the trip suggested that its purpose was also to act as a pacifying agent in the November crisis. The subcommittee remained only five days, however, and therefore played no part in the December negotiations. At one point in these negotiations, when the resistance of the armed forces was at its peak, Dr. Fiallo sent a telegram to the Sanctions Committee requesting "its urgent presence."[40] Since there was little or no support for this in the OAS, it was not seriously considered. The Latin American states were not prepared to go quite that far in stretching the non-intervention doctrine, and the United States feared that the presence of the OAS would limit its freedom of maneuver in the delicate negotiations. Also, the additional publicity that the presence of an OAS team would have focused on the negotiations might have made it more difficult to elicit the necessary compromises from the participants, especially the opposition leaders. The incident illustrates the point that the desirability of "multi-lateralizing" an inter-American problem has its limits, particularly from the viewpoint of the United States.

The subcommittee delayed publishing the report on its third trip until after the formation of the Council of State and President Kennedy's statement supporting the lifting of sanctions. It then reported—prematurely as it turned out—that the armed forces had ceased their obstructionist tactics and henceforth would stay out of politics, clearing the way for the formation of a coalition government and the holding of free elections in the near future. As a result, the committee concluded, the Dominican Republic had "ceased to constitute a danger to the peace and security of America," and the sanctions should be discontinued.[41] On January 4, 1962, the Council voted unanimously—save for Cuba's abstention—to do so,[42] whereupon the United States promptly resumed diplomatic relations with the Dominican Republic, resumed purchases of Dominican sugar, and announced the dispatch of an economic aid mission.[43]

After the installation of the moderate Rafael Bonnelly as head of the Council of State, the United States used its diplomatic influence and economic and military assistance programs in an attempt to rebuild the Dominican economy, reform the army into a non-political, antiguerrilla force, and insure the holding of free elections and compliance with their results.[44] With the inauguration of Juan Bosch, considered by the Kennedy administration to be an idealistic social democrat deeply committed to the goals of the Alliance for Progress, the active role of the United States in Dominican politics temporarily ended.

A closer examination of United States objectives during the transition between the assassination of Trujillo and the elections of 1962 may help shed light on its actions in this period.[45] The interpretation that seems most plausible and consistent with the events is that the United States sought to achieve two proximate objectives: the maintenance of order and the attainment of democracy. The ultimate objective was the creation of a stable and non-Communist government. The maintenance of order was considered crucial, on the assumption that in the short run the chances of a Communist take-over would be increased if chaos and a breakdown of police and army control were to follow the assassination of Trujillo. In the long run, the reduction of Communist influence was thought to depend upon the creation of a democratic government capable of meeting the legitimate demands of a people oppressed thirty years by one of the worst totalitarian regimes of this century. Although over time the objectives of order and democracy may have been perfectly compatible, in the short run there obviously was considerable tension between them. The requirements of a policy that sought to maximize only order would have demanded the complete support of the United States for Balaguer and his *Trujillista* supporters in the armed forces, for they were probably capable of suppressing Communist activities by brute force. A policy, however, that sought to promote only democracy would have demanded immediate United States pressures to break the power of the army and to force out Balaguer and the Trujillos, as well as complete support for the anti-Trujillo forces that came out into the open after the assassination. This was the policy that Venezuela and spokesmen for the Dominican exiles urged on the State Department.

Faced with this dilemma, the administration split the difference. From the evidence now available, it cannot be ascertained with certainty whether this was a conscious decision of a united administration aware of the risks of emphasizing one element to the exclusion of the other or whether in fact it was a non-decision, the mere product of differing opinions within the administration.

One of the crucial questions was how to evaluate Balaguer. Could he be counted on to bring democracy to the Dominican Republic? Or, for that matter, was he capable of maintaining order? Or both? Or neither? Faced with these uncertainties, it is not surprising that the administration exhibited a certain amount of ambivalence toward the Balaguer regime and, whether consciously or inadvertently, opted for *both* order and democracy.

Until the events of mid-November, 1961, it was the policy of the United States to work *with* the existing power structure—Balaguer and the armed forces—but to attempt to induce it by means of economic pressures and diplomatic persuasion to liberalize the worst features of the Trujillo era and to prepare for democratic elections. Balaguer was to be a transitional figure, essential for the maintenance of order until the country could be prepared for further democratization. After the departure of the Trujillos, the United States decided to help *destroy* the existing power structure by supporting the opposition. This decision undoubtedly was not merely the next phase in a preconceived plan but was also a response to the growing strength of the internal Dominican opposition to Balaguer and the increasing evidence that Balaguer either had no intention of seriously negotiating his own removal or was prevented from doing so by the armed forces. That is, the Department became convinced that in fact Balaguer no longer represented either order or democracy.

The activist United States policy in 1961-62 and the subsequent course of Dominican events illustrate both the uses and the limitations of direct intervention as a technique of United States foreign policy. In the short run, the objectives of the United States were realized. The Bosch government was democratically elected and had begun a broad program of social and economic reform within a democratic framework. The military coup against Bosch in September, 1963, however, underlines the fact that in the long run the creation of a stable and democratic Dominican Republic depends on internal Dominican developments that are largely, although not entirely, beyond the control of the United States.*

---

*At the time the above paragraph was written, I had not, of course, anticipated that in 1965 the United States would actively assist the forces of militarism in the Dominican Republic instead of the forces of democracy. Along these same lines, I used the term "direct intervention" to refer to intervention on behalf of democracy, not against it.

Given, then, the inherent limitations on the ability of the United States to influence the political structures of other nations, the United States strategy in the Dominican Republic in 1961–62 must be regarded as remarkably successful. Besides the administration's generally skilful policy execution and good sense of timing, a number of elements were crucial. First, the policies of the United States were generally understood and popularly welcomed in the Dominican Republic. The appearance of the Navy off the coast of Santo Domingo was wildly cheered in that city, and in the United Nations the Dominican foreign minister, in response to a Cuban attempt to have the United States labeled an aggressor, replied: "Blessed be the moment when the American fleet came to Dominican waters."[46] Second, the existence of an organized, articulate, democratic, and responsible opposition group provided the United States with an increasingly attractive alternative to the existing regime. Third, the economic vulnerability of the Dominican Republic to the sugar sanctions was compounded by the psychological vulnerability of the remainder of the Trujillo family to these and other pressures—it is unlikely that Trujillo, Sr., would have been so quickly overcome. Fourth, the Latin American states generally supported, or at least tacitly acquiesced in, the United States intervention. Even the naval show of force did not arouse public or private protests of Latin American governments or non-governmental political groups. The widespread hatred of Trujillo, particularly in the articulate sectors of public opinion, outweighed the Latin American sensitivity to United States intervention. Finally, it had been possible to involve the OAS, and its actions complemented those of the United States.

In view of the success of the United States pressures in 1960–62, and given the apparent depth of the United States commitment to the creation of a democratic and stable Dominican Republic, the relatively mild response of the Kennedy administration to the right-wing military coup that deposed Bosch in September, 1963, was somewhat puzzling. It is perhaps best explained by the disappointment and even alarm felt by most United States officials over Bosch's performance in his seven-month stint in office. To be sure, the immediate suspension of diplomatic relations with the new junta and the cutting off of economic and military assistance indicated the continued United States concern for democracy in the Dominican Republic, but far stiffer measures might have been applied. Direct United States military intervention was perhaps out of the question in view of Bosch's failure to request it, but sugar purchases might again have been stopped. In any event, with the coming to office of the Johnson administration, the democratization of the Dominican Republic ceased to be an operational objective of the United States, and in December, 1963, diplomatic relations with the military junta were resumed.

The part played by the OAS in the Dominican situation in 1961–62 calls for further evaluation. Although its activities were peripheral to that of the United States and although it could have done even more, the role of the OAS, viewed in its totality, was not inconsiderable.

The most important contribution of the inter-American body was its provision of legitimacy for the actions of both the United States and the Dominican opposition groups. Although the United States was concerned with the Dominican internal situation and the OAS was theoretically concerned only with Dominican international actions, there was no real difference, for by means of the convenient fiction that the continuation of dictatorship in the Dominican Republic was prima facie evidence of an intent to pursue an aggressive international policy, the oas was able to continue its Dominican role after the assassination of Trujillo and thereby give the essentially unilateral United States actions a multilateral character. This in turn had the effect of reducing a possible nationalistic and anti-American reaction in Latin America and the Dominican Republic itself and thus greatly enhanced the effectiveness of United States policy.

Similarly, by making the economic pressures of the United States a legitimate exercise of the peace-keeping functions of an international organization, the oas gave the Dominican opposition leaders—whose strategy was to bring to bear a maximum of outside as well as internal pressures on the Balaguer regime—a degree of maneuver that nationalistic pride might otherwise have denied them. It was one thing for the Dominicans to plead repeatedly with the oas to maintain sanctions against their own nation and against the wishes of their government, but it would have been quite another had they been forced to direct their appeals to the United States without an oas "screen."

The oas made other significant contributions, for its collective intervention in Dominican internal politics was not limited to the actions of the Sanctions Commitee. In October, 1961, the Inter-American Commission on Human Rights, after receiving numerous complaints about violations of human rights, requested and received permission from the Balaguer government to visit the Dominican Republic. The Commission traveled throughout the country, interviewed opposition leaders, labor leaders, and private individuals, and personally informed

Balaguer of numerous cases of police repression, including murder and torture. Although the Commission had no power to enforce its recommendations, some remedial action was taken.[47] The reason is not hard to find. Although the Commission was theoretically an independent organ with no connection to the Council, it was obvious that Balaguer and the armed forces had consented to the investigation only because of their interest in ending the sanctions and more generally because of the combined United States–OAS pressures. The strategic role of these pressures in the success of the Commissions' investigation was indirectly indicated by the subsequent rebuffs of attempts to take similar action in Nicaragua, Paraguay, and Haiti, which were under no such pressures.[48]

Still another element in the OAS intervention was the role of a "technical assistance" mission to the Dominican Republic in the fall of 1961. In August, 1961, Balaguer, eager to demonstrate his democratic intentions, requested OAS assistance in drawing up new electoral legislation. The OAS Secretariat complied with this request under a flexible interpretation of its authority to extend technical assistance for economic and social development. Also interpreting its mandate broadly, the three-man OAS mission made detailed criticisms of the existing Dominican laws and practices and drew up recommendations on suffrage, political parties, voter registration, campaigns, and the conduct of elections. The mission returned to the Dominican Republic in June, 1962, at the request of the Dominican Council of State, to help draft legislation that incorporated most of their original recommendations.[49]

The final role of the OAS was the observation of the December, 1962, elections by a distinguished group of hemispheric academicians, jurists, and public servants, including a seven-man Pan American Union delegation headed by Secretary-General José A. Mora. The team, appointed by, and acting under, the OAS, split into small groups to observe the elections from vantage points all over the country. Their presence undoubtedly was an important factor in the honesty, orderliness, and freedom of the elections.[50]

Beyond its concrete contributions, the OAS became the symbol of hope for the Dominican people. Its presence in the Dominican Republic in its various manifestations — sanctions subcommittees, Human Rights Commission, technical assistance and electoral observation missions—helped deter the government from repressive measures against opposition elements and at the same time stimulated and lent psychological support to that opposition. The OAS personnel who served on these missions all reported the scenes of jubilation that greeted their arrival in the Dominican Republic and the willingness of a long-silent people to vent their grievances as they gradually became confident that this was not just another trick of the regime.[51] As the Dominican foreign minister told the 1962 Punta del Este Conference, the Dominican people were inspired by the presence of the OAS, which told them "that there finally had appeared a power capable of effectively contributing to the tyranny's downfall."[52]

In view of the long tradition of non-intervention, the deep involvement of the OAS in Dominican internal matters was remarkable. As subsequent developments in the OAS have indicated,[53] the role of the OAS reflected less a radical change in policy than an *ad hoc* reaction to some very special circumstances.

First, Trujillo had made a grave mistake in getting caught in the attempted assassination of Betancourt. This was a most serious violation of the principle of non-intervention, and some kind of OAS action was almost unavoidable, particularly in view of the close ties between Betancourt and the Kennedy administration. Had Trujillo continued to confine his aggressions to his own people, there almost certainly would have been no OAS action.

Second, an opportunity for further international action was created by the assassination of Trujillo and the subsequent internal fluidity in the Dominican Republic.

Third, strong leadership in the OAS was provided by two of its most influential members, the United States and Venezuela, whose own national interests were thought to require a solution of the Dominican problem.

Fourth, Trujilloism was a symbol of evil in Latin American eyes, and the actions of the United States and the OAS were apparently quite popular in hemispheric public opinion. Any state attempting to invoke the principle of non-intervention would therefore have risked serious political consequences at home and abroad.

Fifth, the involvement of the OAS was increased gradually over an eighteen-month period. Had it been foreseen at San José in 1960 that the imposition of sanctions was to become a lever to force internal change in the Dominican Republic, it is highly improbable that sanctions would have been imposed; Herter's proposal that the sanctions be used precisely in that manner had been summarily dismissed as a clear violation of the non-intervention principle. Nonetheless, the original sanctions constituted a foot in the door, and thereafter the burden was on those who would dislodge it.

Finally, the Latin American commitment to the principle of non-intervention was shown in certain circumstances to be less significant in fact than it was in rhetoric. When political calculations so warranted, the non-intervention principle could be bypassed, particularly if it could be done by more or less devious means, such as the artificial formula linking dictatorship to aggression. In short, non-intervention is not so much a juridical "doctrine" as a political tool capable of being manipulated, stretched, or even ignored. As Talleyrand is said to have noted, "Non-intervention and intervention are two words that in diplomatic discourse mean precisely the same thing."

All in all, the joint United States—oas intervention in the Dominican Republic in 1960–62 must be counted as a noteworthy success, despite the at least temporary reversion to non-democratic practices in the Dominican Republic that followed. The recent setbacks have by no means entirely negated the earlier gains, for the experience with democracy and reform in the Dominican Republic, short-lived as it was, is almost certain to make impossible a return to the full-fledged feudalistic totalitarianism of the past and to increase internal as well as external pressures for a return to progressive government. Moreover, the Dominican case may serve as a precedent and a source of experience for similar collective interventions against dictatorships elsewhere in the hemisphere, should political support for such action develop.

From the point of view of the United States, the requirements of national self-interest and the requirements of more universalist values had happily coincided. Although the United States had helped prevent a return to Trujilloism not so much out of love for democracy as out of fear of communism, the results were in the interests of the Dominican people. Whatever course the Dominican Republic may take, the destruction of the brutal inhumanity of Trujilloism remains as a clear gain for the Dominicans and for the hemisphere as a whole.

1. John C. Dreier, *The Organization of American States and the Hemisphere Crisis* (New York: Council on Foreign Relations, 1962), p. 77.

2. In addition, of course, it was the dictatorial states (Nicaragua, the Dominican Republic, Peru under Odría, Venezuela under Pérez Jiménez, Cuba under Batista, Guatemala after 1954, etc.) that were normally the loudest critics of "communism" and the most reliable supporters of the United States.

3. The United States was represented on the Peace Committee by John Dreier, who has since written that "the changed mood of the United States was to a considerable degree responsible [for the two reports]." (*Hemisphere Crisis,* p. 98.)

4. Inter-American Peace Committee, *Report to the Seventh Meeting of Consultation of Ministers of Foreign Affairs* (Washington, D.C.: Pan American Union, 1960), Appendix E, p. 3. (Cited hereinafter as *Peace Committee, Report to Seventh Meeting.*)

5. *Ibid.,* p. 4.

6. Although the Committee was refused permission to visit the Dominican Republic, it interviewed Dominican exiles and citizens of other countries who had recently been in the Dominican Republic, examined "extensive and reliable press material," and "made wide use of valuable information provided it by certain Representatives of member states." (*Ibid.,* Appendix D, pp. 1-5.)

7. *Ibid.,* pp. 5-6.

8. *Ibid.,* p. 5.

9. *Actas del Consejo,* July 6, 1960.

10. Report of the Investigating Committee, reprinted in *Efforts,* pp. 249-61.

11. Meeting of Consultation of Ministers of Foreign Affairs, 6th, San José, 1960, *Actas y Documentos* (Washington, D. C.: Pan American Union, 1961), Speech of Venezuelan Foreign Minister to the First Session of the General Committee, Document 21. (Cited hereinafter as *6th Meeting, Actas.*)

12. *Ibid.,* Speech of Herter to Second Session of the General Committee, *Document 22.*

13. *Ibid.,* Speech of Herter to Second Plenary Session, *Document 31.*

14. *Ibid.,* *Document 22.*

15. *Ibid.* As John Dreier, a member of the United States delegation, later wrote, this power "would involve far more than merely observing the casting of ballots; the OAS group would virtually have to take control over the political machinery of the Dominican state and superintend the relaxation of police terror, the establishment of political parties, and the conduct of electoral campaigns under proper safeguards." (*Hemisphere Crisis*, p. 100.)

16. *6th Meeting, Actas, Document 22.* (Emphasis added.)

17. Herter, *ibid., Document 31.* (Emphasis added.)

18. No record vote on the Herter proposal was taken. Almost all the speeches of the Latin American foreign ministers emphasized non-intervention, however, and Venezuela opposed the Herter plan because of the delay in the imposition of sanctions. Moreover, a subsequent State Department publication states that the conference received a communication from the Dominican Republic agreeing "under certain conditions" to OAS assistance in and observation of Dominican elections, but that this offer was turned down because "(1) this would constitute OAS intervention in the internal affairs of a member state, (2) this would not be satisfactory to Venezuela, and (3) only those measures listed in Article 8 and none other could be taken." (*Efforts*, p. 69, n. 1.)

19. The imposition of sanctions raised the question of whether Article 53 of the UN charter, requiring prior Security Council authorization of regional "enforcement actions," had been violated. In the Security Council, the Soviet Union introduced a resolution which would have placed the Council on record as "approving" the OAS action. The United States, Argentina, and Venezuela vigorously opposed the Soviet move, however, seeing it as an attempt to gain a veto over future OAS action. Arguing that only military action constituted enforcement, they succeeded in having the Council merely "take note" of the OAS action. (*New York Times*, September 6, 9, 10, 1960; *Hemisphere Crisis*, pp. 28-29.)

20. *6th Meeting, Actas,* Final Act, Resolution 1.

21. The Hearings in the House of Representatives on the President's request clearly demonstrated the marked shift in United States policy toward the Dominican Republic. In a remarkably blunt statement, Undersecretary of State C. Douglas Dillon referred to Trujillo as "a tyrant, a torturer and a murderer," and all but admitted that the objective of the administration's request was to bring down the Trujillo regime, so that "the Dominican Republic will once more, and soon, have

a government that abides by human rights and does not commit aggression against other members of the Organization." (House Committee on Agriculture, *Extension of the Sugar Act of 1948, Hearings,* 86 Cong., 2d sess., 1960, Part II, especially p. 67.)

22. OAS Document C-i-497, 1960, *First Report of the Special Committee of the Council to Comply with the Mandate Received by the Council in accordance with Resolution I of the 6th Meeting of Consultation of Ministers of Foreign Affairs.*

23. *Actas del Consejo,* January 4, 1961. The Council action grew out of a study made by the United States Department of Commerce at the request of the State Department to determine what economic measures would most effectively hurt the Trujillo regime. Moreover, although collective in form, the new sanctions were in essence unilateral, for the United States was the only significant source of the items in question. (Interviews.)

24. There have been persistent reports that the CIA was involved in the assassination, at least to the extent of supplying the arms. (See especially Norman O. Gall, "How Trujillo Died," *New Republic,* April 13, 1963.) More plausible, however, is Tad Szulc's contention that the Kennedy administration knew of the plot but did not discourage it. (*Winds of Revolution* [New York: Frederick A. Praeger, 1963], p. 221.)

25. *New York Times,* June 4, 1961.

26. *First Report of the Subcommittee submitted to the Special Committee to Comply with the Mandate Received by the Council in Accordance with Resolution I of the Sixth Meeting of Consultation of Ministers of Foreign Affairs* (Washington, D. C.: Pan American Union mimeograph, 1961), p. 1. (Cited hereinafter as Subcommittee, *1st Report, 2d Report,* or *3d Report.*)

27. *Ibid.*

28. Subcommittee, *1st Report.*

29. Interview with one of the Latin American representatives on the subcommittee. This same source stressed that throughout the Dominican situation the subcommittee had to tread a very thin line, for there was much covert unhappiness over its actions that might easily have become overt opposition; some Latin American governments, he asserts, were not even convinced that Trujillo had been involved in the assassination attempt against Betancourt until Balaguer himself later confirmed it.

30. Subcommittee, *1st Report*, p. 27.

31. In March, 1961, Congress had granted President Kennedy's request for authority to cut off all purchases of Dominican non-quota sugar, i.e., the Dominican share of the former Cuban quota. (*Bulletin*, January 1, 1962, p. 34.)

32. Subcommittee, *Second Report*.

33. *Ibid.*, p. 26.

34. Interviews; *New York Times*, November 17, 1961. The embassy had been closed when diplomatic relations were broken in 1960, but consular relations had been maintained, a convenient arrangement that combined the symbolic advantages of a diplomatic break with the practical utility of a continued United States presence.

35. United States statement to the Sanctions Committee, reprinted in *Bulletin*, December 4, 1961, pp. 929–32; Statement of United States delegate, *Actas del Consejo*, November 22, 1961.

36. *Bulletin*, December 4, 1961, p. 931.

37. *New York Times*, November 19, 1961.

38. See my "The United States, the Organization of American States, and the Dominican Republic, 1961–63," *International Organization*, Vol. XVIII, No. 2, 1964.

39. *New York Times*, December 17, 24, 1961.

40. *New York Times*, December 4, 1961.

41. Subcommittee, *Third Report*.

42. *Actas del Consejo*, January 4, 1962.

43. *New York Times*, January 5, 7, 1962.

44. See, for example, the announcement of the United States military assistance program to the Dominican Republic (*New York Times*, June 9, 1962); the announcement of a major increase in the Dominican sugar quota (*Bulletin*, August 13, 1962, p. 254); the announcement of a $23,750,000 Alliance for Progress grant just prior to the Dominican elections, "made in recognition of the valiant efforts of the Dominican Government and people to establish a viable, democratic state. . . . " (*Bulletin*, December 24, 1962, pp. 958-59); and a report of United States diplomatic activity on the eve of the elections, designed to convey to the Dominicans that the United States would "fully support" the

constitutionally elected government against any attempt of the losers or of the armed forces to overturn it. *(Washington Post,* December 20, 1962).

45. The following interpretation of United States policy is based on extensive personal interviews on a not-for-attribution basis with most of the key participants in the Dominican drama, both in the Department of State and the OAS. Since there was a great deal of disagreement over the nature of the United States objectives, the reconstruction of events and general analysis that follow are my own.

46. *New York Times,* November 25, 1961.

47. Inter-American Commission on Human Rights, *Report on the Situation Regarding Human Rights in the Dominican Republic* (Washington, D.C.: Pan American Union, 1962); interviews.

48. See below, Chapter VII.

49. See the article by Henry Wells, the United States member on the mission, "The OAS and the Dominican Elections," *Orbis,* Spring, 1963.

50. *Ibid.;* also, a report on the elections was given by H. Field Haviland, Jr., a member of the OAS group, to members of the Brookings Institution in January, 1963.

51. Interviews.

52. Meeting of Consultation of Foreign Affairs, 8th, Punta del Este, 1962, *Documentos de la Reunion* (Washington, D.C.: Pan American Union, 1962), Speech of José Bonilla Atiles, Dominican Foreign Minister, *Document 52.*

53. See below, Chapters VI and VII.

CHAPTER **6**

The OAS as an Antidictatorial Alliance (II):

The Haitian–Dominican Conflict of 1963

THE CONSTRUCTIVE ROLE of the United States and the OAS in the Dominican Republic was not repeated in the Haitian-Dominican conflict two years later, although once again a ready-made opportunity for collective intervention on behalf of democracy was available. The issues, once again, were whether the OAS should ignore the non-intervention principle and directly intervene in the internal affairs of one of its members and, as in previous Caribbean cases, whether the goal of democracy justified ignoring the principle of collective security in cases in which they conflicted. This time the OAS chose to act as an instrument of collective security, emphasizing the maintenance of peace between Haiti and the Dominican Republic rather than acceding to United States–Dominican attempts to have it act as an antidictatorial alliance and help overthrow the Haitian government.[1]

After the election of Juan Bosch as President of the Dominican Republic in late 1962, Haitian-Dominican relations, historically conflict-ridden, worsened considerably. Bosch, a romantic, intellectual reformer, was the very antithesis of the Haitian ruler, François Duvalier, a totally corrupt and vicious dictator who rivaled the worst of the long line of Haitian oppressors. Within a short time, exiles from each regime found refuge in Port-au-Prince and the familiar Caribbean pattern of propaganda, plotting, and sabotage began.

The situation came to a head in late April, 1963, when the Dominican government learned that members of the Trujillo family were gathering in Port-au-Prince,[2] apparently as a forerunner of an effort to assassinate Bosch and return the Dominican Republic to Trujilloism. As relations between the two neighboring countries rapidly deteriorated, the Bosch government apparently decided that the security of the democratic experiment in the Dominican Republic required drastic action, for in late April the Dominicans seized upon a relatively minor incident in a clear attempt to overthrow the Duvalier regime, hopefully by collective action but perhaps even unilaterally.

On the morning of April 27, two Haitian policemen broke into and searched the Dominican Embassy in Port-au-Prince, which had been serving as an asylum for Haitian opponents of Duvalier. Reacting harshly, the Bosch government immediately demanded an urgent meeting of the OAS Council to consider Haitian "threats to the peace and security of the Continent," and simultaneously warned Haiti that if it did not cease its harassing of the Dominican Embassy within twenty-four hours, the Dominican Republic would "at any price [take] . . . the necessary measures to enforce respect for the dignity and sovereignty of the Dominican nation."[3]

The response of the United States to the crisis was conditioned by the Kennedy administration's new policy on dictatorship. Just before the crisis, this policy was spelled out in a major speech by Assistant Secretary of State Edwin Martin, in which the United States made its most sweeping attack on the principle of non-intervention since it had accepted it in the 1930's. Calling for a change in traditional Latin American attitudes, Martin quoted approvingly Panamanian President Roberto Chiari's recent charge that

> the principle of nonintervention, carried to its most extreme interpretation, becomes a universal condemnation . . . [of those] brother peoples who within their own national boundaries are deprived by force of all chance of self-determination . . . to live forever subject to . . . oppression.

The recent recognition of the interdependence of the hemispheric states in economic matters, Martin went on, had not been paralleled by a similar recognition of the "mutuality of interest in promoting representative democracy":

> If the inter-American community can discuss and make recommendations on how to improve economic and social conditions, it should be able under the proper circumstances to consider the conditions of the democratic process of the hemisphere and the means for improving it.

To be sure, he admitted, there had been some progress in the "political-security field," since throughout the hemisphere it was now understood that the principle of non-intervention could not be allowed to cloak international subversion or prevent collective action to fight communism; but the Latin Americans had not fully accepted the United States position that the attainment of democracy was the best defense against communism and that the "failure of the democratic process in any one of the member states . . . [was] a matter of concern to the entire community." The principle of non-intervention, he concluded, should no longer be allowed to "close the door to possible collective measures intended to assure all the peoples of the Americas, within their own boundaries, of their freedom."[4]

The United States concern over Duvalier, then, as it had been in the Dominican Republic over Trujilloism, was primarily a reflection of its new anti-Communist strategy in Latin America. Until the end of 1961, the United States had managed to live with the Duvalier regime and had even included it in its economic assistance program on the familiar assumption that in the absence of an alternative, the collapse of Duvalier might lead to complete chaos and an opportunity for a Communist take-over. That is, in the incredibly backward and traditionally anarchistic Haitian context, Duvalier represented "stability."

Under the Kennedy administration, however, United States policy began to harden, as it did toward other Latin American dictatorships. Diplomatic relations became increasingly strained, and in May, 1962, the United States embassy boycotted Duvalier's celebration of the first anniversary of his "re-election"; several months later most of the economic assistance program was suspended, ostensibly for "technical" reasons.[5]

When the Haitian-Dominican conflict broke out, the

Dominicans sought to capitalize on the United States preoccupation with communism by charging that Haiti was establishing secret relations with the Soviet bloc and seeking economic assistance in exchange for Haitian assistance in Communist infiltration of the Caribbean.[6] Also, at about the same time, reports appeared indicating the arrival in Cuba of "a wave of French-speaking Africans," mainly from Guinea, destined to infiltrate Haiti.[7] No evidence was offered to substantiate either of these claims, and State Department officials dismissed both; but, nonetheless, the Kennedy administration *was* concerned with the potentially explosive combination of abysmal poverty, nearly total illiteracy, and brutal dictatorship.[8] Thus, although the Communist threat was considered more potential than immediate, it was thought serious enough to warrant an attempt to bring down Duvalier when the opportunity presented itself in the Haitian-Dominican crisis.

The United States, then, hoped to use the Dominican request for oas action as an opening wedge for a collective effort to force at least a moderation of Duvalier's repression of the Haitian people and, optimally, get rid of Duvalier altogether.

At the Council meeting of April 28 the Dominican delegate demanded that the oas take action to halt the violations of its embassy, terroristic tactics against Haitians seeking asylum from Duvalier, and the Trujillo-Duvalier plot against the life of President Bosch. The Haitian delegate, denying everything, charged in turn that the Dominican government was interfering in Haitian internal affairs and was preparing military action against his country. Neither country requested the application of the Rio Treaty, but the President of the Council (Gonzalo Facio of Costa Rica) did so on his own initiative. The Council then voted 16-0 to appoint a committee to investigate the situation.[9]

As the Investigating Committee, composed of Colombia, Bolivia, Chile, Ecuador, and El Salvador, arrived in Haiti, the situation was worsening.[10] Haiti had broken diplomatic relations with the Dominican Republic, ostensibly in response to the Dominican ultimatum but also, it was feared, in order to force the closing of the Dominican embassy and thereby cut off anti-Duvalier Haitians from Dominican protection. On April 29, however, as Dominican troops began massing along the Haitian border, Haitian officials told the Investigating Committee that it would grant "safeguards" to fifteen of the twenty-two refugees in the Dominican Embassy and would allow the others to be transferred to some other embassy.[11] Several days later, acceding to the demands of the Dominican Republic and the pleas of the Investigating Committee, Haiti gave the Committee "ample and complete assurances" that it would guarantee fully the safety of all diplomatic embassies and refugees in them and would issue safeguards for all refugees who wanted to leave the country.[12] Apparently on the strength of this promise, the Investigating Committee decided to terminate its investigation in Haiti and proceed to the Dominican Republic, although not without a scarcely veiled warning to the Haitian government that while it naturally gave "full credence" to its promises, it "feels certain that the provisional organ of consultation [the OAS Council] . . . will follow with undiminished zeal the evolution of the existing situation."[13]

The Committee, in its initial investigation, had interpreted its task in the narrowest possible terms, to the dissatisfaction of both Haiti and the Dominican Republic, as well as other members of the OAS, including the United States. On the one hand, the Haitian government had demanded that the Committee investigate its own as well as the Dominican charges, especially its allegations that the Dominican Embassy was "a center of intrigues against the Haitian Government" and that the Dominican government was "liquidating" the Haitian colony in the Dominican Republic, was giving material support to Haitian exiles planning to attack the Duvalier government, and was carrying on "a constant campaign of defamation" against Duvalier.[14] To this the Committee replied that its mandate was limited to that stated in the council's resolution of April 28, i.e., to investigate "the events denounced by the Dominican Republic."[15] On the other hand, the Committee, by initially confining the scope of its activities to the diplomatic-asylum question, in effect rejected the Dominican demands that it examine its accusations concerning the plot to assassinate Bosch and the presence in Haiti of numerous members of the Trujillo family and other "dangerous elements" formerly associated with the Trujillo regime.[16]

However, a deeper OAS involvement was necessitated by the failure of the Investigating Committee to achieve even its modest objectives—cessation of Haitian harassment of the Dominican Embassy and a safe passage for the twenty-two refugees out of the country. Despite the Haitian promises, safeguards to the refugees were not issued, and the Dominican Embassy was surrounded by soldiers and machine gun emplacements. Ignoring pleas by the President of the Council to refrain from military action, the Dominican Republic continued its military buildup along the Haitian border, and Bosch bluntly warned that he would use "whatever means necessary" to protect the embassy and the refugees in it.[17]

As a result, on May 8 the Council decided to broaden

the mandate of the Investigating Committee by an 18-0 vote, authorizing it to return to the Caribbean "to make an on-the-spot study of the situation existing between Haiti and the Dominican Republic and to offer the parties its services for the purpose of finding a prompt solution to the conflict."[18] Under this broader phrasing, the Committee could examine the conflict in its entirety, not simply the immediate events that had precipitated the crisis and merely reflected the more general conflict.

The Committee was not able to begin this second phase of its activities until May 13, however, for the Duvalier regime initially refused to allow it to re-enter Haiti and finally succumbed only after heavy pressure from the OAS, especially from the United States and the Council President, Gonzalo Facio.[19] The Committee spent the next ten days traveling back and forth between Haiti and the Dominican Republic, before issuing its second and final report in early June.

The report was very nearly as critical of the Dominican Republic as it was of Haiti, and it was of no comfort to those OAS states who had hoped that the Committee might, under its broader mandate, bring real pressure to bear on Duvalier. With regard to the refugee problem, the immediate cause of the dispute, the Committee verified that the Haitian police had indeed briefly violated the Dominican Embassy, but it added that no refugees had been molested and implied that the incident had been minor and exaggerated by the Dominican Republic.[20] Moreover, it specifically supported the Haitian accusation that Haitian exiles in the Dominican Republic were engaging in "subversive" activities against the Duvalier regime, unimpeded by Dominican authorities, and also confirmed that high Dominican officials had publicly "defamed" the Duvalier regime.[21]

The Committee verified that three members of the Trujillo family were in Haiti but said that it had no evidence of any plot against Bosch.[22] Although admitting that the Dominican Republic's "uneasiness" over the Trujillos was justified, the Committe implied that the Haitian complaints against exile activity in the Dominican Republic were equally justified when it stated that the best solution was for *both* governments to comply with existing agreements requiring all hemispheric governments to control the activities of resident exiles.[23] Moreover, it noted that the Bosch government had turned down Haiti's offer to enter into a new agreement to regulate the activities of exiles on the basis of "strict reciprocity."[24]

Finally, although expressing its "profound pleasure" over the withdrawal of Dominican troops from the Haitian border, the Committee recommended to the Council that it reiterate to both governments its "plea" that they refrain from "the threat or use of force" and that it "express to the Dominican Government the concern" caused by its mobilization measures.[25]

The Dominican Republic had also charged that the violation of human rights in Haiti was one of the main factors responsible for the tensions between the two countries, pointing out that among the repercussions was an increasing flow of Haitian refugees into its territory. In a concession to the cause of democracy, the Committee did point out that it had "trustworthy information" confirming the Dominican charges and, citing the Peace Committee's 1960 finding that there was a close relationship between violations of human rights and international tensions, asserted that this relationship "undeniably" had contributed to the Dominican-Haitian tensions.[26] Nonetheless, while this represented some progress, especially compared with the first decade of the OAS when the very idea that the organization could legitimately concern itself with such matters was denied, the failure of the Committee to condemn Haitian repression specifically, let alone suggest concrete collective measures, was a blow to the United States and the pro-democratic Latin American nations.

In its conclusions the Committee did not condemn either side, hint at any sanctions, or even suggest a continued role for the OAS to assist in bilateral negotiations or observe fulfilment of its recommendations—the threat of a Dominican invasion had passed, and clearly the Committee wanted to disengage the OAS as rapidly as possible. As a result, it recommended merely that the Council make a new "plea" to both governments to refrain from the use of force and to submit their disputes to pacific settlement procedures, "urge" Haiti to grant safe-conducts to refugees still in diplomatic asylum in Port-au-Prince, "appeal" to Haiti to observe human rights, "express concern" over the presence in Haiti of members of the Trujillo family and others associated with them, and "urge" both governments to observe the various inter-American agreements on territorial asylum and control of illegal exile activities.[27] In its plague-on-both-your-houses attitude, the Investigating Committee had refused to give much weight to the Dominican foreign minister's reminder "that the Dominican Republic has a democratic government, elected by the people . . . whereas the Haitian Government is a dictatorship which continually violates human rights."[28]

The pro-democratic forces took even a worse beating, however, in the Council meeting of July 16 that was called to consider the Committee's report. Of all the recommendations of the Investigating Committee, only the expression of concern over the Trujillos in Haiti was controversial. Although the United States and a number of Latin American states fought for its adoption, primarily as a symbolic gesture of sympathy with the Dominican Republic, which had fared badly in the whole affair, the recommendation fell one short of the thirteen affirmative votes required for adoption.[29]

The effect of the OAS in the situation had not been very great. It may have played some role in the departure of the Trujillos from Haiti, the cessation of police activities against foreign embassies, and the slow releasing of refugees from their virtual imprisonment in them,[30] although Dominican military threats and United States pressures were probably just as persuasive. It may have also been influential in preventing a Dominican invasion (at one point the Investigating Committee warned Bosch that if his army moved against Duvalier he could be found guilty of aggression);[31] but once again other factors may have been more important.[32] Finally, the OAS had done nothing at all to ease the torments inflicted by Duvalier and his cohorts on the Haitian people; the murdering, torturing, and looting continue unabated in Haiti today.

The OAS, then, had refused to take advantage of an international crisis to bring pressures to bear on a hemispheric dictatorship as it had done in the Dominican Republic in 1961. At first glance, the Haitian situation appeared to parallel closely the Dominican one: a transgression against inter-American norms by a widely detested dictator creates the opportunity—or pretext—for collective action to bring him down. But there were considerable differences.

To begin with, in the Haitian situation, unlike the Dominican case, the requirements of democracy clashed with the requirements of collective security. Democracy could be brought to Haiti only by large-scale intervention *against* the Duvalier regime, whereas under the Rio Treaty that regime was entitled to collective *protection* from the threatening moves of the Dominican Republic. In the Dominican case, on the other hand, the initial OAS involvement was easily justified as required by collective security. The well-documented pattern of Dominican involvement in Venezuelan affairs in the 1958–60 period, culminating in the assassination attempt against the Venezuelan President, was a flagrant violation of the nonintervention principle. The situation was far more ambiguous in the Haitian-Dominican conflict, however. Duvalier had carefully refrained from meddling in the politics of other nations, and no evidence was presented to the OAS supporting Bosch's charge of an assassination plot. Moreover, the Dominican reaction to the Haitian violation of its embassy in Port-au-Prince was so disproportionate that, within the narrow perspectives of collective security, it was the Dominican Republic that became the "aggressor." It could even be argued, in fact, that only the unpopularity of the Duvalier regime spared the Dominican Republic from the Council's condemnation. In this light, the whole affair may be more noteworthy for what the OAS did not do about the Dominican Republic than for what it did not do about Haiti.

Still, there is no doubt that, once involved, the OAS could have done far more than it did in bringing pressure to bear on Duvalier to moderate his dictatorship. The precedent linking violations of human rights to international tensions were available, and although the OAS gave it lip service, it did not use it to justify the imposition of sanctions, as it had against Trujillo and his successors. The reasons for this reflect no credit on the Latin Americans; most of them were simply indifferent to the fate of Haiti, which was generally regarded as a counterpart to the Congo, populated by hopelessly ungovernable savages whose problems were of little consequence to the hemisphere. Even the Haitian elites were either Negro or mulatto and therefore did not arouse the same sympathy in Latin America as had the Castilian Dominican aristocracy under Trujillo. Moreover, the French Haitians, unlike the Spanish Dominicans, shared neither language, history, nor culture with the rest of Latin America. Thus, although the Latin Americans were willing (or thought it prudent) to make an exception to the nonintervention principle on behalf of the Dominicans, it was business as usual for the Haitians.

In any event, the oas had less leverage over Haiti than it had had over the Dominican Republic. To all appearances, Duvalier was even more ruthless and determined to remain in power at any price than the Trujillo family had been; probably nothing short of military invasion would have forced Duvalier out, a course that was not necessary in the Dominican Republic.

As a result of these factors, only Venezuela and Costa Rica actively aided the United States–Dominican attempt to maneuver the oas into forceful action against Haiti. Venezuela favored the strongest possible action against Duvalier, even including collective military action.[33] Costa Rica also vigorously supported strong action, and its delegate to the Council used his position as Council President to deliberately bait the Haitian delegate, hoping to push Duvalier into defiance of the oas and thereby "internationalize" the situation as a pretext for collective intervention in Haiti's internal affairs. But all the maneuverings ended in failure when it became clear that at least half the Council—including the "Big

Four" of Mexico, Brazil, Argentina, and Chile — were adamantly opposed to further pressures, including even so minimal a gesture as a collective break in diplomatic relations. Thus, tentative plans of the United States and the anti-Haitian Latin American group to ask the Council for sanctions had to be dropped.[34]

At several points during the crisis the United States considered the possibility of direct military intervention in Haiti. Although the Kennedy administration wanted to avoid such intervention, troops would have been landed in the event of a complete collapse of the Duvalier regime or widespread violence involving attacks on foreigners inside Haiti. There was indeed good reason for fear. In late April, Duvalier officials direly warned that should the Dominicans invade Haiti a bloodbath aimed at foreigners, including even diplomatic officials, would result. In view of the ruthless nature of the Duvalier regime, this threat was taken with deadly seriousness and a United States Navy task force with a Marine detachment aboard was rushed to Haitian waters. In the event the threatened reign of terror materialized, contingency plans called for the United States to land the Marines and, perhaps with the assistance of the Dominican troops poised at the border, restore "order," a task which would necessarily entail the dismantling of the entire Duvalier structure. In short, although the United States hoped to avoid armed intervention, should it have proved necessary to employ force to protect U.S. citizens, the opportunity almost certainly would have been seized to throw Duvalier out and begin steps toward the creation of a responsible and progressive Haitian government.[35]

A second contingency plan involved a more active role for the OAS. In mid-May the United States was told by apparently reliable sources that Duvalier planned to flee Haiti on May 15. In this event, it was feared, anarchy would ensue, with Haitians and foreigners alike at the mercy of the undisciplined and murderous "Ton-ton Macoute," Duvalier's private militia. In such circumstances, the OAS Council would be asked by the United States to authorize United States and Dominican forces, perhaps augmented by Venezuelan and other Latin American units, to act as an international "police" force in order to lend "assistance" to a new OAS-sponsored Haitian regime composed mainly of anti-Duvalier Haitian army officers and perhaps certain exile groups specially selected for this purpose and landed along with the international forces. Once order had been restored, the OAS, in the guise of "technical assistance," hopefully would continue to play an active role in Haitian affairs, exercising what would amount to a de facto OAS trusteeship until a responsible regime was established and firmly in control.

Although it was not possible to get an advance commitment from the Latin Americans to support such a radically interventionist scheme, it was expected that under the conditions specified a two-thirds majority could be obtained for at least a stop-gap action. The Latin American diplomatic corps in Port-au-Prince were in real terror for their lives, and had an attack on the embassies occurred, the situation would have had an "international" aspect that would have legitimized OAS action. On the night of May 14, the Council President, Gonzalo Facio of Costa Rica, a leader in the various attempts to carve out a more active role for the OAS in Haiti, assembled his staff in the Pan American Union, ready to call for an urgent Council meeting upon Duvalier's anticipated departure. But Duvalier did not flee, and the plan collapsed.[36]

In the absence of wholesale violence against foreigners,

two other possible ways of getting rid of Duvalier were briefly considered by the United States. One involved clandestine support for some or all of the numerous Haitian exile groups, most of them based in the Dominican Republic, that were ready to invade their homeland. This traditional "Caribbean solution" was rejected, however, partially because after the Bay of Pigs the administration was leery of getting involved in similar operations, partially because the State Department argued that there were no organized groups that were much of an improvement over Duvalier or capable of gaining the support of the Haitian people, and partially because the administration doubted the ability of the various disorganized, quarreling, and generally incompetent exile groups to mount a successful invasion against Duvalier's tough militia.[37] As a result, the United States rejected a rather Byzantine plan developed by a well-known high OAS official involving the financing and arming of an exile expedition that would attempt to establish a beachhead on the Haitian coast, proclaim itself the de facto government of Haiti, receive quick diplomatic recognition from the United States and sympathetic Latin American governments, and then ask for an international police force as well as economic support and "technical assistance" to maintain itself against the "renegade" Duvalier forces.[38]

The most direct method of getting rid of Duvalier would have been an outright invasion of Haiti either by the United States or the Dominican Republic, or both. The costs of such a drastic "solution" to the Haitian problem, however, were considered prohibitive. Military action, except in response to a Duvalier attack on foreign embassies, would have been a blatant violation of inter-American norms and perhaps might have resulted in an official condemnation by the OAS. The support of the Haitians themselves, even the exiles, by no means would have been assured, particularly if the Dominicans had been involved; Haitian hatred of the Dominicans was historically intense, especially after Trujillo's infamous massacre of thousands of Haitian laborers in 1937. Moreover, international conse quences might not have been limited to the Western Hemisphere, for a white invasion of a Negro republic, no matter how humanitarian the reasons or the effects, would have furnished much ammunition to the Communist bloc and might have been bitterly opposed by the sensitive and nationalistic African states. Even at home, because of the domestic racial crisis, a United States invasion might not have had much popular support and furthermore would have been bound to increase demands for similar action against Cuba, seemingly a far greater threat to United States interests. Finally, in view of Duvalier's threat to massacre all foreigners should the United States or the Dominican Republic intervene, an invasion might have been costly in human terms as well.

But even if an invasion could have been brought off with a minimum of bloodshed and undesirable political consequences at home and abroad, the headaches of the United States would have just begun. In view of the chaotic nature of Haiti's economy, the total absence of established political institutions or even of a trustworthy police force, and the vacuum of responsible or effective Haitian leadership, the United States in effect would have been saddled with an indefinite trusteeship, an experience that had not proved a happy one in the past and which predictably would have been even less so in a nationalistic, race-conscious, and anticolonial world.

In view of all these factors, the United States never seriously considered an invasion, barring the contingencies of either an attack on United States citizens or an open Communist take-over in Haiti. Moreover, heavy United States pressure was brought to bear successfully to dissuade Bosch from acting on his own, if indeed that had ever been his intention.[39]

By the end of the spring of 1963, it became apparent that Duvalier had weathered the crisis and that his regime would not collapse under merely psychological pressures. The OAS having refused to act as an antidictatorial alliance and unilateral measures having been rejected, the United States moved to re-establish more "normal" relations with Haiti. In early June the Navy task force departed from Haitian waters, and diplomatic relations (suspended three weeks earlier as a symbolic gesture) were resumed.

Under the Johnson administration, the United States has returned to the stability-first policy of the 1950's in Haiti, as well as in its over-all Latin American policy. Although the United States has no continuing economic assistance program to Duvalier and is attempting to discourage arms shipments to him, a tight curb has been placed on the activities of anti-Duvalier exile groups living in the United States; and, on the diplomatic level, the present United States Ambassador to Haiti has sought to encourage United States private investment, has cut himself off from non-governmental contacts in Port-au-Prince, and maintains cordial relations with Duvalier. This abandonment of an anti-Duvalier posture, it is reported, has created widespread bitterness and scorn for United States policy among Duvalier's numerous opponents inside and outside Haiti.[40]

1. Nonetheless, because of the United States effort to turn the OAS into an antidictatorial alliance, the case is treated here rather than in the chapters on collective security.

2. OAS Document C-i-624, June 10, 1963, *Second Report of the Committee of the Council of the OAS Acting Provisionally as Organ of Consultation, Prepared in Compliance with the Resolutions Adopted on April 28 and May 8, 1963*, p. 10. (Cited hereinafter as *Haiti, Second Report.*)

3. Dominican note to OAS, OAS Document C-i-618, May 13, 1963, *Primer Informe de la Comisión del Consejo de la Organización de los Estados Americanos Actuando Provisionalmente Como Organo de Consulta, en Cumplimiento del Párrafo 1 de la Resolución Aprobada el 28 Abril de 1963* (cited hereinafter as *Haiti, First Report*), Annex A.

4. *Department of State Bulletin,* May 6, 1963, pp. 710-15.

5. *New York Times,* May 23, August 1, 1962.

6. *New York Times,* April 29, 1963.

7. See especially Adolf A. Berle, "Is Haiti Next?", *Reporter,* May 23, 1963.

8. Interviews.

9. *Actas del Consejo,* April 28, 1963. Brazil and Bolivia abstained, ostensibly because of lack of instructions.

10. The United States was originally named to the Committee, as is customary, but asked to be excused, citing its strained relations with the Duvalier regime. No doubt the United States also felt that its own freedom of maneuver would have been constrained by participation in the OAS action.

11. *Haiti, First Report,* pp. 8-9.

12. *Ibid.,* Annex H, p. 29.

13. *Ibid.*

14. *Ibid.,* pp. 6-7; OAS Document C-d-1069, April 30, 1963, *Telegram from Duvalier to the President of the Council.*

15. *Haiti, First Report,* p. 6; *Actas del Consejo,* May 8, 1963.

16. *Haiti, First Report,* pp. 11-12.

17. OAS Documents C-d-1066, April 30, 1963; C-d-1072, May 7, 1963; C-d-1074, May 7, 1963. (Exchange of Telegrams between the President of the Council and President Bosch of the Dominican Republic.)

18. *Actas del Consejo,* May 8, 1963.

19. Interviews.

20. *Haiti, Second Report,* pp. 8-9. The United States, along with the Dominicans, took a more serious view of the incident. The Haitian violation of the embassy, although minor in itself, may have been designed to test the Dominican reaction; if it had been weak, then Haitian forces might have gone in after the refugees. (Interviews.)

21. *Ibid.,* pp. 16–17.

22. *Ibid.,* pp. 10–11.

23. *Ibid.,* p. 16.

24. *Ibid.,* p. 5.

25. *Ibid.,* p. 18.

26. *Ibid.,* pp. 12–14.

27. *Ibid.,* pp. 18–19.

28. *Ibid.,* p. 2.

29. The vote was twelve in favor; Peru and Brazil against; Guatemala, Mexico, and Paraguay abstaining; Nicaragua absent. Mexico led the opposition, arguing that Haiti, like other states, had a sovereign right to admit anyone it chose and that in any event the resolution was superfluous since the Trujillos had recently departed. (*Actas del Consejo,* July 16, 1963.) One high State Department official privately asserted that Nicaragua and Paraguay had been prepared to vote in favor until Bosch had made the tactical error of attacking the dictatorial methods of the Shick-Somoza and Stroessner regimes, just two days before the vote. (Interview.)

30. For the next year and a half a small OAS committee continued to negotiate with the Duvalier government for safe-conducts for the exiles and an easing of Haitian-Dominican tensions.

31. Interviews.

32. See below, footnote 39.

33. Interviews.

34. Interviews.

35. Interviews.

36. Interviews. See also reports of the *New York Times* during the period.

37. Interviews.

38. This plan, and the United States reaction to it, was described to me by its initiator. During the summer of 1963 an exile force in fact did invade Haiti, but when the United States refused its plea for immediate recognition and other forms of support, the rebellion collapsed. Had the rebels succeeded in gaining firm control of a substantial part of Haiti, however, and had they been amenable to a United States–directed major effort to reconstruct the Haitian economic and political structure, the United States was prepared to offer its support. (Interviews.)

39. A number of Latin American and United States policymakers asserted in interviews that in view of the Dominican Army's low state of military preparedness and the lack of enthusiasm of military leaders for the whole affair, Bosch would have been extremely reluctant to order his forces to invade. It is possible that Bosch was only bluffing in an attempt to bring pressure on Duvalier or even to divert the attention of his military leaders from their domestic grievances.

40. See especially Richard Eder, "Haiti: Land of the 'Big Tontons'." *New York Times Magazine,* January 24, 1965.

*   *

CHAPTER 7

The OAS and Democracy:

Institutionalizing the Role

THE RESPONSE OF THE OAS to the Haitian-Dominican conflict of 1963 made it clear that the great majority of the Latin American states had no intention of abandoning non-intervention and allowing the inter-American system to become transformed into an antidictatorial alliance. Although ostensibly the OAS has an important role to play in promoting democracy and human rights in the hemisphere, the reality has been somewhat different. As has already been pointed out, the OAS has not only ignored its Charter, which proclaims that the "solidarity of the American States and the high aims which are sought through it require the political organ-

239

ization of those States on the basis of the effective exercise of representative democracy," but in fact the OAS has often *impeded* the development of democracy in Latin America.

A few years ago it seemed that significant changes might be forthcoming, especially when, in order to justify collective action against Trujillo, the Peace Committee developed the formula linking dictatorship to international tension. However, the OAS has stopped short of accepting the doctrine that *all* dictatorships are "aggressive" and therefore are a legitimate object of multilateral action under the inter-American collective security system. It is now clear that if the Peace Committee formula should again be applied, it will be on an *ad hoc* basis so that action may be taken against *specific* dictatorships when political considerations so dictate, while others may be ignored. To preserve this flexibility, the majority in the OAS have resisted the occasional attempts of the United States and pro-democratic Latin American states to institutionalize a role for the OAS in Latin American political processes. There are no provisions in the OAS for collective action to facilitate internal political change; in a hemisphere divided between the left and the right, the dictatorships and the democracies, the military and the civilians, there is no agreement on what kinds of change to hinder and what kinds to assist.

The attitude of the majority of Latin American states was made clear soon after the end of World War II, when Uruguayan Foreign Minister Eduardo Rodriguez Larreta formally proposed that the inter-American system take collective action to restore democracy and human rights whenever they were violated in any hemispheric state. The Larreta Doctrine, as it was known, was carefully grounded on the principle of collective security. Larreta argued that dictatorships are inherently expansionist and based on "ideologies of force." Therefore, peace was safe only when democracy prevailed: "the parallelism between democracy and peace must constitute a strict rule of action in inter-American policy."[1]

The new doctrine was quickly and enthusiastically accepted by the United States, which, under the influence of Assistant Secretary of State Spruille Braden, was following a strongly pro-democratic policy. Secretary of State Byrnes announced the "unqualified adherence" of the United States, agreeing with Larreta that "violations of the elementary rights of man by a government of force . . . [are] matters of common concern to all the republics . . . [and] justify collective multilateral action."[2] Other high officials linked the very fate of the inter-American system to the democracy issue:

> Our concern for the development and strengthening of the inter-American system cannot be separated from our concern for the maintenance and development of democratic ideals and practices in all the American Republics. Democracy and the inter-American system . . . are bound to stand or fall together.[3]

Although the United States argued that "the necessity for intervention by the use of force would *rarely* occur . . . [and that] you wouldn't have to go that far in a *majority* of cases,"[4] the implication that the United States would be willing to contemplate the use of armed force to implement the Larreta Doctrine in *some* cases was clear.

The Larreta Doctrine was developed in the context of World War II, in which neo-fascist Latin American regimes were the main obstacle to inter-American co-operation. In addition, both Uruguay and the United States undoubtedly intended the doctrine to apply primarily to Argentina; Uruguay felt threatened by the neighboring Perón regime, and Spruille Braden of the United States was engaged in his well-known attempt to bring down the Argentine dictator.

Not surprisingly, the Larreta Doctrine was overwhelmingly rejected by Latin America, only six states qualifiedly supporting it.[5] Clearly the doctrine, which was widely viewed as being inspired by the United States in order to legitimize its Argentine policy, was a sweeping repudiation of the principle of non-intervention.

The democracy issue came up again at the Bogotá Conference, at which the Charter of the OAS was promulgated. The major battle was fought over a Guatemalan proposal that the hemispheric states agree to withhold recognition from "antidemocratic" regimes, on the grounds that they deny human rights, they are a danger to the "unity, solidarity, peace and defense" of the continent, and that they would not effectively co-operate in inter-American common efforts.[6] Ecuador countered with a proposal embodying the famous Estrada doctrine,[7] which would abolish the practice of diplomatic recognition altogether on the grounds that recognition is per se an intervention in the internal affairs of the government in question. The Guatemalan proposal had no chance for success and was not even brought to a vote. The dictatorships and conservative oligarchies (Argentina, Bolivia, Colombia, Dominican Republic, El Salvador, Haiti, Honduras, Nicaragua, Panama, and Paraguay) were of course opposed, and Ecuador (which had just experienced a coup d'état), Mexico, and Chile were traditionally against the use of recognition as an instrument of policy. The United States opposed the Guatemalan proposal for several reasons:

(1) having unsuccessfully supported the Larreta proposal, the State Department did not intend to associate itself with another losing cause;[8] (2) a number of United States policymakers were convinced that as a practical matter recognition ought to be maintained with all governments, since the removal of United States diplomatic missions historically had accomplished little, but had cut off both a source of information and potential United States influence;[9] (3) in any event, the attainment of democracy in Latin America had ceased to be an operational goal of United States policy.

The recognition controversy was solved along the lines suggested by the United States, ostensibly a compromise between the Guatemalan and Ecuadoran proposals, but in fact much closer to the latter. Resolution 35 of the Final Act declared that "continuity of diplomatic relations among the American states is desirable," that "the right of maintaining, suspending, or renewing diplomatic relations with another government shall not be exercised as a means of individually obtaining unjustified advantages under international law," and that "the establishment or maintenance of diplomatic relations with a government does not imply any judgment upon the domestic policy of that government." The last phrase, in particular, could be, and in fact was, later used to legitimize United States diplomatic recognition of Latin American dictatorships coming to power in coups against democratic governments.[10]

A second attempt to instil democratic content into the OAS was a Brazilian-Uruguayan proposal that the Charter include a "Declaration of the Rights and Duties of Man," to be enforced by an International Court of Human Rights.[11] The first part of the proposal was defeated in a close vote, the United States and most dictatorships voting against it. The proposal for protection of human rights by an International Court was also rejected, ostensibly because such rights were not yet "codified."[12] It is part of the operating principles of the inter-American system, however, never fully and finally to reject pro-democratic proposals, so by resolution the foreign ministers directed the Inter-American Juridical Committee to prepare a draft statute on an International Court for submission to the next inter-American conference.[13] It is by this time-honored method that such proposals are quietly interred rather than rejected outright.

Finally, Brazil and Uruguay wished to include a statement listing the basic elements of democracy in Article 5 of the Charter, in which the American states "reaffirmed" the traditional inter-American "principles," but even this mild proposal was rejected on the grounds that it was too difficult to define "the essentially dynamic characteristics of democracy."[14]

As a result, the practice of democracy is not required of OAS members. There are, to be sure, a whole series of pious paper commitments to democracy and human rights, beginning with a statement of "principles" in the Charter and continuing through the "Declaration of Santiago" in 1959, but none of them are deemed to have the force of law.

Ostensibly in response to this "gap" in the inter-American system, the foreign ministers at the Santiago Conference (1959) directed the Council to prepare "a draft convention on the effective exercise of representative democracy and the establishment of the procedures and measures applicable thereto."[15] In late 1959 a committee of the Council (consisting of Argentina, Brazil, Mexico, Nicaragua, Peru, Uruguay, and Venezuela) duly submitted its draft convention, outlining the "attributes" of democracy and providing for the collective non-recognition and exclusion from the OAS of any regime established by the forcible overthrow of a freely elected government or otherwise violating the various requirements.[16]

Naturally no one took this impossible recommendation seriously, apparently not even its own drafters, who declared in their report that the proposed treaty did not "necessarily" represent the views of the governments of the committee members![17] Still, the prescribed procedures had to be followed, and the draft convention was submitted to the governments for their comments.

The first to reply was the United States, which stated that its federal structure made its participation in an international treaty of this kind impossible.[18] As of 1965, only six other states—Mexico, Brazil, Chile, Argentina, Guatemala, and the Dominican Republic—had bothered to comment officially, all of them objecting on one ground or another.[19] There the matter stands today. It is clear that nothing will become of the convention, which on its face is unenforceable. In any event, the obstacles to firm OAS action on behalf of democracy are political, not legal.

The OAS and Antidemocratic Coups

Other, more serious attempts to carve out an active role for the OAS in Latin American politics have been made. In late July, 1962, after the Argentine and Peruvian military coups, the Dominican Republic, Venezuela, Honduras, and Costa Rica joined in requesting a meeting of the foreign ministers "to consider the attitude that the governments of the member states should adopt toward regimes arising from coup d'états."[20] The request was made under Article 39 of the Charter, providing for foreign ministers' meetings "to consider problems of an urgent nature and of common interest to the American States," rather than under the Rio Treaty, indicating that the sponsors intended to press for a general revision of OAS policy rather than immediate sanctions against the Argentine or Peruvian military juntas.

At the Council meeting of July 30, 1962, it became clear that the sponsors had nothing less in mind than a sweeping revaluation of the non-intervention principle. Democracy, not non-intervention, must be the cornerstone of the inter-American system, they argued: "The exercise of representative democracy and respect for human rights has ceased to be an internal matter of each state but has become an international obligation."[21]

The four-nation move put the United States in a delicate position. In the first place, the proposal, which would have worked a revolutionary change in the nature of the inter-American system, had no chance at all. Normally the United States does not like to become associated with hopeless ventures that succeed only in demonstrating hemispheric divisions, preferring instead to seek "practical" compromises. Moreover, the timing of the proposal clearly suggested it was aimed at the Peruvian coup; and the Kennedy administration, which was having second thoughts concerning the wisdom of its own strong reaction to that event, undoubtedly considered that an OAS conference would accomplish nothing useful. Finally, the United States had reservations about the broad nature of the proposal. The sponsors intended to press for the establishment of a general policy of non-recognition of all military coups, a matter that the United States preferred to decide on its own and on an *ad hoc* basis. As a result, the United States successfully pressed for a delay in consideration of the proposal, asserting that it "understands and sympathizes with the reasons which motivate the four co-sponsoring governments," but adding that "in these areas we believe we must move with a judicious combination of resolve and restraint."[22]

Ten days later the Council voted to reject the four-nation proposal, seven favoring it (Colombia, Honduras, Dominican Republic, Venezuela, Bolivia, Costa Rica, Ecuador), five opposed (Paraguay, Peru, Uruguay, Argentina, Haiti), the United States and the remaining Latin American states abstaining.[23] In its stead, however, the United States submitted an alternative proposal, hoping to demonstrate that its abstention had not indicated a lack of concern over the problem. The United States, asserted its delegate, agreed with the pro-democratic Latin American states that

> with all due regard to all the principles embodied in inter-American instruments, the nullification or thwarting of the practice of representative democracy in any American state is properly a matter of concern to all the American states.

Moreover, it agreed with the four governments that "priority attention" should be given this matter. On the other hand, the United States believed that the OAS ought not to be called upon "to review the past or condemn particular events, regrettable as these may have been." Thus the United States proposal, while reflecting the "same concern" and pursuing the "same objectives" as the original, differed "in a certain degree both in the procedures and in the timing of the approach."[24]

Under the United States resolution, the Council would (1) "agree to the desirability of a Meeting of Consultation of Ministers of Foreign Affairs to consider the general problem posed in the four-country request";

(2) appoint a committee to suggest a date and agenda for the meeting, "in the light of the general trends in the hemisphere affecting the effective exercise of representative democracy which *might* warrant the immediate convocation of the Meeting"; (3) "urge" the member states to use the facilities of the oas, including those established by Resolution IV of the Santiago Conference, "whenever freely elected governments are endangered."[25]

Although tortuously phrased, the United States proposal appeared to differ from the original in two important ways. There would be no oas meeting now, but only in the event of future coups. Furthermore, even in such an event there would be no automatic commitment to oas action, that being left to the later determination of the Council.

Nonetheless the United States version apparently aroused as much opposition as the original; Mexico, for example, found it "clearly interventionist."[26] After several weeks of informal consultations the United States offered some modifications, dropping its suggestion that a committee be chosen to recommend a date and agenda for a possible future meeting and even its reference to Resolution IV of the Santiago Conference, which established merely that the governments could ask the Peace Committee to "study" the problems arising from the "non-compliance" with the principles of democracy and human rights.

Thus, the United States proposal now merely asserted that it was "desirable" to hold a meeting to consider the general problem of coups, leaving the actual convocation and date to be decided later "in light of the general tendencies . . . in the Hemisphere that affect the exercise of democracy."[27] Even in this new and toothless form, however, the proposal lacked majority support, and in order to forestall a losing vote the United States suggested that its proposal be sent to the General Committee of the Council for "further study." This being the standard procedure for burying embarrassing problems, the proposal quietly passed away.[28]

A year later, after the resurgence of militarism in Latin America had claimed the Guatemalan, Ecuadoran, Honduran, and Dominican governments, Venezuela and Costa Rica renewed the battle. In October, 1963, they once again proposed a Foreign Ministers' Conference under Article 39 to consider what the OAS should do about military coups.[29] With the forcible removal of Ecuador, the Dominican Republic, and Honduras from the ranks of its supporters and the apparent continuing dilution of United States concern over the problem, the proposal clearly had even less of a chance than it had in 1962. In the ensuing month, after informal consultations, the proposal was modified twice. First, all reference to OAS action against coups was dropped, the new wording providing merely for a conference "to consider the problem of the preservation and strengthening of representative democracy."[30] When this still proved to be unpalatable, the reference to the "preservation" of democracy was eliminated. In this emasculated form, the OAS voted 18-1 (Guatemala opposing) to call a meeting at a date to be later determined "to consider the strengthening of representative democracy on the Continent."[31]

The vote signified nothing, for the wording was hopelessly vague—even Haiti could vote yes! Although the United States was not enamored with the idea and continued to oppose any proposal that would limit its freedom of action, such as an automatic break in diplomatic relations and suspension of economic assistance to governments created by military coups, the State Department decided to go along with the proposed meeting, safe in the knowledge that if it were ever held, nothing of substance would be accomplished. The meeting however was never convoked, and the entire matter has been buried.

The OAS and Disarmament in the Western Hemisphere

The question of hemispheric arms control and disarmament is indirectly related to the democracy issue, for the Latin American armed forces have normally been a major obstacle to democratic reform and economic and social progress. Inter-American lip service to the principle of arms control dates back to Resolution X of the Final Act of the Rio Conference of 1947, which stated that

> no stipulation of the [Rio] Treaty nor any of the obligations created under it should be interpreted as justifying excessive armaments or may be invoked as a reason for the creation or maintenance of armaments or armed forces beyond those required for common defense in the interest of peace and security.

With the commencement of the United States military assistance program in 1951 and the general expansion and modernization of the Latin American armed forces, nothing more was heard of this until 1955, when Ecuador suggested the desirability of a foreign ministers' meeting to deal with the "improvement of the systems for the control of traffic in arms and ammunition and . . . the effective application of the recommendation contained in Resolution X [of the Rio Conference]."[32] The "armaments race," pointed out the Ecuadoran delegate, is clearly out of proportion to the requirements of Hemisphere defense . . . and, if it continues in the future, can become an incalculable danger not only to the solidarity and unity of the Hemisphere, but also to the economic and social stability of the peoples of the Hemisphere.[33]

Ecuador never actually proposed such a conference, however, and the subject did not come up again for several years.

On March 5, 1958, Costa Rica, a nation which had abolished its own armed forces as a means of preserving its democratic experiment, proposed to the Council the establishment of a committee to study the possibility of a Latin American arms control agreement along the following lines: (1) a Latin American agreement not to buy or manufacture nuclear arms; (2) a United States pledge not to give or sell nuclear arms to Latin America; (3) a Latin American agreement not to buy conventional weapons from countries outside the hemisphere; (4) a Latin American agreement not to acquire conventional weapons beyond the requirements considered necessary for internal security, *as determined by the* OAS; (5) the establishment of a system of arms control and inspection in the hemisphere; (6) a greater emphasis on civil engineering and public works functions for the Latin American armed forces. The inter-American system, argued Costa Rica, had made both intra- and extrahemispheric aggression practically impossible and therefore had made large national forces unnecessary. The money saved on armaments would be far better spent on a massive economic development effort.[34]

This revolutionary proposal was nothing short of a frontal attack on Latin American national pride, and the Latin Americans reacted accordingly. Mexico led the vociferous opposition. The Costa Rican proposal would limit the sovereignties of the Latin American states, it argued, particularly if the OAS rather than the states themselves were to determine the levels of national armaments and the point at which they ceased to serve genuine military purposes; only each individual state *and particularly the armed forces themselves* were qualified to determine such matters. Moreover, it noted, the plan limited Latin America but not the United States, thereby raising serious questions about the continued existence of the inter-American system of *collective* security.[35]

The reaction of the United States was also markedly cool. After all, the United States, with its military assistance programs, its bolstering of the military as a stabilizing element in the Latin American political process, and its attempts to bring the OAS into the cold war had had a prime responsibility in the growth of the Latin American armed forces and the spread of national arms races. The United States, asserted its delegate, was against "unnecessary" diversions of resources from economic development to armaments, but only "so long as the basic requirements for national and collective defenses under present world conditions were still adequately met." Underlining this point, he added that it was "of first importance . . . that the requirements for the defense of the American continent . . . be recognized and fulfilled."[36]

On March 6 further discussion of the Costa Rican proposal was suspended, "in order to give the delegations an opportunity to consult their governments."[37] The Chairman of the Council was directed to call a new meeting when the members desired to present further "observations." As an OAS document later succinctly noted, "no observation having been presented, the proposal has received no further consideration."[38]

In 1959 and again in 1960 Chile renewed the call for an arms control plan for the Western Hemisphere arguing, as did Costa Rica, the priority of economic development. On April 6, 1960, Chile proposed the calling of an OAS conference to take up the matter. Details of the Chilean plan, if they existed, were not made public, but in a general way Chile indicated that arms should be limited to those necessary to maintain internal order and the territorial integrity of each state, as well as those necessary for the collective defense of the continent. Thus, unlike the offensive Costa Rican proposal, no mention was made of an international control mechanism nor were the military roles of the Latin American armed forces to be disposed of. As a result, the United States and most of the Latin American states, including Mexico, Argentina, and Brazil, were able to lend at least verbal support to the holding of a conference. A committee was thereupon appointed to study the Chilean proposal;[39] as of 1966, however, the "study" was apparently still in progress, for nothing more had been heard of the matter.

It is quite clear that in the context of Latin American politics, "arms control" refers primarily to the reduction of the capability of the Latin American armed forces to intervene in the political process. For this very reason, as long as the armed forces continue to play a major political role in Latin America, there is no prospect for meaningful arms control.

The OAS and Human Rights

Only in the area of human rights has even modest— very modest—progress been made in creating a permanent role for the OAS in the domestic politics of hemispheric states. As with the related question of the promotion of democracy, the establishment of collective procedures to protect individuals from the depredations of repressive governments has been a perennial issue in the OAS. Nothing concrete was done until recently, however. Not only the dictatorships and the non-interventionist states but the United States as well vigorously opposed the establishment of even token collective mechanisms. The United States posture was a reflection of its own domestic problems and its general Latin American policies of non-intervention, support for existing regimes, and the maintenance of hemispheric unity.

At the Bogotá Conference in 1948, once the United States had helped defeat the troublesome Guatemalan, Uruguayan, and Brazilian efforts to create machinery for the enforcement of human rights and democracy, it was willing to agree to the vague and unenforceable "Declaration of the Rights and Duties of Man." In a related matter, however, it unsuccessfully opposed an almost equally harmless resolution directing the Inter-American Juridical Committee to prepare a draft statute on an Inter-American Court to Protect the Rights of Man.[40]

Two years later the Juridical Committee reported that "it was not feasible" to create such a court, correctly noting that it "would involve a radical transformation of the constitutional systems of the American States."[41] At the Washington Conference of 1951, El Salvador made a determined effort to resurrect the issue, but the United States joined with the Latin American dictatorships in voting that the matter was not relevant to the topic of the conference.[42]

The issue came up once again at the 1954 Caracas Conference in the form of a Uruguayan proposal that the Council (rather than the Juridical Committee) immediately undertake the task of preparing a draft convention on an International Court. Since, however, "a majority of the delegations [including the United States] considered . . . this somewhat premature,"[43] a more innocuous resolution was substituted which, "without pre-judging whether it was desirable" to create a Court, called upon the Council to

> continue its studies on the jurisdictional aspects of the pro-tection of human rights . . . analyzing the possibility of the creation of an Inter-American Court for the Protection of Human Rights in order that the matter be considered at the Eleventh Inter-American Conference.[44]

There the matter rested until the Santiago Conference in 1959. The overthrow of a number of Latin American dictatorships in the late 1950's and the Caribbean tur-moil in the spring of 1959 had created pressures for a reopening of the human rights question. As a result, the foreign ministers directed the Inter-American Coun-cil of Jurists to try again to prepare a draft convention on an Inter-American Court. Moreover, the Council was directed to create an Inter-American Commission on Human Rights to assist in "furthering respect" for human rights.[45] Once again, even this modest step forward was too much for the United States, which, arguing that its federal structure made impossible its participation in any international body concerned with human rights, abstained.[46]

The Inter-American Court still remains a dead letter. Although the Council of Jurists has duly prepared an elaborate convention on human rights, featuring the Court as its main enforcement body, only three states (not includ-ing the United States) favor its adoption.[47] There is no prospect that the Court will come into existence in the foreseeable future.

The Inter-American Commission on Human Rights

is in existence, however, despite early United States efforts to emasculate it. After the Santiago Conference, the OAS appointed a committee to draw up statutes for the proposed Rights Commission. In its initial report, submitted to the Council in October, 1959, the committee recommended the creation of a Commission of seven distinguished citizens of America, elected and functioning in their individual capacities rather than as representatives of their countries. The function of the Commission, an "autonomous entity" of the OAS, would be "to promote respect for human rights," by (1) formulating recommendations to the governments to help them incorporate human rights into their national laws; (2) preparing whatever studies, reports, and projects it considered necessary to further its objectives; and (3) examining complaints of any government, group, or individual alleging the violation of human rights. Upon receiving a complaint, the Commission would investigate and, if the case so warranted, would submit a report to the offending government recommending corrective measures. If remedial measures were not adopted, the Commission could make the report public. Other than this, the Commission would have no powers of enforcement.[48]

Six months later, after receiving the comments of the member states on their initial draft, the committee submitted a revised and watered-down version to the Council, designed to pacify the objections of the United States and the non-interventionist bloc. Under the new statutes, the Rights Commission would act only when it judged that reported violations were serious and when all domestic remedies had been exhausted or denied. Moreover, the Commission could publish its report only by an absolute majority vote and in cases of "eminently serious" violations. Finally, at the request of the United States, it would be made explicit that the Commission could make only recommendations "compatible with the constitutional law of the country to whose government they were sent"[49]—the United States was clearly concerned over the potential embarrassment of an international condemnation of violations of Negro rights in the South, remedies for which were complicated by the federal structure of the United States.

Even as modified, however, the United States still had objections to the proposed statutes. According to the Santiago resolution, the United States argued, the function of the Rights Commission should be merely to *promote* human rights, the actual *protection* of those rights awaiting the completion of the formal convention being drafted by the Council of Jurists. As such, the Commission's authority should be confined to the preparation of studies, reports and recommendations "of a general nature," and the statutes authorizing it to review specific cases and publish reports on them should be dropped. "If these powers to intervene in the internal affairs of member Governments are accepted," the U.S. bluntly warned, "they will likely give rise to serious problems with respect to the future operation of this Commission."[50]

In May, 1960, the Council voted on the second draft of the statutes. Only the section authorizing the Commission to examine and report on specific complaints was controversial. There were two versions: the first and most controversial would allow not only individuals and private groups but governments as well to submit complaints to the Commission. This, feared some states, would result in the Commission's becoming a political football between traditional rivals. As a result, a second version authorized only private individuals or groups to submit complaints to the Commission.

The United States continued to oppose both versions.

While asserting its "deep sympathy" with "the movement to enlist the active participation of the oas in
furthering human rights and in promoting representative
democracy," the United States insisted that constitutional
problems and respect for the principle of non-intervention
required that the Commission be confined to reliance on
"moral force" and "dramatization" of the problem. If either
version were approved, the United States would vote against
the statute as a whole.[51] Both versions were defeated. Thus
emasculated, the remainder of the statute, confining the
Commission to general studies and reports, was approved
20–0.[52]

Despite, however, the apparently successful efforts of
the United States and the non-interventionist bloc to
restrict the Rights Commission to an all but ceremonial
role, the Commission has managed to resurrect itself.
Contrary to the clear intention of the Council, the
Commission has decided that Article 9b of its statutes,
authorizing it "to make recommendations to the Governments of the member states in general . . . for the
adoption of progressive measures in favor of human
rights," also authorizes it to investigate reported violations
of human rights and make "recommendations" to *individual*
states, even against their wishes.[53] Moreover, under an
equally broad interpretation of Article 11c of its statutes
("The Commission may move to the territory of any American State when it so decides by an absolute majority of
votes and with the consent of the government concerned"),
the Commission proceeded to obtain the "consent" of the
Dominican Republic for a temporary "move" there in
1961,[54] whereupon it investigated the Dominican government's violations of human rights and issued a detailed and

critical public report on its findings.[55] In addition, the Commission has prepared critical reports on violations of human rights in Haiti and Cuba and has pointedly made public Nicaragua's and Paraguay's persistent refusals to permit the Commission to examine numerous complaints of violations of human rights in those states.[56]

Since 1960 the United States has dropped its opposition to the Rights Commission, partially because of its change of heart over the democracy issue in general, but equally as important because the Commission has carefully avoided involvement in the United States civil rights problems and in general has exercised "discretion" and "responsibility" in confining its activities to the most notorious (and incidentally the smallest) of the Latin American dictatorships. For similar reasons, and because of the great amount of favorable publicity that the Rights Commission has received in Latin America, the major Latin American states have also refrained from objecting to the Commission's flagrant bypassing of the Council's original restrictions.

In 1962, at the Punta del Este Conference, the United States joined with the Latin American states in unanimously recommending to the Council that the Rights Commission statute be broadened "to permit it effectively to further respect for [human] . . . rights in the countries of the hemisphere."[57] Nothing has come of this, however, because of the dilatory tactics of some Latin American states in the Council. However, neither the Commission nor its supporters on the Council have felt it necessary to exert any pressures, since the Council would be highly unlikely to grant the Commission any more authority than it already has granted itself. As with other OAS activities, the Latin Americans prefer to allow the Rights Commission to exercise more political authority unofficially than they will formally agree to.

In any event, the actual results of the Commission's activities, despite its noble efforts, have been marginal. As has been recounted, the Commission played a role in the Dominican Republic in 1961 that supplemented the more important activities of the Special Committee of the Council and the technical assistance missions of the Pan American Union. The Commission was refused permission to go to Haiti, Nicaragua, Paraguay, and Cuba, however, although the Commission unofficially claims that in the latter three countries some remedial measures were taken after the Commission made public statements on reported violations.[58] Another potential role for the Commission was pointed up by the Dominican government's 1963 request that the Commission investigate complaints of the Dominican opposition parties of violations of human rights.[59] The Commission did not support these complaints and thereby in effect presented the Bosch government with a certification of purity, useful both for international and domestic purposes.

Beyond these instances, the Commission has been limited to its "general" and largely meaningless "studies" on human rights. While the Commission's activities undoubtedly constitute progress, it is clear that as long as the maintenance of "sovereignty" is considered by the Latin Americans to be the primary function of the inter-American system, neither the Commission nor any other organ of the OAS can play a truly significant part in the advancement of democracy and human rights in the hemisphere.

1. Larreta note reprinted in *Department of State Bulletin,* November 25, 1945, p. 864. (Cited hereinafter as *Bulletin.*)

2. *Bulletin,* December 2, 1945, p. 892.

3. Ellis O. Briggs, *Bulletin,* April 27, 1947, p. 769.

4. Briggs, *Bulletin,* January 13, 1946, p. 31. (Emphasis added.)

5. Costa Rica, Cuba, Guatemala, Nicaragua, Panama, and Venezuela.

6. International Conference of American States, 9th, Bogotá, 1948, *Handbook for Delegates* (Washington, D.C.: Pan American Union, 1947), p. 89. (Cited hereinafter as *Bogotá Conference.*)

7. Foreign Minister Genaro Estrada of Mexico in 1930 had argued that recognition of new governments "is an offensive practice which, besides wounding the sovereignty of other nations, lays them open to having their domestic affairs judged in one sense or another by other governments." (Quoted in Roy C. Macridis [ed.], *Foreign Policy in World Politics* [Prentice-Hall, 1962], p. 322.)

8. Interviews.

9. *Ibid.*

10. Cf. United States recognition later that same year of the Venezuelan military government after the coup against the Gallegos-Betancourt government and of the Odría junta in Peru after the coup against the democratic Bustamente government.

11. Bogotá Conference, *Diario,* pp. 418-19. An "American Declaration of the Rights and Duties of Man" was agreed to as a set of "principles," without treaty status and with no enforcement machinery. (Resolution XXX, Final Act.)

12. Bogotá Conference, *Diario,* Doc. CB-10-E, Report of Committee on Organiation.

13. Bogotá Conference, *Final Act,* Resolution XXXI. The United States opposed even this meaningless gesture as "premature." (Manross, *op. cit.,* p. 53.)

14. Bogotá Conference, *Report of the Delegation of the United States* (Washington, D.C.: Government Printing Office, 1948), p. 35.

15. Meeting of Consultation of Ministers of Foreign Affairs, 5th, Santiago, Chile, 1959, *Actas y Documentos* (Washington, D. C.: Pan American Union, 1959), Resolution IX, Final Act.

16. OAS Document C-i-447, 1959, *Report of the Special Committee to Study Resolutions IX and X of the Fifth Meeting of Consultation of Ministers of Foreign Affairs.*

17. *Ibid.*

18. OAS Document C-d-792, 1962, *Observations of the Governments on the Draft Convention on Democracy.*

19. *Ibid.*

20. Joint note to the Council, in *Actas del Consejo,* July 30, 1962.

21. *Actas del Consejo,* July 30, 1962.

22. *Ibid.*

23. *Actas del Consejo,* August 10, 1962.

24. *Actas del Consejo,* August 8, August 10, 1962.

25. *Actas del Consejo,* August 10, 1962. (Emphasis added.)

26. *Ibid.*

27. *Actas del Consejo,* August 22, 1962.

28. Interviews.

29. *Actas del Consejo,* October 3, 1963.

30. *Actas de Consejo,* November 4, 1963.

31. *Actas del Consejo,* November 12, 1963.

32. Pan American Union, *Applications of the Inter-American Treaty of Reciprocal Assistance* (Washington, D.C.: Pan American Union, 1957), Reservation of Ecuador to the Report of the Investigating Committee in the Costa Rican–Nicaraguan case of 1955, p. 190.

33. *Ibid.*

34. *Actas del Consejo,* March 5, 1958. (Emphasis added.)

35. *Ibid.*

36. *Ibid.*

37. *Actas del Consejo,* March 6, 1958.

38. Pan American Union, *The Organization of American States, 1954-1959* (Washington, D. C.: Pan American Union, 1959), p. 35.

39. *Actas del Consejo,* April 6, 1960.

40. Inter-American Conference, 9th, Bogotá, 1948, *Diario*

(Washington, D.C.: Pan American Union, 1948), pp. 576–91; Inter-American Conference, 9th, Bogotá, 1948, *Report of the United States* (Washington, D.C.: U.S. Government Printing Office, 1948), p. 82.

41. Pan American Union, *Report of the Activities of the Organization of American States, 1948–1953* (Washington, D.C.: Pan American Union, 1953), p. 75.

42. Meeting of Consultation of Ministers of Foreign Affairs, 4th, Washington, 1951, *Documents* (Washington, D.C.: Pan American Union, 1951), Document 159, Minutes of the 7th Meeting of Committee II.

43. Inter-American Conference, 10th, Caracas, 1954, *Report of the Delegation of the United States* (Washington, D.C.: U.S. Government Printing Office, 1955), p. 30; Inter-American Conference, 10th, Caracas, 1954, *Diario* (Washington, D.C.: Pan American Union, 1954), Document 489, Minutes of the 9th Plenary Session.

44. Inter-American Conference, 10th, *Diario,* Resolution XXIX, Final Act.

45. Meeting of Consultation of Ministers of Foreign Affairs, 5th, Santiago, Chile, 1959, *Actas y Documentos* (Washington, D. C.: Pan American Union, 1961), Resolution VIII, Final Act.

46. *Ibid.,* Document 100, Minutes of the 5th Session of the General Committee. The vote was 15 in favor, 4 (Mexico, Dominican Republic, Uruguay, Brazil) opposed, 2 (Bolivia, United States) abstaining.

47. See the debates, *Actas del Consejo,* May 6, 1964.

48. The report is contained in *Actas del Consejo,* October 29, 1959. The members of the committee of the Council were Colombia, Cuba, Chile, Ecuador, El Salvador, Honduras, and the United States.

49. *Actas del Consejo,* March 16, 1960.

50. *Actas del Consejo,* April 6, 1960.

51. *Ibid.*

52. *Actas del Consejo,* May 25, 1960.

53. Inter-American Commission on Human Rights, *Report on the Work Accomplished during Its First Session, October 3–28, 1960* (Washington, D.C.: Pan American Union, 1960).

54. See above, Chapter V.

55. Inter-American Commission on Human Rights, *Report on the Situation Regarding Human Rights in the Dominican Republic* (Washington, D.C.: Pan American Union, 1962).

56. Inter-American Commission on Human Rights, *Report on Human Rights in Cuba* (Washington, D.C.: Pan American Union, 1962); *Report on Human Rights in Haiti* (Washington, D.C.: Pan American Union, 1964); *Reports on the Work Accomplished during Its Second–Ninth Sessions* (Washington, D.C.: Pan American Union, 1961–64.)

57. Meeting of Consultation of Ministers of Foreign Affairs, 8th, Punta del Este, 1962, *Documentos de la Reunion* (Washington, D.C.: Pan American Union, 1962), Resolution IX, Final Act.

58. Interviews.

59. Reported to the Council by Manual Bianchi, President of the Inter-American Commission on Human Rights, in *Actas del Consejo,* May 23, 1963.

*

Conclusions

Integrative Forces in the OAS

PAN AMERICANISM, or "the Western Hemisphere Idea,"
is often thought to be the major integrative force in the
inter-American system. According to this view, the Americas have, in the past, been bound together by the
common acceptance of the idea that "the peoples of
this Hemisphere stand in a special relationship to one
another which sets them apart from the rest of the
world . . . born . . . of the determination to insulate
America from Western Europe and its perpetual broils."[1]
Recently, however, the Western Hemisphere Idea has
lost much of its cementing power as technological progress
has shattered the isolation of the hemisphere, the United
States has become a global power with global commitments,
and continued authoritarianism in Latin America has ren-
dered absurd the "traditional dichotomy" between American democracy and European dictatorship.[2]

Moreover, there is a school of thought in Latin America—perhaps a growing one—that argues that Pan
Americanism has never existed, at least insofar as it
signifies "a strong feeling of unity or belonging that
transcends state lines . . . [and] includes a strong senti-
mental, cultural, or racial bond among several peoples

who wish for union or reunion."[3] Rather, it is argued, Pan Americanism has no roots in public opinion, being merely a creation of the United States and the reactionary ruling oligarchies of Latin America designed to perpetuate their unholy alliance.[4] In short, "Pan Americanism is an illusion at best and a hoax at worst."[5]

Both the lyrical panegyrics of the proponents of Pan Americanism and the conspiratorial theories of its critics seem overstated. The Western Hemisphere Idea has never been an emotional force in the lives of ordinary Americans, North or South. On the other hand, it is apparent that the political leaders of the Americas have indeed felt some kind of genuine commitment to Pan Americanism beyond that dictated by calculations of *raison d'état*. It is impossible to go through the records of any inter-American gathering without finding repeated eulogistic references to Pan Americanism; although much of this, of course, can be discounted, it seems plausible that at least to some extent obeisance to Pan American unity becomes self-fulfilling and affects the actions of statesmen. The ideology of Pan Americanism, then, must still be counted as an integrating force in the inter-American system.[6]

Nonetheless, it is clear that inter-American unity has primarily depended on the degree to which the national objectives of the United States and of the Latin American states have been similar or at least compatible. As has been indicated, the crucial United States objective in its Latin American policies is the maintenance of stability. Secondarily, the United States has sought the support of Latin America in its global cold war activities.

The OAS has contributed to the realization of both these ends, generally following the United States lead. In the 1950's, when the United States was primarily concerned with the maintenance of the status quo in Latin America, the OAS gave its active support; more recently it has, at least to some degree, gone along with the United States concern with the twin threats of communism and reaction. In its capacity as a system of collective security the OAS has helped end numerous outbreaks of interstate conflict in the Caribbean, and no doubt it has deterred others. In its capacity as an anti-Communist alliance, it has lent at least verbal support to the Korean War effort and more than that to United States activities to meet the Communist threats in Guatemala and Cuba. Finally, on one occasion it acted as an antidictatorial alliance, helping the United States to destroy Trujilloism in the Dominican Republic (and thereby, presumably, heading off a Communist threat).

Moreover, the OAS has bestowed its collective blessings on what have been essentially unilateral United States undertakings, thereby helping to legitimize them in the eyes of the highly nationalistic Latin American people. Sometimes this legitimacy has been merely symbolic, as in the OAS support of the Korean War effort, its "authorization" of the Cuban missile blockade, and its recent trade embargo against the Castro regime. On other occasions, however, multilateral support has been quite crucial to the successful outcome of United States undertakings, as in the pacification of the various Caribbean conflicts in the 1950's and in the United States intervention in the Dominican Republic in 1961.

Until the 1930's, the United States was content to employ its vast power unilaterally to achieve its objectives in Latin America, even when this involved outright military force. Since then, however, the United States has decided that the moral, political, and in some cases even military costs of naked unilateralism are too high, except in what have been thought to be extreme circumstances, as in the Guatemalan and Cuban crises. Insofar as the OAS has been willing to support United States policies, then, it has helped disguise the important role of the United States and has made the open threat or actual employment of United States power unnecessary.

However useful the OAS may be to the United States, its continued viability has depended equally on its utility to the Latin Americans. The Latin American states, all of them relatively weak, historically have been preoccupied with the maintenance of their "sovereignty." In this respect, the inter-American system has been of great value to them, for its primary effect has been to protect their political independence and territorial integrity against external threats. In its capacity as a collective security system, the OAS has protected the Latin Americans against internecine conflict. In its capacity as an anti-Communist alliance, it has helped protect them against the actual, potential, or assumed dangers of Communist expansionism.

Moreover, the participation of the United States in the OAS has given the Latin Americans leverage over United States policies that they otherwise would lack, no small benefit considering their historical fear of the "Colossus of the North" as the primary threat to their independence. It would be an error to take an overly "realistic" view and assume that the power of the United States renders it invulnerable to OAS pressures. In fact, the commitment of the United States to the inter-American system has acted as an important constraint on United States power. In the 1964 conflict over the Panama Canal, for example, OAS pressures and mediatory efforts played a signficant role in inducing the eventual United States concessions. Insofar, then, as the United States values multilateral support and hemispheric solidarity, the bargaining power of the Latin Americans is increased, a resource which is often used to exact political concessions and occasionally even economic rewards.

Finally, the OAS has been useful to all its members not only in their relations with each other but also in their relations with their own publics. In particular, the commitment to multilateral action on hemispheric problems has enabled governments to resist emotional demands for the unilateral "solution" of problems for which no acceptable solutions are immediately obtainable. That is, the OAS can be used, as it has been in the Cuban problem, to bury problems and legitimize inaction.

Disintegrative Forces

Despite the existence of strong cementing elements in the inter-American system, there are a number of fragmenting forces at work as well. The political objectives of the hemispheric states by no means have been invariably compatible or the benefits of multilateral co-operation symmetrical; when they have not been, the OAS has naturally failed to function effectively. Normally, the United States concern for non-Communist stability and the Latin American concern for sovereignty have been perfectly compatible, since both have usually required the maintenance of the political status quo in the hemisphere and the effective functioning of a system of collective security. In the Guatemalan and Cuban cases, however, when the status quo was a Communist one, the two principles sharply conflicted, for the restoration of stability required that the principle of national sovereignty be ignored. In those cases, especially the former, the OAS was sharply split and relatively ineffective, neither unqualifiedly supporting the efforts of the United States and some Latin American states to overthrow the status quo nor, conversely, protecting the targets of those efforts.

More generally, the Latin Americans have been reluctant to actively support the United States in its global anti-Communist struggle, except when the hemisphere has been directly threatened. The involvement of the United States in the cold war is often seen in Latin America as directly conflicting with the proper functioning of the inter-American system, which was originally designed to insulate rather than involve the hemisphere in overseas conflicts. Moreover, the greater the proportion of economic and military resources the United States devotes to the rest of the world, the less there is available for Latin America.

Thus, most Latin American states refused to go along to any substantial degree with United States economic and military mobilization efforts in the Korean War, and many of them have not accepted the United States contention that communism in Guatemala and Cuba was an alien system "imposed" on those countries by the forces of "international communism."

Differing perceptions of the proper role for the inter-American system have not been limited to the Communist problem. The absence of a genuine hemispheric political community has sometimes limited the effectiveness of the collective security mechanism as well. Enthusiasm for collective security has varied according to the nature of the governments involved in interstate conflicts. The system has been most effective when there has been least conflict of values, as in purely territorial disputes or attacks upon democracies by dictatorships. When collective security has clashed with democracy, however, as when Nicaragua and the Dominican Republic were attacked by pro-democratic exile groups in the 1950's, OAS action has been hesitant and half-hearted, and there probably would have been none at all but for the insistence of the United States.

Moreover, geography has played a role. In general, the South American states have shown far less interest in OAS involvement in hemispheric conflict than have the United States and the Caribbean countries, because most of the conflicts since the creation of the OAS have taken place in the Caribbean. With the exception of Mexico, for historical reasons traditionally non-interventionist, the firmest supporters of non-intervention and the most vociferous critics of OAS "superstatism" have been the non-Caribbean South American nations of Argentina, Brazil, Chile, Peru, Uruguay, and Paraguay.

Given, in fact, the wide political, ideological, economic, and cultural differences in the hemisphere, one might argue that the really striking fact is that the OAS has worked as well as it has. "Realistic" assessments of international politics, stressing the narrowly conceived "national interest" as the prime mover in state behavior, cannot adequately account for the inter-American system, in which states sometimes support or at least acquiesce in collective action even when it is counter to their immediate interests. They may go along for fear that their open opposition might destroy the system or render it ineffective in future operations; that is, if they consider that, in more cases than not, collective action is consistent with their objectives, they are sometimes willing to sacrifice short-term for long-term considerations. Furthermore, states generally respond to a wide and complex variety of motivations, not merely to the cynical demands of unmitigated egotism. Although initially derived from a convergence of interests, solemn and highly formalized organizational commitments tend to take on an independent existence of their own, which few states lightly disregard.

Nationalism, as manifested by the concern for "sovereignty," is another disintegrative factor in the OAS. However, sovereignty has not been as much of a constraint on OAS action in actual fact as it has been on paper. There have been occasions when the majority have been willing to allow the OAS to exercise informally and on an *ad hoc*, temporary basis far greater political authority than formal OAS treaties and regulations provide. Still, the doctrine of non-intervention and the fear that the OAS will develop into a "superstate," both reflections of the concern for sovereignty, have kept the political capabilities of the OAS limited to the minimum required for preserving the peace and normally have prevented the OAS from playing a meaningful role in hemispheric conflicts not involving actual armed hostilities between states. Thus, with the exception of the Dominican case, the OAS has been largely excluded from internal Latin American conflicts, particularly the continuing struggle between popular democratic movements and traditional civil-military elites, and has played only a peripheral role in interstate conflicts waged by subversion, infiltration, and propaganda.

To some extent, Latin American legalism, traditionally a refuge of weak states, is another impediment to a more effective OAS, although from another perspective legalism helps maintain the system. Political conflicts in the OAS are normally waged by indirect methods, in long-winded, hair-splitting "juridical" debates. For example, for the record, Mexico and other Latin American states based their opposition to the removal of Cuba from the OAS on the grounds that the organization did not have the "juridical competence" to take such action. While legalism functions, then, as a device to purposely inhibit action and to avoid or at least cloak potentially disruptive political conflicts, there does seem to be a residual degree of genuine Latin American concern for juridically "proper" procedures. This penchant for technicalities often leads to absurd scholastic haggles and, more to the point, inhibits the ability of the OAS to respond flexibly to new contingencies.

A frequently cited weakness in the OAS is the vast disparity of power between the member states, the United States having far greater economic and military strength than all of the Latin American states together. As a result, the United States is immune to collective action going beyond mere diplomatic pressures and normally plays the major role in any OAS enterprise involving the application of economic or military coercion.

The problems created by this power asymmetry are indicated in the belief of many Latin Americans that the OAS merely institutionalizes and legitimizes United States domination of the hemisphere. There is no question that Castro's sardonic reference to the OAS as the State Department's "Ministry of Colonies" touched a sensitive nerve in Latin America, as did former Guatemalan President Juan José Arévalo's book, *The Shark and the Sardines*. In Arévalo's view, the inter-American system and the Western Hemisphere Idea are merely "instruments at the service of the Shark":[7]

The greatest diplomatic success—let us call it diplomatic—of the Empire has been that of collective authorization to act— that is to say, to take, to remove, to buy and to sell without hindrance. From that instant, piracy is not piracy. Every holdup, every banquet, every crime is discussed around a table of brothers, around the table of twenty smaller brothers, deprived of sovereignty, and a big brother, hyper-sovereign.[8]

Such views partially account for the reluctance of the nationalistic, sensitive Latin American states to expand the scope of OAS political action, for fear they might merely open the door to increased United States interference in Latin American domestic affairs.

In actuality, the United States has not "dominated" the OAS. Since one of the major values of the organization to the United States is its ability to legitimize and evoke widespread consent for United States policies and operations in Latin America by enveloping them in a multilateral framework, an OAS obviously under Washington's thumb would be dysfunctional. As a result, deliberate constraints have been placed on the employment of United States economic and military power in inter-American diplomacy. With the single exception of the Haitian incident at Punta del Este, for example, there is no evidence that the United States has ever tied economic assistance to support of its political policies in the OAS. On the contrary, some of the most consistent opponents of recent United States anti-Communist policies (Brazil under Goulart, Argentina under Frondizi) have received the lion's share of United States economic assistance.

While the United States obviously exercises great influence in the OAS and occupies a central role in the collective decision-making process, then, it does not *dictate* policy. Rather it bargains, negotiates, and compromises, and although it can usually in effect veto action it strongly opposes, it by no means invariably gets its own way. For example, the United States has been maneuvered into anti-

Communist conferences that it wasn't sure it wanted; it has received only limited support for its own anti-Communist initiatives; and it failed outright to gain OAS support for collective action against Duvalier in 1963.[9]

Moreover, insofar as the United States exercises leadership in the OAS, it usually acts as the broker of the organization, seeking consensus and leaning over backward to bring its position into line with the majority of the Latin American states. In potentially disruptive conflicts the avoidance of anti-American antagonism and the maintenance of the system frequently take precedence over substantive considerations or the amassing of support for United States views. Thus, in the controversy over Cuba, the United States has become increasingly willing to subordinate collective action against the Castro government to the goal of avoiding a serious split and perhaps even a permanent disruption of the system.

In brief, as a result of the limitations the United States normally has placed around the uses of its power in the inter-American system since the Good Neighbor Policy, the asymmetries of *potential* power are usually far greater than the asymmetries of *applied* power. Nonetheless, to the extent that the United States is still perceived by many Latin Americans to be dominant, the capability of the OAS to influence political processes in the hemisphere is reduced.

Intrahemispheric conflicts and divisions are by no means limited to those between the United States and Latin America; there are important, bitter, and often violent conflicts among the Latin American states themselves. As has been discussed, ideological conflicts between the dictatorships and the democracies have continually riven the hemisphere. More recently, conflicts between radical movements and traditionally conservative oligarchies, as between Guatemala and its neighbors and Cuba and the other Caribbean states, have erupted. Moreover, territorial conflicts continue, still embittering, for example, the relations between Peru and Ecuador as well as Bolivia and Chile. Such intrahemispheric conflicts weaken the OAS and inhibit the expansion of its political functions.

From 1948 through 1964 every Latin American state but Chile, Mexico, and Uruguay had at least one illegal change of government. By complicating the task of obtaining an enduring consensus on new policies, this continuing Latin American political instability also weakens the OAS. Military coups in the Dominican Republic and Honduras in 1963, for example, removed those countries from the ranks of the OAS members favoring a more vigorous role for the inter-American system in the promotion of democracy in Latin America and thereby seriously set back that cause at a time when it seemed some real progress was finally being made. Moreover, as has been described, political instability often increases interstate conflict, for exiles find their way to sympathetic countries and launch campaigns against their homelands.

Still another fragmenting force is endemic anti-Americanism, which although greatest in the 1950's, is again on the rise, particularly among intellectuals and emerging leftist, nationalistic groups. The causes are manifold. The very fact of overwhelming United States power grates on Latin American pride, especially when that power is used to intervene in Latin American politics, as in Guatemala, Cuba, and recently the Dominican Republic. Moreover, except under Kennedy, the United States has been associated in Latin American minds with militarism and right wing dictatorship and, in general, with the conservative elites that in many nations still maintain a tight grip on political power, material wealth, and social status. There are economic factors as well, notably the refusal of the United States until recently to grant large-scale economic assistance to Latin America or to participate in price-stabilization programs for Latin American exports; although much more economic aid was granted in the postwar period than in the halcyon Good Neighbor days, the immensely larger economic assistance to United States allies in Europe and Asia aroused bitter Latin American resentment. Finally, the widely differing economic ideologies, social structures and cultural traditions of the United States and Latin America contribute to misunderstandings and resentments.

It is possible that the increasing intensity of nationalism in Latin America will further fragment the OAS, especially insofar as it feeds on anti-Americanism and leads to demands for "independent" or even neutralist foreign policies, à la Brazil under Goulart. One manifestation of this has been the development of "Pan Latin Americanism" or "Hispano Americanism" as alternative organizing principles to Pan Americanism. One writer professes to note an already strong trend "towards a strengthening of the solidarity of the Latin American group and a weakening of the group's ties with the United States."[10]

On the other hand, the experience of the Organization of Central American States (OCAS) indicates that real Latin American unity is no less difficult to attain than is hemispheric unity. Although the political unification of Central America has been a dream of intellectuals and statesmen of that region for more than a century, it was not until the formation of the OCAS after World War II that even symbolic progress was made. Moreover, the OCAS has proved to be a disappointment, being "at most a loose cooperative arrangement among states retaining full sovereignty."[11] No attempt has been made to give it political content, and even economic, social, and cultural measures can be adopted only by unanimous vote. The existence of the Organization did not prevent the conflict between Honduras, Nicaragua, and Guatemala in 1954 nor between Costa Rica and Nicaragua in 1955. Although there have been some mutual tariff reductions in the area, it seems clear that nationalism, political instability, ideological differences, and traditional interstate rivalries still are frustrating hopes for meaningful Central American co-operation.

The Central American experience and the difficulties encountered in the recent South American experiment in regional economic integration suggest that grandiose schemes for complete Latin American unity will face even more insuperable obstacles, and it is unlikely that the trend toward neutralism and disassociation from the United States will go so far as to seriously disrupt the OAS. As long as United States economic, political, and military power continues to influence developments in the hemisphere, the Latin American states are not likely to forego the influence they gain over United States policy from their participation in the inter-American system in favor of unrealistic dreams of Latin American unity.

The Political Capacity of the OAS: A Summary

An evaluation of the effectiveness of the OAS must depend on the assumptions that are made about its proper role in hemispheric political conflict. If its primary role is to control overt interstate conflict and to maintain the territorial integrity of each of the member states, there is little question but that the OAS has been quite effective. Unlike any other region in the world, the Western Hemisphere has seen no major conflagration in several decades. Given the numerous political, ideological, and territorial conflicts in the hemisphere, this is no minor accomplishment. Although the OAS rarely removes the underlying causes of disputes, it has insured that most of them have been fought out by relatively non-violent methods; and it is plausible that in the absence of the deterring presence of the OAS, there would have been many more outbreaks of interstate conflict. Moreover, the OAS has generally played a major role in the peaceful termination of the relatively few open conflicts that have erupted, acting, variously, as an impartial fact-finding agency, a peace-keeping force separating belligerents and preventing further armed conflict, a communications network between disputants and a forum for the conciliation and negotiation of their dispute, and an arbitral board with the authority and capability to enforce its decisions.

In what sense can OAS action be considered truly collective? The United States plays the key role in most OAS actions, providing leadership, logistical services, economic pressures, and, when necessary, military force. Still, the importance of the Latin American contribution should not be underestimated: the Latin Americans provide political and diplomatic skills for negotiating, conciliating, and mediating; but most of all, they provide legitimacy. Collective action requiring economic and military sanctions may be essentially United States action, but it is action given an all-important symbolic multilateral character by the authorization of the OAS.

There is an alternative perspective on the effectiveness of the oas, however. If its role is considered to be that of helping the Latin Americans free themselves from the burden of corrupt, reactionary, and brutal government, then not only has it failed, it has often helped perpetuate such governments by insulating them from external political pressures. The oas has intervened in political conflict in the hemisphere only when conflict has cut *across* state boundaries. With the single exception of the Dominican case of 1960–62, it has been unconcerned with conflicts not involving the Communist issue that have been fought out *within* state boundaries. The most important and explosive political conflicts in the Western Hemisphere, however, have been intra- and not interstate in nature. Moreover, it is nearly certain that Latin American political instability, ideological conflicts, and civil wars will be intensified in the future, for most of the area is being painfully transformed from traditional agrarian, oligarchical societies to modern urban, industrial, and pluralistic ones. Unless the oas can play a constructive role in this transitional process, it may become increasingly irrelevant to the most important political problems of the hemisphere.

Some Recommendations

It has been demonstrated that the inter-American system has had enough utility to warrant continued United States efforts both to expand the scope of its operations and to associate the Latin American states as closely as possible with United States objectives. This will be particularly important if the United States defines its primary goal as that of helping restructure Latin American society and guiding Latin American change along non-Communist but progressive lines. The ability of the United States to control events unilaterally in Latin America, as elsewhere, is rapidly diminishing, and traditional foreign policy weapons, such as military displays, economic penalties and rewards, and the like, will become increasingly futile in dealing with leftist and nationalistic regimes resting on a broad base of mass support. As a result, the importance of the OAS to the execution of United States policy is likely to increase in the future. In the massive undertaking represented by the Alliance for Progress and associated political action, the primary task for the United States will be that of engineering genuine Latin American consent. It is precisely in this area that potentially the OAS can be most useful.

Whether the OAS will be willing to play a major role in hemispheric problems is another question, however. Compromise, delay, and half-measures are serious drawbacks in the inter-American system. This is, of course, true of any collective decision-making institution, but it is particularly serious in the OAS, where the invariable pursuit of unity typically results in inter-American policy formulated on the basis of the lowest common denominator of agreement. While this has the important function of reducing conflict and thereby helping to stabilize and maintain the system, it also may result in an inadequate response to problems on which there is little or no consensus. The more serious the problem, the more likely it is that the existing area of agreement will be too narrow to support an effective and meaningful policy.

This has been particularly true with regard to the Latin American social, economic, and political revolution, the major problem now facing the hemisphere. The doctrine of non-intervention and the presence in the OAS of a number of Latin American states under the control of conservative minorities that are unenthusiastic about assisting in their own demise have prevented the OAS from playing a major role in the process of political change in Latin America.

There has been, it is true, some Latin American recognition that the non-intervention doctrine is an anachronism and a major obstacle to the development of a more useful OAS. In recent years a number of Latin American presidents have openly called for a repudiation or at least modification of the doctrine. Presidents Echandi and Orlich of Costa Rica, Betancourt of Venezuela, Bosch of the Dominican Republic, and Villeda Morales of Honduras, all repeatedly called upon the OAS to intervene actively in Latin America on behalf of democracy and human rights. President Chiari of Panama bluntly told the Council in 1962 that the non-intervention doctrine had been "drifting toward a new formula of eyes shut and hands off, which . . .[was] not exactly . . . [its] original meaning . . . " and that the doctrine must be "reviewed" to allow for the taking of "collective measures intended to assure all the peoples of the Americas, within their own boundaries, of their freedom and their right to control their own destiny."[12] But perhaps the most significant breakthrough was the announcement by President Kubitschek in 1960 that Brazil was considering the relaxation of her traditional opposition to collective intervention and would consider favorably "any proposals . . . for the strengthening of democracy, including those relative to adoption of multilateral sanctions in cases that are well-defined and circumscribed to be violations of political and human rights."[13]

However, Latin American foreign policies are no

noted for their continuity. Kubitschek was replaced by the nationalistic Goulart, and Brazil returned to an extreme non-interventionist position. Bosch and Villeda Morales fell prey to reactionary militarism, with obvious consequences for Dominican and Honduran support of pro-democratic intervention. Even the Venezuelan regime of Raul Leoni has recently shown indications of a retreat from the vigorous Betancourt support of punitive measures against military coups d'état.

Moreover, sometimes the loudest critics of non-intervention are motivated primarily by a desire for action against a specific regime rather than by a general commitment to a more vigorous OAS. As C. Neale Ronning has pointed out:

> When a government feels threatened by a neighboring regime with an antagonistic ideological and political orientation (or when its domestic and foreign interests make it convenient to picture such a regime as a threat), there is a growing tendency to insist on a right of collective intervention.[14]

Thus, Uruguay's support of multilateral sanctions against dictatorships waned after the collapse of the Perón regime in Argentina; Venezuela's pro-democratic policy was largely aimed at the Trujillo regime in the Dominican Republic; and the Central American states have been primarily concerned with Cuba.

In short, it is apparent that only slight progress has been made in revising the non-intervention doctrine. Prospects for future collective action on behalf of democracy rest in the first instance on a relaxation of Latin American distrust of the United States, but even more fundamentally on a continuing decline in the power of conservative oligarchies in Latin America, the main beneficiaries of the non-intervention doctrine.

Collective Intervention for Democracy: Pro and Con

Even if collective intervention should prove possible in the future, its desirability has been frequently questioned.[15] Although the arguments against multilateral intervention to assist the development of democracy in Latin America are powerful, they are not, I believe, conclusive.

First, it is argued that democracy is only relative, that nearly all states diverge to a greater or lesser degree from the ideal. How then can objective criteria be developed to guide collective action? The problem is particularly difficult when openly authoritarian regimes using traditional *caudillist* methods persecute minorities and trample on civil liberties but nonetheless enjoy majority support and are engaged in economic and social modernization programs; the Perón and Castro regimes would perhaps be examples.

Moreover, it can be argued that authoritarian methods are inevitable if real economic and social progress is to be made in societies long dominated by small oligarchies with vested interests in the status quo. Put another way, political democracy may be incompatible with economic and social democracy when small minorities make use of the democratic process to veto change. As Tad Szulc has pointed out, the democratic revolutions in Latin America in the 1950's "halted at the line of social change."[16] When, then, authoritarian regimes are engaged in efficient modernization programs that are necessary both for their own sake as well as to lay the basis for more meaningful political democracy in the future, they may well merit inter-American support, not condemnation.

On the other hand, there have been and still are a number of Latin American dictatorships that are both brutal and reactionary and have nothing at all to recommend them: Trujillo's Dominican Republic, Somoza's Nicaragua, Duvalier's Haiti, Stroessner's Paraguay, for example. In such cases, the argument for collective intervention is powerful.

A second objection to a policy of collective intervention, though, is that it would be carried out only against the smallest and weakest states, although they have no monopoly on undemocratic practices; it is hardly conceivable that the United States would permit the OAS to examine its failings, nor is it very likely that the OAS could play any role in Argentina, Chile, Brazil, or Mexico.

Although it is true that nothing much can be done about undemocratic practices in large states, at least not in the foreseeable future—that is one of those unfortunate realities of power—surely any expansion of human rights and freedom in this hemisphere is to be welcomed. Moreover, most of the worst dictatorships in recent hemispheric history have in fact been in the smallest states.

Third, it is argued that OAS intervention would be collective in name only; hemispheric power realities would dictate that any intervention would have to be acceptable to the Colossus of the North and would be dominated by it. The OAS would be converted into an instrument of United States foreign policy.

It is obviously correct that the United States would dominate any collective intervention involving severe economic sanctions or large-scale military operations, as in the event of intervention against Cuba. On the other hand, smaller operations could be genuinely collective. For example, it would certainly not be beyond the capabilities of the Latin American members of the OAS to organize a multilateral military expedition to overthrow the Duvalier regime in Haiti and establish a provisional government under the direction of the OAS Secretariat. It is not the lack of human and material resources but the doctrine of non-intervention that is the real constraint.

Furthermore, the issue of United States domination of collective intervention could become irrelevant. In the early 1960's, the United States demonstrated that in certain circumstances it was prepared to intervene unilaterally in Latin American domestic affairs against both governments of the extreme left and extreme right. It is possible, for example, that the 1961–62 United States intervention in the Dominican Republic would have been paralleled by similar action in Venezuela had there been either a right wing military or a left wing Castroite coup against the Betancourt government. To the extent, then, that the United States finds it necessary to take forceful action in the future, a continued Latin American influence over United States policy will depend in large part on the degree to which the Latin Americans permit the OAS to play a role in hemispheric political problems.

Fourth, it could be argued that collective interventions, like unilateral United States interventions in the past, would be more likely to strengthen the antidemocratic forces than control them. The interventions in Nicaragua, Haiti, and the Dominican Republic in the 1920's ended in the creation of a predatory and reactionary militarism that has continued to plague those countries ever since. United States diplomatic intervention in Argentina in 1946 probably strengthened rather than hurt Perón.

The experience of the UN in the Congo and Cyprus demonstrates that collective intervention is by no means free from the problems of unilateral intervention. Nationalistic resentment may *strengthen* local rulers and allow them to institute even more authoritarian measures. Even if collective pressures succeed in overthrowing one dictatorship, there is no guarantee that a democracy will take its place. Right-wing authoritarianism may only be replaced by left-wing authoritarianism or even by near anarchy, as perhaps in Katanga. In short, it could be concluded, democracy can only come from within.

It is true that the evidence from history generally indicates the inadequacy of outside intervention as a means of fostering democracy, but against that is the partially successful example of the Dominican Republic in 1961-62 (and perhaps even the Congo). Although there was a reversion to non-democratic procedures in the Dominican Republic, this does not prove the inherent futility of intervention but, on the contrary, demonstrates that the intervening powers must be prepared, if necessary, to reapply strong pressures until democracy is firmly established. Moreover, setbacks do not by any means entirely negate earlier gains. The experience with democracy and reform in the Dominican Republic, short-lived as it was, is almost certain to make impossible a return to the feudalistic totalitarianism of Trujillo and to increase internal as well as external pressures for a return to progressive government.

This should not be read, however, as a plea for indiscriminate intervention (and least of all for the ill-considered 1965 Dominican type). Certainly interventions must be skilfully executed and limited to situations in which the circumstances are favorable. They would be most likely to succeed in highly fluid situations in which assistance is given to a democratic opposition group with broad local support in revolt against a narrowly based dictatorship or, conversely, to a popular social democratic regime threatened by extremists. It is quite possible that such situations will develop in the future—perhaps in Venezuela, Argentina, or Peru, for example.

For United States policy-makers, the attraction of a program of collective action on behalf of democracy would probably rest on the argument that the removal of obstacles to change in Latin America would dilute the appeal of communism. It is my view, however, that the case for pro-democratic intervention should rest more on its moral validity than its anti-Communist utility. The comforting assumption that the promotion of change in Latin America is in the best interests of the United States might easily be incorrect. The Alliance for Progress, for example, might well facilitate the emergence of leftist, nationalistic, and anti-American groups in Latin America. Thus, a coldly cynical policy might dictate support for those reactionary dictatorships, such as Nicaragua and Paraguay, that have demonstrated an ability to maintain the status quo indefinitely and repress potentially radical populist movements. The defense of an activist OAS—United States policy must therefore ultimately rest on the conviction that although it may or may not prove to be good for the United States, it will almost surely be good for the long-repressed peoples of Latin America.

1. Arthur P. Whitaker, *The Western Hemisphere Idea* (Ithaca: Cornell University Press, 1954), pp. 1, 5; see also J. Fred Rippy, "The Western Hemisphere Concept: Permanent or Fleeting?" *Inter-American Economic Affairs,* Spring, 1957.

2. Whitaker, *op. cit.,* pp. 154–55, 170–77.

3. René de Visme Williamson, *Culture and Policy* (Knoxville: University of Tennessee Press, 1949), p. 56.

4. The major spokesman for this view is Jorgé Castañeda. See his "Pan Americanism and Regionalism: A Mexican View," *International Organization,* August, 1956.

5. Williamson, *Nationalism,* p. 57.

6. For a similar view see Northwestern University, "The Organization of American States," in *United States–Latin American Relations,* United States Senate Committee on Foreign Relations, 86th Cong., 2d sess., 1960, p. 206.

7. Juan José Arévalo, *The Shark and the Sardines* (New York: Lyle Stuart, 1961), p. 13.

8. *Ibid.,* p. 113.

9. In this connection, the OAS has been accused of acting as a United States "puppet" in the 1965 Dominican crisis. To some extent, of course, the OAS *was* presented with a *fait accompli,* but it should not be overlooked that the OAS today contains a great many conservative, militaristic regimes, most of which are quite happy to support anti-"subversion" operations. Once again, it is a coincidence of interests rather than United States "domination" that best explains OAS action.

10. Whitaker, *Nationalism,* p. 67.

11. Norman J. Padelford, "Co-operation in the Central American Region: The Organization of Central American States," *International Organization,* Winter, 1957, p. 43.

12. *Actas del Consejo,* June 13, 1962.

13. *New York Times,* January 31, 1960.

14. C. Neale Ronning, "Intervention, International Law, and the Inter-American System," *Journal of Inter-American Studies,* April, 1961, p. 269.

15. See especially Castañeda, *op. cit;* Laurence Duggan, *The Americas* (New York: Henry Holt & Co., 1949); Luis Quintanilla, *Pan Americanism and Democracy* (Boston: Boston University Press, 1952); Sumner Welles, "Intervention and Interventions," *Foreign Affairs,* October, 1947; Ninth International Conference of American States, Bogotá, 1948, *Opinion of the Inter-American Juridical Committee on the Project Submitted by Guatemala to the Inter-American Conference on Problems of War and Peace,* Document CB-4-D, Chronological Collection of Documents (Washington, D. C.: Pan American Union, 1948).

16. Tad Szulc, *Winds of Revolution* (New York: Frederick A. Praeger, 1963), p. 98.

Selected Bibliography

*

Selected Bibliography

THE BEST SOURCES on United States policy in the OAS are still the primary materials. The most important OAS documents are the transcriptions of the proceedings of the Inter-American Conferences and the Meetings of Consultation of Ministers of Foreign Affairs; the minutes of Council meetings (*Actas del Consejo*); the reports of the Inter-American Peace Committee, the Inter-American Commission on Human Rights, and the Special Consultative Committee on Security; and the Annual Reports of the Secretary General. A number of publications of the Pan American Union are very useful, especially the detailed summaries of inter-American action taken in hemispheric conflict contained in *Aplicaciones del Tratado Inter-Americano de Asistencia Reciproca, 1948–1960* (Washington, D.C., 1960) and its 1960–61 *Suplemento* (an English-language edition, *Applications of the Inter-American Treaty of Reciprocal Assistance,* is complete only through 1956); *Annals of the Organization of American States, 1949–1958*; and three summaries of all OAS activities: *Report on the Activities of the Pan American Union, 1938–1948* (Washington, D.C., 1948), *Report on the Activities of the Organization of American States, 1948–1953* (Washington, D.C., 1953), and *The Organization of American States, 1954–1959* (Washington, D.C., 1959).

The most useful State Department publications are the following: *Bulletin of the Department of State; A Case History of Communist Penetration: Guatemala,* (Washington, D.C.: U. S. Government Printing Office, 1957); *Cuba*

(Washington, D.C.: U. S. Government Printing Office, 1961) ; *Inter-American Efforts to Relieve Tensions in the Western Hemisphere, 1959–1960* (Washington, D.C.: U. S. Government Printing Office, 1962) ; *Intervention of International Communism in Guatemala* (Washington, D.C.: Government Printing Office, 1954) ; *Report of the Delegation of the United States on the Inter-American Conference for the Maintenance of Continental Peace and Security* (Washington, D.C.: U. S. Government Printing Office, 1948); *Report of the Delegation of the United States on the International Conference of American States, 9th, Bogotá* (Washington, D.C.: U. S. Government Printing Office, 1948) ; *Report of the Delegation of the United States on the Inter-American Conference, 10th, Caracas* (Washington, D.C.: U. S. Government Printing Office, 1955) ; *Report of the Secretary of State on the Meeting of Consultation of Ministers of Foreign Affairs of the American States, 4th, Washington* (Washington, D.C.: U. S. Government Printing Office, 1953) .

Finally, the *New York Times* often has excellent coverage of major inter-American conferences and crises.

The best secondary sources are the following:

BOOKS AND MONOGRAPHS

ARÉVALO, JUAN JOSÉ. *The Shark and the Sardines.* New York: Lyle Stuart, 1961.

BALL, M. MARGARET. *The Problem of Inter-American Organization.* Stanford: Stanford University Press, 1944.

———. "Recent Developments in Inter-American Relations," in *The Yearbook of World Affairs.* London: Stevens & Sons, 1949.

BERLE, ADOLPH A., JR. *Latin America—Diplomacy and Reality.* New York: Council on Foreign Relations, 1962.

DOZER, DONALD. *Are We Good Neighbors?* Gainesville: University of Florida Press, 1959.

DREIER, JOHN C. *The Organization of American States and the Hemisphere Crisis.* New York: Council on Foreign Relations, 1962.

DUGGAN, LAURENCE. *The Americas*. New York: Henry Holt & Co., 1949.

FENWICK, CHARLES G. *The Inter-American Regional System*. New York: Declan X. McMullen Co., 1949.

———. *The Organization of American States*. Washington, D.C.: Charles G. Fenwick, 1963.

FREEMAN, ALWYN V. "The Political Powers of the OAS Council," in *Law and Politics in the World Community*, ed. GEORGE H. LIPSKY. Berkeley: University of California Press, 1953.

GRABER, D. A. *Crisis Diplomacy*. Washington, D.C.: Public Affairs Press, 1959.

———. "United States Intervention in Latin America," in *Yearbook of World Affairs, 1962.*. London: Institute of World Affairs, 1962.

HULA, ERICH. "Pan Americanism: Its Utopian and Realistic Elements," in *Problems of Post-War Reconstruction*, ed. HENRY JORDAN. Washington, D.C.: American Council on Public Affairs, 1942.

HUMPHREY, JOHN P. *The Inter-American System*. Toronto: Macmillan Company of Canada, 1942.

LLERAS, ALBERTO. *The Inter-American Way of Life*. Washington, D.C.: Pan American Union, 1951.

———. *The Organization of American States*. Lewisberg, Pa.: Bucknell University Press, 1954.

MANGER, WILLIAM. *Pan America in Crisis*. Washington, D.C.: Public Affairs Press, 1961.

MECHAM, J. LLOYD. *The United States and Inter-American Security, 1889–1960*. Austin: University of Texas Press, 1961.

MORRISON, DELESSEPS S. *Latin American Mission*. New York: Simon & Schuster, 1965.

NORTHWESTERN UNIVERSITY, *The Organization of American States*. United States Senate Committee on Foreign Relations, Study No. 3 of *United States–Latin American Relations*, 86th Cong., 2d sess., 1960.

PAN AMERICAN UNION. *The Meetings of Consultation*. Washington, D.C.: 1962.

———. *The Organization of American States and the United Nations*. Washington, D.C., 1960.

QUINTANILLA, LUIS. *A Latin American Speaks.* New York: Macmillan Co., 1943.

———. *Pan Americanism and Democracy.* Boston: Boston University Press, 1952.

RONNING, C. NEALE. *Law and Politics in Inter-American Diplomacy.* New York: John Wiley & Sons, 1963.

———. *Punta Del Este: The Limits of Collective Security in a Troubled Hemisphere.* New York: Carnegie Endowment for International Peace, 1963.

TAYLOR, PHILIP B., JR., *Hemispheric Security Reconsidered.* New Orleans: Tulane University Press, 1957.

THOMAS, ANN VAN WYNEN and A. J., JR. *Non-Intervention.* Dallas: Southern Methodist University Press, 1956.

———. *The Organization of American States.* Dallas: Southern Methodist University Press, 1963.

WHITAKER, ARTHUR P. "The Organization of American States," in *The Yearbook of World Affairs, 1959.* London: Stevens & Sons, 1959.

———. *The Western Hemisphere Idea.* Ithaca: Cornell University Press, 1954.

WOOD, BRYCE. *The Making of the Good Neighbor Policy.* New York: Columbia University Press, 1961.

ARTICLES

ARANHA, OSWALD. "Regional Systems and the Future of the UN," *Foreign Affairs,* April, 1948.

BALL, M. MARGARET. "Issue for the Americas: Non-Intervention vs. Human Rights and the Preservation of Democratic Institutions," *International Organization,* Winter, 1961.

CASTAÑEDA, JORGE. "Pan Americanism and Regionalism: A Mexican View," *International Organization,* August, 1956.

CLAUDE, INIS L. "Multilateralism—Diplomatic and Otherwise,"*International Organization,* Winter, 1958.

———. "The OAS, the UN, and the United States," *International Conciliation,* March, 1964.

CUEVAS, FRANCISCO. "The Bogotá Conference and Recent Developments in Pan-American Relations: A Mexican

View," *International Affairs,* October, 1948.

DREIER, JOHN C. "The Council of the OAS: Performance and Potential," *Journal of Inter-American Studies,* July, 1963.

———. "The Organization of American States and United States Policy," *International Organization,* Winter, 1963.

FENWICK, CHARLES G. "The Inter-American Peace Committee," *American Journal of International Law,* October, 1949.

———. "Inter-American Regional Procedures for the Settlement of Disputes," *International Organization,* February, 1956.

———. "The Inter-American Regional System: Fifty Years of Progress," *American Journal of International Law,* January, 1956.

———. "Intervention and the Inter-American Rule of Law," *American Journal of International Law,* October, 1959.

———. "The Meeting of Consultation of Foreign Ministers as a Procedure of Inter-American Collective Security," *American Journal of International Law,* April, 1955.

———. "The Ninth International Conference of American States," *American Journal of International Law,* July, 1948.

———. "The Unanimity Rule in Inter-American Conferences," *American Journal of International Law,* April, 1948.

FITZGIBBON, RUSSELL H. "The Organization of American States: Time of Ordeal," *Orbis,* Spring, 1961.

FURNISS, EDGAR S., JR. "The Inter-American System and Recent Caribbean Disputes," *International Organization,* November, 1950.

———. "Recent Changes in the Inter-American System," *International Organization,* September, 1948.

———. "The United States, the Inter-American System, and the United Nations," *Political Science Quarterly,* September, 1950.

GILLEN, JOHN, and SILVERT, K. H. "Ambiguities in Guatemala," *Foreign Affairs,* April, 1956.

GUERRANT, EDWARD O. "The Council of the Organization of American States," *World Affairs Quarterly,* January,

1956.

HAAS, ERNST B. "The Challenge of Regionalism," *International Organization,* Autumn, 1958.

———. "Regional Integration and National Policy," *International Conciliation,* May, 1957.

HANSON, SIMON G. "Failure at Punta del Este," *Inter-American Economic Affairs,* Spring, 1962.

HERRERA, ROBERTO. "Evolution of Equality of States in the Inter-American System," *Political Science Quarterly,* March, 1946.

KUNZ, JOSEF L. "The Bogotá Charter of the Organization of American States," *American Journal of International Law,* July, 1948.

———. "The Idea of 'Collective Security' in Pan-American Developments," *Western Political Quarterly,* December, 1953.

———. "The Inter-American Treaty of Reciprocal Assistance," *American Journal of International Law,* January, 1948.

MORA, JOSÉ A. "The Organization of American States," *International Organization,* Autumn, 1960.

PADELFORD, NORMAN J. "Regional Organization and the United Nations," *International Organization,* May, 1954.

PIKE, FREDERICK B. "Guatemala, the United States, and Communism in the Americas," *Review of Politics,* April, 1955.

RIPPY, J. FRED. "The Western Hemisphere Concept: Permanent or Fleeting?" *Inter-American Economic Affairs,* Spring, 1957.

RONNING, C. NEALE. "Intervention, International Law, and the Inter-American System," *Journal of Inter-American Studies,* April, 1961.

TAYLOR, PHILIP B., JR. "The Guatemalan Affair: A Critique of United States Foreign Policy," *American Political Science Review,* September, 1956.

TRAVIS, MARTIN B. "The Organization of American States: A Guide to the Future," *Western Political Quarterly,* September, 1957.

WELLS, HENRY. "The OAS and the Dominican Elections," *Orbis,* Spring, 1963.

WHITAKER, ARTHUR B. "Development of American Regionalism: The Organization of American States," *International Conciliation,* March, 1951.

———. "Guatemala, OAS, and US," *Foreign Policy Bulletin,* September, 1954.

———. "Rio and Bogotá: Pan American Perspective," *Inter-American Economic Affairs,* December, 1947.

*

Index